CW01168544

the cruel hunters
SS-Sonderkommando Dirlewanger
Hitler's most notorious
anti-partisan unit

the cruel hunters

SS-Sonderkommando Dirlewanger Hitler's most notorious anti-partisan unit

French MacLean

Schiffer Military History
Atglen, PA

Book Design by Robert Biondi.

Copyright © 1998 by French MacLean.
Library of Congress Catalog Number: 97-80402.

All rights reserved. No part of this work may be reproduced or used in any forms or by any means - graphic, electronic or mechanical, including photocopying or information storage and retrieval systems - without written permission from the copyright holder.

Printed in China.
ISBN: 0-7643-0483-6

We are interested in hearing from authors with book ideas on related topics.

Published by Schiffer Publishing Ltd.
4880 Lower Valley Road
Atglen, PA 19310
Phone: (610) 593-1777; Fax: (610) 593-2002
E-mail: Schifferbk@aol.com
Please visit our web site catalog at

In Europe, Schiffer books are distributed by
Bushwood Books
6 Marksbury Avenue Kew Gardens
Surrey TW9 4JF England
Phone: 44 (0) 20-8392-8585; Fax: 44 (0) 20-8392-9876

This book may be purchased from the publisher.
Include $3.95 for shipping. Please try your bookstore first.
We are always looking for people to write books on new and related subjects.
If you have an idea for a book please contact us at the above address.

PREFACE

This was a difficult book to write. Difficult, because it is a story, in part, of the deaths of many innocent men, women and children. The work did not start out that way. I chose the subject of the Dirlewanger unit for two reasons – first, because so little has been written about this unusual formation, and second, because I found a unique record of the unit's battle reports which enabled a definitive book to finally be written.

For me, writing about a subject that little has been previously written is much like solving a detective story. There is a general understanding that something took place, but the scope of the undertaking and the persons involved are a mystery at the outset. If I can shed light on this particular subject, it may, in turn, help another historian solve a different mystery. That is why I chose this peculiar story.

All this would not be possible if I did not stumble on the operational records of Dirlewanger's unit available at the National Archives. After World War II, Army historians collected literally tons of captured German records concerning both military and political life in the Third Reich. Some years later the United States returned these records to the Federal Republic of Germany – they are now housed at various locations of the Bundesarchiv-Militärarchiv to include Freiburg and Koblenz. Prior to this, however, the National Archives microfilmed all records; these microfilms now reside in Washington, D.C. More importantly, the archivists compiled extensive guides to these rolls of film, explaining the content of each in great detail. While working on a different project I happened by chance to find mention of Dirlewanger and his unit in one of these guides to the microfilm. A review of these few rolls convinced me a book could be done.

The work was difficult in another, more personal arena. In previous writings I have addressed many aspects of the German military in World War II, aspects – that although we may condemn the politics behind the military – which were outstanding feats of martial achievement and leadership under fire. In researching these subjects, I had the opportunity of meeting several distinguished old soldiers – several of whom have become warm friends of my wife and mine. To a man, they represent the finest virtues of chivalry in combat, fought in units which conducted themselves honorably in action, and served to rebuild Germany in a more peaceful tradition after the war. They were never involved in anything remotely like what you will read about in the upcoming story. I hope they understand my choice of subjects for this work.

To the thousands of innocent victims who fell in this true story and to those soldiers on all sides who conducted themselves honorably, this book is dedicated.

CONTENTS

Preface 5
Acknowledgments 9
Introduction 12

Chapter 1   A Monster is Born 21
Chapter 2   The Anti-Partisan Years, 1942 69
Chapter 3   The Anti-Partisan Years, 1943 106
Chapter 4   Farewell to Russia, 1944 151
Chapter 5   Warsaw 175
Chapter 6   The Monster Dies 199
Chapter 7   Judgment at Nuremberg 229

Epilogue 249

Appendices
Appendix 1: SS Ranks 266
Appendix 2: Sonderkommando Officers 267
Appendix 3: Sonderkommando Enlisted Personnel 269
Appendix 4: Fate of Dirlewanger Protagonists 276
Appendix 5: Dirlewanger Unit Designations 279
Appendix 6: German Anti-Partisan Operations
    with Sonderkommando Dirlewanger 280
Appendix 7: Compostion of Sonderkommando Dirlewanger 282
Appendix 8: Glossary 283

Sources 286
Index 299

Index of Maps

Sachsenhausen	44
Poland 1940	60
White Russia 1942	70
White Russia 1943	107
White Russia 1944	152
Retreat from White Russia 1944	171
Wola, Warsaw Uprising 1944	181
Old Town, Warsaw Uprising 1944	190
Inner City, Warsaw Uprising 1944	192
Slovakia – Hungary 1944	200
Germany 1945	215
Altshausen 1945	224

ACKNOWLEDGMENTS

I could not have completed this work alone. First, I must go back some fifty-five years and credit numerous individuals I have never met – the hundreds of faceless personnel recorders, stenographers, typists, law clerks, bookkeepers, radio operators, teletype supervisors, mid-level bureaucrats, file clerks, regulation writers, couriers and military historians of the Waffen-SS. You may not have written and filed your myriad of reports for the sake of posterity, but, because of your otherwise admirable trait of German thoroughness and efficiency in all matters paper, you left a trail. It was a cold trail – but a trail nonetheless.

Skipping forward to the present, I would like to thank Marianne K. Driscoll, who spent painstaking hours translating extensive German personnel record documents. While I am comfortable reading and understanding operational reports and summaries done in German – when I needed a word-by-word, complete translation of letters, efficiency reports and recommendations for awards I asked for her assistance. She always came through, no matter how busy she was.

Jim Kelling, Niels Cordes, Bang Tran and the staff at the National Archives II came to anticipate my Saturday morning visits with good cheer and helpfulness. They invariably provided timely assistance in finding specific rolls of microfilm, as well as help me operate the different types of viewers and copiers. When a writer is pursuing a train of thought, the last thing he needs to worry about is paper supply and toner fill or how the microfilm viewer is supposed to operate. However, they do much more than that. Niels has reviewed hundreds of rolls of microfilm and has almost a photographic memory – many times he was able to recall documents he had seen in his reviewing process.

Teresa Amiel Pollin, Aaron Kornblum, Ron Kurpiers and the research assistants at the United States Holocaust Memorial Museum opened their extensive photograph files on many aspects of this story which relate to the Holocaust. It is an important segment which helps remind us of the fragility of individual rights and freedoms we often take for granted. The photographs provided by this fine institution are labeled (USHMM) throughout the book.

To Frau Wieck and Frau Hoffmann of the *Bundesarchiv-Militärarchiv* at Koblenz I extend my gratitude. They provided a great deal of assistance in my search for additional photographs relating to this work – by their own nature difficult to find. Without these photographs this enterprise would not have been possible in its current form. These illustrations are designated (BAK) in this work.

I must also recognize Herr Rudolf Multer of Altshausen, Germany for his extensive assistance and photographs concerning Oskar Dirlewanger during the immediate post-war period. Rudolf must certainly be considered the expert on the mysterious fate of the leader of this unit.

High on the list of contributors also stands Christoph Schottes and the publishers at *Edition Temmen* in Bremen, Germany. They graciously permitted four photos from one of their works, *Antifaschisten in SS-Uniform*, by Hans-Peter Klausch, to appear in this work. I look forward to the day when many of the books from this fine company are translated into English.

Back in this country, I must also thank Ray Embree who provided several photographs of very rare insignia attributed to the Dirlewanger unit.

The publishers at Schiffer also deserve a great deal of appreciation. Robert Biondi is the type of publishing executive that most writers only hope to encounter. Their most beneficial capacity has been to let me organize the structure of the book in a way I desired. They are without a doubt

Acknowledgments

one of the most prolific publishing firms on World War II subjects in this country.

To Dr. Tom Veve, a dedicated historian and college administrator, goes a special word of appreciation. A friend of over twenty years, he painstakingly read every word of multiple drafts of this work, offering critical comments and improvements, which have undoubtedly made this a better product. At his urging and mentoring, I attempted to convert this book from just another military history reference on World War II, to that of the definitive source on the Dirlewanger saga. I will let the reader be the judge of the success of this attempt.

Finally, I would also like to express gratitude to my wife Olga. In addition to her normal high level of tolerance for my historical pursuits to include trips to Germany and spending numerous hours in front of the computer, she read my draft cover to cover and provided much needed constructive suggestions for making the book better. It is easy for a historian to get immersed into the details of his or her work and forget that the lay reader will require certain explanations of events, that the author will not. Without a honest read by others before the manuscript goes to print, a work of history can easily get bogged down in so many details, so that only another historian can read and understand it. This is too important a story to permit that to happen.

French MacLean
Falls Church, Virginia

INTRODUCTION

*The occupied territories are seething with discontent.
The time has come for decisive action.*
- Heinrich Himmler, August 1942.[1]

This is a brutal story – but, from the safety of fifty years distance in time – it is an extremely compelling one. It is also an enduring lesson that a military unit, formed under an evil ideology, led by a social outcast and composed of vicious criminals, will sink to its lowest common denominator – hate.

The Dirlewanger Battalion, also known as "*Sonderkommando* (special commando) Dirlewanger" was perhaps the most little understood, but at the same time the most notorious, German SS anti-partisan unit in World War II.[2] German propaganda correspondents and wartime photographers did not follow them in action. And for good reason. Wherever the Dirlewanger unit – named for and led by Oskar Dirlewanger – operated, corruption and rape formed an every-day part of life and indiscriminate slaughter, beatings and looting were rife.[3]

Formed as a battalion of convicted poachers in 1940, the unit operated in Poland until 1942, guarding Jews in forced labor camps and making life miserable for Poles in Lublin and Cracow. From there Dirlewanger spent two years combating partisans in central Russia, giving no quarter and expecting none in return, during vicious fighting against an elusive foe in the midst of inhospitable swamps and dismal forests. In 1944 Dirlewanger savaged Warsaw during the Polish Uprising, before moving to Slovakia to crush another rebellion there. The end of the war saw the

Introduction

unit, which was now a division in size, fighting for its life south of Berlin against the Soviet Army.

After the war, when Dirlewanger disappeared and it was widely believed that the entire *Sonderkommando* had been put to the sword by the Soviets in a fit of revenge, the exploits of the unit were used as an example of SS unlawful and inhumane behavior. During the International Military Tribunal at Nürnberg, the prosecution presented the conduct of Dirlewanger as evidence to declare the Waffen-SS to be a criminal institution. The defense countered with an argument that has existed to this day in many history books – that the *Sonderkommando* was not really an element of the Waffen-SS at all. The record shows differently.

This Waffen-SS formation consisted not only of common criminals, but also disgraced army and SS officers, reduced in rank and now serving as privates. However, not all officers and non-commissioned officers were sent to the unit as punishment. Many had been previously assigned to the SS main headquarters and were transferred to the *Sonderkommando* to gain front-line combat experience and perhaps an award or two before returning to Berlin. Foreigners comprised the ranks as well and included Ukrainians, Croatians, Austrians and Spaniards. Discipline for all within the *Sonderkommando* was brutal. Offenders were beaten with clubs and some were shot without benefit of any judicial proceeding.[4] Superiors were permitted to strike subordinates without needing to justify it to Dirlewanger. One form of punishment was known as the "Dirlewanger Box" borrowed from the concentration camp "standing coffin" punishment. In this punishment the victim was placed in an upright closed coffin for extended periods of time. It was said that one would come out of the box either dead or as a killer.[5]

The *Sonderkommando* was an effective partisan hunting element, defeating many enemy bands throughout the vast expanse of White Russia. Unfortunately, Dirlewanger did not confine himself to combating an armed foe. No one can accurately say how many men, women and children were killed by this renegade unit in Poland and Russia, but the total certainly was in the tens of thousands.[6] Dirlewanger was not shy about broadcasting his successes, and any analyst reading his battle reports cannot but come to the conclusion that many of his victims were non-combatants.

The Cruel Hunters

Oskar Dirlewanger, the leader of this renegade outfit, was a complex character. Besides severe deficiencies in personal character, he – in his own mind at least – was a warrior for Germany. He served the German cause in four conflicts. In World War I he was wounded six times, decorated for bravery and rose to be the acting commander of a battalion. Shortly after the war he fought the communists in essentially a civil war in Germany; and from these exploits – where he was wounded again – was made an honorary citizen of a town he had liberated. In the mid 1930s, Dirlewanger went to Spain with the German Condor Legion, fought on the side of Franco's Nationalists and again was decorated. Finally, in World War II he rose to the rank of *SS-Oberführer*[7] and commanded first a battalion, regiment and finally an SS division.[8]

In many respects Dirlewanger was a lightning rod in the Byzantine power struggles inside the SS. He was constantly praised by the likes of *SS-Obergruppenführer* Gottlob Berger one of the most powerful men in the SS main headquarters. He received glowing efficiency reports from *SS-Brigadeführer* Odilo Globocnik, an architect of the "Final Solution" – the Nazi plan to exterminate the Jewish people. *SS-Obergruppenführer* Erich von dem Bach-Zelewski, the SS chief of all anti-partisan forces, submitted Dirlewanger for the German Cross in Gold, a prestigious military award. Yet there were enemies. *SS-Gruppenführer* Friedrich Krüger, the Higher SS and Police Leader for occupied Poland wanted to throw Dirlewanger in jail in 1942. Wilhelm Kube, the Reichs Commissioner for White Russia, and an honorary *SS-Gruppenführer,* was abhorred by a report of hogs devouring half-burnt human bodies – after the *Sonderkommando* set fire to a barn full of captured partisans. In another incident, a tenacious SS investigator, who had brought about a conviction and subsequent execution of a concentration camp commander, stalked Dirlewanger for almost the entire war attempting to prove a case of race defilement against him. Yet, *SS-Brigadeführer* Franz Breithaupt, who was later promoted to *SS-Gruppenführer* and chief of the SS Legal Department – under whose auspices these investigators operated – recommended Dirlewanger for promotion. Earlier, an angry *Gauleiter* dismissed him from the Nazi Party during his prosecution for statutory rape in the mid-1930s. Yet several short years later, the Lord Mayor of his hometown of Würzburg publicly praised Dirlewanger for his wartime exploits.

Introduction

Some high ranking Nazis, especially at the Nürnberg Trials, claimed they did not really understand the mission or the organization of the unit. But the SS was proud of Dirlewanger, a convicted sex offender, while the army – traditionally a bastion of proper conduct and decorum – often looked the other way with regard to Dirlewanger and his unique combat unit. Adolf Hitler, *SS-Reichsführer* Heinrich Himmler and other Nazi leaders developed and supported the *Sonderkommando* and frequently mentioned Dirlewanger's exploits to other Nazi leaders. The following is part of a speech Himmler gave in 1944 to his assembled *Gauleiters* (Nazi district leaders) in the city of Posen in occupied Poland:[9]

> In 1941 I organized a 'poacher's regiment' under Dirlewanger...a good Swabian fellow, wounded ten times, a real character – bit of an oddity, I suppose. I obtained permission from the Führer to collect from every prison in Germany all the poachers who had used firearms and not, of course, traps, in their poaching days – about 2,000 in all. Alas, only 400 of these 'upstanding and worthy characters' remain today. I have kept replenishing this regiment with people on SS probation, for in the SS we really have far too strict a system of justice...When these did not suffice, I said to Dirlewanger...'Now, why not look for suitable candidates among the villains, the real criminals, in the concentration camps?'...The atmosphere in the regiment is often somewhat medieval in the use of corporal punishment and so on...if someone pulls a face when asked whether we will win the war or not he will slump down from the table...dead, because the others will have shot him out of hand.

This was high praise indeed from the most powerful man in the SS. However, such was the nature of the shifting sands of power in Nazi Germany that one day later, the *SS-Reichsführer* issued a written letter of reprimand to Oskar Dirlewanger.

The German people knew of Dirlewanger and the activities of his unit, to a degree, simply by reading the newspaper. For example, the *Schwarze Korps*, a German wartime magazine which reported on the activities of the Waffen-SS, published this article about him on November 16, 1944:[10]

> The road of the 49-year old *SS-Oberführer* Oskar Dirlewanger was always the battle against destruction and Bolshevism. He fought in several *Freikorps*, led the armored train against Max Hölz and belonged to the Condor Legion. When you see him you cannot tell that he has been wounded eleven times, once very severely during World War I. In this war he has been so successful in leading his unit against Bolshevik bandits that the Soviets put a high price on his head. When the insurrection in Warsaw started, *SS-Oberführer* Dirlewanger led his men in the battle for houses and streets of the city with unbelievable severity and tenacity. The Führer rewarded their fighting and the personal combat of their commander by awarding the Knight's Cross of the Iron Cross to *SS-Oberführer* Dirlewanger.

As alluded to above, Hitler knew of the activities of the Dirlewanger *Sonderkommando*, and talked about these exploits with other Nazi leaders. On August 20, 1942, for example, the Führer ate lunch with Dr. Hans Lammers, State Secretary in the Reich Chancellery, and Dr. Otto Thierack, the Reich Minister of Justice. During the mid-day discussions Hitler stated:[11]

> A poacher kills a hare and goes to prison for three months! I myself should have taken the fellow and put him into one of the guerrilla companies of the SS. I am no admirer of the poacher, particularly as I am a vegetarian; but in him I see the sole element of romance in the so-called sport of shooting. Incidentally, there is no doubt that we number quite a few poachers among the most stalwart adherents of the Party.

Introduction

Later in the war, during the Warsaw Uprising, Hitler again publicly discussed the *Sonderkommando*. Colonel General Heinz Guderian, then Chief of the General Staff, had received reports that Dirlewanger and his men had committed horrible atrocities in quelling the revolt. At a staff meeting Guderian urged Hitler to withdraw the unit from the fight. Hitler refused to accept Guderian's advice even after an SS general, Hermann Fegelein, corroborated the reports.[12] This is a strong indicator that Hitler did not disapprove of Dirlewanger's conduct during the Uprising. Days later Hitler displayed even more support by giving final approval for the issue to Dirlewanger of the Knight's Cross, Germany's highest award for bravery and military achievement – the award of which, incidentally, had been endorsed by several army generals in the chain of command of Army Group Center.

The Dirlewanger unit was mentioned in the daily reports of the Wehrmacht only twenty-three times during the entire war; twice in November 1944, fifteen times in December 1944, five times in February 1945, and once in April 1945.[13] This is not many entries considering the *Sonderkommando* was in existence for over twelve hundred days during the war. Despite the periodic reports in newspapers, most of the activities of the unit, like those of the SS mobile killing squads were not publicized. They were not publicized because Hitler, Himmler and other Nazi leaders did not want them to be. In a speech made at Posen on October 4, 1943 to a select audience of SS leaders, *SS-Reichsführer* Himmler stated why not:[14]

> I also want to talk to you quite frankly on a very grave matter. Among ourselves it should be mentioned quite frankly and yet we will never speak of it publicly...I mean the evacuation of the Jews, the extermination of the Jewish race. It is one of the things it is easy to talk about. 'The Jewish race is being exterminated', says one party member, it is quite clear, it is in our program – elimination of the Jews; and we are doing it, exterminating them...Most of you know what it means when a hundred corpses are lying side by side or five hundred or a thousand. To have stuck it out and at the same time

– apart from exceptions caused by human weakness – to have remained decent men, that is what has made us hard. This is a page of glory in our history which has never been written and is never to be written.

Himmler was wrong concerning the forbidden written history. The Germans kept meticulous records, and it is this documentation that survived the war, which forms the basis of this book. The German organizations created and filed hundreds, thousands and even tens of thousands of documents describing all facets of the war. And these records, which undoubtedly would have horrified Heinrich Himmler, had he survived – fell for the most part intact to the allies.

Three sets of records in particular form the basis for this work. Microfilmed after the war, and currently on file in the National Archives of the United States in Washington D. C., the first set is known as microfilm set T-175, *Records of the Reich Leader of the SS and Chief of German Police*. Four records from this set detail the activities of the *einsatzgruppen* – the mobile SS death squads who killed hundreds of thousands on the eastern front, and which the Dirlewanger unit assisted, as well as records of the Higher SS and Police Leader for whom Dirlewanger worked. They include daily status reports, daily orders, personnel transfers, logistics requests and awards presentations. The terms that appear in these reports are at first glance benign – "cleansed", "handled", "special action", etc. But the meanings are the same – murder.

The next set of records is known as Microfilm Publication A3343, *Records of SS Officers from the Berlin Document Center*, Series SSO. These SS officers' service records consist of the personnel dossiers for more than 61,000 SS officers with the rank of second lieutenant and above. The date span of the records contained in the dossiers extends from 1932 to as late as March 1945 in some cases. While there are nine-hundred and nine rolls in this set, parts of forty-eight detail the lives of every officer known to be assigned to the unit and the lives of higher SS officials who came in contact with both the organization and Dirlewanger. These records are truly an open book into the careers of these men and include court-martial proceedings, promotions, recommendations for awards, transfers, assignment instructions, letters of reprimand, medical histories and family background.

Introduction

The last set of records contain three rolls of film that are particularly applicable to Dirlewanger and his unit – but despite their small size, they are the most important of all. Known as Microfilm T-354, *Records of the Waffen-SS*, reels 648, 649 and 650, they consist of daily reports, radio messages, telegrams to and from the unit, logistics correspondence, battle reports, casualty lists, personnel rosters and details information – from how many partisans or "suspects" were killed in a certain fight, to how many guard dogs were required to track the enemy, to how many bottles of schnapps Dirlewanger charged for shipping captured Russian girls to SS officials in Berlin. In short, they are the wartime operational diary of the *Sonderkommando*. These reports start in 1940 and end in 1944 just before the Warsaw Uprising.

The gaps which exist between the actual German files are filled quite accurately with material from many sources; but three stand out. Matthew Cooper's *The Nazi War Against Soviet Partisans* presents an excellent backdrop to the German anti-partisan effort in Russia. *Der Warschauer Aufstand 1944*, by Hanns von Krannhals, is one of the most complete sources on the 1944 Warsaw Uprising in print. Finally, the premier source for the Nürnberg War Crimes Trial is obviously the *Trial of the Major War Criminals before the International Military Tribunal*, published by the Allied Control Authority for Germany in Nürnberg, Germany in 1948.

For fifty years the exploits of Oskar Dirlewanger and his unique anti-partisan unit lay dormant in the dark recesses of history. It is time they saw the light of day.

ENDNOTES

[1] Cooper, Matthew. *The Nazi War Against Soviet Partisans*. (New York: Stein and Day, 1979), p.98.

[2] This work will generally use the term Sonderkommando as the designation for Dirlewanger's unit; the formation underwent seven name changes throughout the war (see Appendix 5).

[3] Ibid. p.98.

[4] Stein, George H. *The Waffen-SS: Hitler's Elite Guard at War, 1939-1945*. (Ithaca, N.Y: Cornell University Press, 1966), p.268.

[5] Meyer, Gertrud. *Nacht über Hamburg*. (Frankfurt/Main, FRG: Röderberg Verlag, 1971), p.125.

[6] Some Russian sources put the figure as high as 150,000.

[7] As this work is primarily a story about the SS, all SS ranks will be presented in their German form. All other ranks will appear in English. For definitions of these SS ranks see Appendix 1.

[8] The 36th Waffen-SS Grenadier Division was created in February 1945 from SS Sturm Brigade Dirlewanger. See Appendix 5 for various unit designations throughout the war.

The Cruel Hunters

[9] Cooper. *The Nazi War,* p.88.

[10] Personalakt Oskar Dirlewanger, Washington, D.C: National Archives Microfilm Publication A3343, Records of SS Officers from the Berlin Document Center, Roll SSO-154.

[11] Trevor-Roper, H. R. ed. *Hitler's Table Talk, 1941-1944.* (London, England: Weidenfeld and Nicolson, 1953), p. 640.

[12] Guderian, Heinz. *Panzer Leader.* (Washington, D.C.: Zenger Publishing Company, 1979), p.356.

[13] November 23 and 24, 1944, December 3, 10, 11, 12, 14, 15, 18, 21, 22, 23, 24, 26, 27, 28, 31, 1944, February 14, 15, 16, 17, 18, 1945, and April 15, 1945.

[14] Reitlinger, Gerald. *The SS: Alibi of a Nation 1922-1945.* (London: Arms and Armour Press, 1984), p. 278. The best account of the secrecy surrounding the Final Solution, and how this policy came into being, is found in Richard Breitman's *The Architect of Genocide: Himmler and the Final Solution.*

1

A MONSTER IS BORN

"Better to shoot two Poles too many than two too few."
- Gottlob Berger, June 1942.[1]

The story of Oskar-Paul Dirlewanger and his unique unit did not begin in World War II or the years leading up to it, but rather at the end of the 19th century in central Germany. Dirlewanger – the central character in this story – was born September 26, 1895 in Würzburg, Germany. He was the son of August Dirlewanger, an attorney, and Pauline Herrlinger Dirlewanger. The Dirlewanger family had four children and seemed quite typical for the time. Young Oskar attended grade school and high school and passed the matriculation examination known as the *Abitur*. There is no record in his SS personnel file of any juvenile disciplinary problems he may have experienced.[2]

Dirlewanger had an outstanding military record in World War I. Entering the Army in 1913, he was assigned to the machine-gun company of the 123rd Infantry Regiment and was posted to the front in Belgium at the beginning of the war in 1914. He was wounded twice on August 22, 1914, shot in the foot and sabred in the chest. On August 23, 1914 he was again wounded, receiving shrapnel wounds to the head. Dirlewanger received the Iron Cross 2nd Class on August 28, 1914 and spent almost four months in various field hospitals recovering. On April 14, 1915 Dirlewanger was promoted to lieutenant and subsequently served as a platoon leader until November of 1916. On September 7, 1915 he was shot in the hand and bayoneted in the right leg. On October 4, 1915

Dirlewanger was awarded the Württemburg Bravery Medal in Gold. As a result of these many wounds, he spent five months in several military hospitals at Trier and Esslingen. On July 13, 1916 he received the Iron Cross 1st Class. During December of 1916 Lieutenant Dirlewanger served on the staff of the 7th Infantry Division. The first three months of 1917 saw Dirlewanger back at the front-lines as the commander of the assault company of the 7th Infantry Division before moving to take command of the 2nd Machine-gun Company of the 123rd Infantry Regiment. He would lead this unit until October 1918. On April 30, 1918 he was shot in the left shoulder. By this time the unit was in southern Russia and served in the occupation of the Ukraine. At the end of the war he was placed in temporary command of the 2nd Battalion 121st Infantry Regiment. Following the official end of hostilities, he led his unit from southern Russia through Romania, Hungary and Austria to Germany.[3] This was indeed an impressive military record for a junior officer.

After the war, Dirlewanger continued his military ways when he joined the *Freikorps* (Free Corps). The paramilitary *Freikorps*, composed of former officers, demobilized soldiers, military adventurers, fanatical nationalists and unemployed youths, vowed to combat Social Democrats and Communists believed responsible for Germany's postwar plight. While receiving no official support or designation from the former Imperial Army, the various *Freikorps* frequently assumed the name of their commanding officer. By this time, Dirlewanger was twenty-three, a heavy drinker who smoked twenty cigarettes a day. At this point in his life, fighting may have been the only "career" he felt comfortable with. He fought against the Communist general strike in 1919, fought in civil actions in the cities of Backnang, Kornwestheim, Esslingen, Untertürkheim, Aalen, Schorndorf, and Heidenheim near Stuttgart, in the Ruhr at Dortmund and Essen in 1920 and in eastern Germany in 1920 and 1921. During this period Dirlewanger committed several offenses which twice landed him in jail. He served in *Freikorps Epp*, *Freikorps Haas*, *Freikorps Sprösser* and *Freikorps Holz* during this period and was once again wounded (this time in the head) on April 12, 1921. That year he was the commander of an armored train that helped in the liberation of the town of Sangerhausen.[4]

Dirlewanger also resumed his studies after World War I, returning to a trade school in Mannheim for a time in 1919, and seemingly balancing his studies with his service in the *Freikorps*. He took his graduate exam there in March 1921 and then transferred to the University of Frankfurt. His personnel file states he received a doctorate degree in economics from this prestigious institution. Dirlewanger originally joined the Nazi Party in October 1922 with a party number of 12,517. During the November 1923 Beer Hall Putsch, Dirlewanger attempted to drive some armored cars, owned by the Stuttgart police authorities, from Stuttgart to Munich. Shortly after the putsch, he allowed his membership in the party to lapse. He rejoined the party for the second time in 1926 with a new party number of 13,566. However, he subsequently joined a Jewish-owned clothing firm in Erfurt from 1928 to 1931 and left the party once again. In 1931 Dirlewanger became a tax accountant. He rejoined the Nazi Party for a third time on March 1, 1932 and received a party number of 1,098,716 and later in the year joined the SA (*Sturmabteilung*), the Nazi Storm Troops, holding several low level positions in this organization. The following year he began work in the employment office at Heilbronn.[5] This was probably a position reserved for a combat veteran, which certainly qualified Dirlewanger for the post.

Dirlewanger's reputation from the *Freikorps* years continued not only to follow him, but also to bring him renewed accolades. In 1934 Dirlewanger became an honorary citizen of Sangerhausen due to his exploits there in 1921 during an attempted Communist takeover of the town. The *Heilbronner Stadt-Chronik*, a local newspaper, reported the event on May 31, 1934.[6]

PARTY DIGNITARY DIRLEWANGER NAMED HONORARY CITIZEN OF THE TOWN OF SANGERHAUSEN

In many circles, people nowadays hardly remember the times when the Red Bandits and Communists were present in our country. On Easter Saturday of 1921, the Communist leader Max Hölz established the dictatorship over the citizens of Sangerhausen. This dictatorship first consisted of stealing from all public banks, establishing new laws, taking prisoners and removing numerous hostages. Under threat of death, all citizens of Sangerhausen were ordered to hand over all weapons, motorized vehicles and bicycles. In case of resistance from the police, it was warned that the town be burnt down.

The administration of that time, which was practically powerless against these bandits as is well known, remember fondly in such cases old officers who had served at the front and were proven fighters. And in those days, the Armored Train Dirlewanger, who by the way was the first military formation with the swastika flag – since 1921, was ordered to advance to Sangerhausen. Dirlewanger made a quick end to the "Dictators of the Proletariat." After heavy fighting with hand grenades and machine guns, during which Dirlewanger himself was wounded and which lasted until 2 o'clock at night, Dirlewanger's troops succeeded to put the Hölz bandits into flight. During this fight, 22 of his 42 comrades were wounded and one was killed.

This extraordinary deed which certainly would have led to the deaths of all his soldiers had they failed, prompted the council of the town of Sangerhausen, with the consent of the Prussian Minister President, to make the leader of the armored train, Party dignitary and retired first lieutenant Dirlewanger an Honorary Citizen. It should be mentioned briefly that Dirlewanger was also badly served, as happened to many fighters for the Fatherland at that time. Shortly after his return from Sangerhausen, this man – who had been wounded three times during the War and also in Sangerhausen, was imprisoned in Mosbach [Baden] because of crimes against the de-armament law. However, such punishment could not deter Dirlewanger from his plans and his firm will to work for the liberation of the Fatherland. Two days after his release from the prison he rushed again to Upper Silesia in order to do his soldier duties as a fighter in the *Freikorps*. It is without a doubt that Dirlewanger has earned everlasting rewards in the post-revolutionary history of Württemberg. Everywhere where trouble with communists sprang up, the armored train of Dirlewanger appeared, fought against them and defeated them. Up to 1933, Dirlewanger served as a simple SA-man in the rows of the Brown Army of Adolf Hitler.

We congratulate our Party comrade on the occasion of his being named Honorary Citizen and hope that for many years to come he will be able to do his duty in the old spirit. It is especially men like him who, when it is necessary to risk their lives and their own existence, we need in order to realize the great aim of our Führer.

Dirlewanger seems to have been successfully settling into middle age by this time. He had risen to deputy director of the labor office. This was a steady job – employment which many Germans did not have during these days of the depression. He was a member of the party and the SA. He had a distinguished military record and was somewhat of a minor celebrity based on his *Freikorps* exploits. All that was about to change. In July, as part of an SA demonstration, he stormed the labor office in Esslingen and was wounded in the ensuing fighting with police. He was subsequently charged with civil disturbance. Dirlewanger appears to have been a disruptive influence not only to the police, but also to the local SA organization, and soon had a run-in with the district leader (*Kreisleiter*). Gottlob Berger, a prominent leader in the SS, described the confrontation during testimony at the Nürnberg Trial after the war.[7]

Then he [Dirlewanger] got into a quarrel with his *Kreisleiter*...These quarrels arose because this *Kreisleiter* directed money from the Winter Aid Scheme for his own purposes...Now Dr. Dirlewanger was hardly a good boy. You can't say that. But he was a good soldier, and he had one big mistake that he didn't know when to stop drinking. On such an occasion in 1935 [sic 1934] the *Kreisleiter* brought him into a very unpleasant situation and he [Dirlewanger] was convicted for indecent assault upon a minor and sentenced to 2 or 2 1/2 years imprisonment.

Party transcripts, however, show a somewhat different story. The police arrested Dirlewanger on the night of July 14/15, 1934, after an alcohol-related binge, for several crimes including having sex with a minor, driving under the influence and leaving the scene of an accident. While we do not know his motivation for this spree, it is possible that Dirlewanger was depressed and confused over the arrest and execution of Ernst Röhm, the national leader of the SA. Röhm was murdered on Hitler's orders on July 1, but initial reports were that he committed suicide. On July 14th the story broke that, in fact, Röhm had been shot and killed during an abortive uprising against Hitler.[8] In any case, Dirlewanger's activities were serious offenses, even for members of the Nazi Party. Almost immediately, even before the judicial proceedings had run their course, the SA moved to expel Dirlewanger from the organization. The following is a transcript of the official recommendation from Dirlewanger's SS personnel file:[9]

SA Group Southwest Stuttgart, August 8, 1934
Reference: Expulsion of Dirlewanger
To Supreme SA Leadership, Munich

The group makes the application for the immediate permanent expulsion from the SA of *Sturmführer* [equivalent to a lieutenant] Oskar Dirlewanger, Heilbronn, be arranged due to violation of Articles 7 e, f and g.

A Monster is Born

REASONS

According to the leader's questionnaire, *Sturmführer* Dirlewanger joined the SA on April 1, 1932. He was the deputy director of the Labor Office of Heilbronn. During the last days of the month of July he was taken into custody by judicial authorities because of a crime against Paragraph 176 of the State Penal Code. Immediately he was relieved from his duties as Deputy Director of the Labor Office. Concurrently there are two further complaints against Dirlewanger pending at the Judicial Offices of Heilbronn because in one and the same night he drove the official car of the Labor Office into a ditch while completely drunk; on this occasion, a female passenger was severely hurt and he fled the scene of the accident.

Several months ago Dirlewanger was granted absence from Brigade 155 and a suit was entered against him because within circles of dissatisfied elements within the SA, he agitated against the commander and the staff of the brigade. Dirlewanger especially got involved with the notorious troop leader Steimle who was sentenced by the courts in Heilbronn to five months imprisonment, and who is currently serving this time in the prison at Ulm. Dirlewanger led a clique of SA-men in Heilbronn who confuse the expression "National Socialism" with "National Bolshevism" and who are not willing to act disciplined. In addition, Dirlewanger immediately agitated against the newly elected *Oberführer* [SA senior colonel] Ziegler in an unbelievable manner and attempted to stir up misgivings against him within the SA. If *Oberführer* Ziegler is supposed to establish some order in Heilbronn, where the circumstances within the SA have not been too pleasant, then Dirlewanger must go. Furthermore, it is not true that within the SA there exist bad feelings against

Oberführer Ziegler and his staff. This bad atmosphere only exists within a small, undisciplined circle around Dirlewanger and Steimle. It is significant to note that Dirlewanger requested through an acquaintance, the Representative of the Leadership Staff of the NSDAP [Nazi Party], Häring, to be promoted to *Standartenführer* [SA colonel] in the then Upper Group V, even though he has only been in the SA since 1932 and even then only doing lax service. Dirlewanger was recently made an honorary citizen by the village of Sangerhausen. Now, Dirlewanger has been taken into custody because he repeatedly had sex in the official car of the Labor Office with girls who were less than 14 years old.

Dirlewanger has become completely unbearable for the reputation and discipline of the SA in Heilbronn. He has set a bad example through his actions so that in the interest of the reputation of the SA he must be immediately expelled. Therefore, the group makes the application to have Dirlewanger removed from the SA and this expulsion decision should be handed down as soon as possible because the matter cannot be postponed in the interest of the reputation of the SA. The trial for moral crimes will soon take place whereby Dirlewanger undoubtedly will be sentenced to several years in prison.

The Führer of SA-Group Southwest

Regardless of the politics involved, the police booked Dirlewanger for the following: During the night from July 14th to July 15th, 1934, he caused two accidents while driving an official vehicle and he behaved immorally with a girl of less than 14 years old, i.e. one Anneliese _____ (last name known but omitted by author). The Higher Court of the State Court in Heilbronn tried Dirlewanger and sentenced him to two years imprisonment by on September 21, 1934. He served his punishment from January 11, 1935 to October 12, 1936 in the state penitentiary

Ludwigsburg. Upon his release on October 12, 1936 Dirlewanger went on parole until October 31, 1939.

While in prison, Dirlewanger was also thrown out of the Nazi Party. Morals violations with minors were substantial crimes in the Party, which otherwise often tolerated other excesses. These proceedings occurred in February 1936 and are documented once again in his SS file:[10]

> Party District Court Stuttgart, February 26, 1936
> Württemberg-Hohenzollern
> of the NSDAP
>
> In the case under investigation against: Dr. Oskar Dirlewanger, former director of the Labor Office of Heilbronn, presently in the State Penitentiary of Ludwigsburg former party member number 1,098,716, because of violation of Paragraph 4 Article 2a & c of the Law, the third chamber of the Party District Court has today been in session, participants were: E. Fischer, E. Angst and Th. Stöckler.
>
> **RESOLVED**
>
> 1.) The person charged has violated Paragraph 2a and c of the Law.
>
> 2.) The District Court requests that the former disposition of the *Gauleiter* of August 1, 1934 be maintained.
>
> **REASONS**
>
> The person charged has filed his protest, correct in form and in timely fashion. However, the protest has no foundation. In the prior proceedings, the person charged was accused of the following:
>
> 1. He used the official vehicle of the Labor Office of

Heilbronn for private use for which he was not authorized.

2. During the night from July 14th to July 15th, 1934, he caused two accidents while driving the official vehicle.

3. He has displayed undignified behavior towards female farm hands during the time between July 12th and 15th, 1934.

4. At the occasion of a social evening of the Labor Office on July 15, 1934, he violated the curfew.

5. He knowingly has made false statements to the criminal police of the State Police and to the chief of the examining board of the State Labor Office.

6. He attempted to coerce the female, who was hurt in the car accident on July 15, 1934, to make false witness statements.

7. He has behaved immorally with a girl of less than 14 years old, i.e. Anneliese _____, of Heilbronn, which is interpreted as a crime by the provisions of Paragraph 176 Article 3, State Penal Code.

The most severe accusation is 7 above, together with 2 above the subject of criminal proceedings at the ordinary court.

Even before these criminal proceedings were completed, the SA Special Court of the Highest SA Leadership has ordered that effective August 30, 1934 Dirlewanger be relieved of his duties and stripped of his rank, thereby permanently excluding him from the SA, with the justification that he was proven guilty of immoral behavior and that for this reason he had already lost his position as Director of the Labor Office in Heilbronn. His bad conduct and his punishable actions – a car accident in drunken state, while causing a passenger to become hurt, and leaving the scene of the accident make him unworthy to be a SA leader.

The proceedings of the District Court were binding until the legal proceedings of the criminal court were concluded. With a sentencing by the Higher Court of the State Court of Heilbronn dated September 20/21, 1934, the accused was sentenced to two years imprisonment because of a crime of morality with persons under 14 years of age. His protest was rejected by the State Court. Therefore, the sentencing of the Higher Court stands.

On the basis of this sentence, it is clear that the accused who had not had a prior record has used Anneliese _____, born on _____, 1920, from Heilbronn, four or five times in the period of February to mid-July 1934 in order to satisfy his sexual appetite. On one of the car rides which led to sexual activities, she was wearing her *Jungmädel* uniform (member of the youngest female party cadets) as a member of the *BDM (Bund deutscher Mädel)*. In addition to this, the accused led an immoral life. He had maintained relations, which led to sex, with several other women, among them the 20-year old leader of the *BDM* group of Heilbronn.

In the legal sentencing it is further stated that during several trips in the night of 14th/15th of July 1934, he caused no less than five injuries to persons and a series of damages due to the effect of alcoholic beverages. There was no punishment for this since the suit was halted by the use of the law for granting freedom from punishment as of August 7, 1934. With this, it is proven that the accused violated items 2 and 7 of the party laws. In view of the severity of the punishable action and the lowly nature of the crimes, as well as inferior character which shows from his action, the accused – despite his unquestionable efforts for the NSDAP – could not be granted mitigating circumstances. Whoever sins against our female youth in such shameful way has no longer any place in the NSDAP. Besides these severe moral sins, the items under 1, 3, 4, 5 and 6 of the prior disposition have no weight any longer. Therefore, the District Court has decided not to further examine these points and to end the investigation.

This decision may be questioned in front of the Highest Party Court. The reclamation must be made within eight days, starting from the day of issue, at the Party District Court Württemburg/Hohenzollern, Stuttgart, Kronprinzstrasse 2a, and must be justified within these eight days. If no application is made, the decision becomes legally binding.

With the hindsight of many years it appears as though the actions against Dirlewanger were a reasonable response to serious infractions of the law. But not everyone felt offended by Dirlewanger's outrageous conduct. Berger again commented on the affair at the Nürnberg Trial:[11]

The condemnation was absolutely unjust. Scarcely was he [Dirlewanger] out of jail when he reported to me at the Ministry of Education. He blew his stack. It was in 1937. I explained to him quite clearly, "This is the last time. All this comes from your drunkenness." He had not left me very long without news when I heard from someone else that he had been arrested again and jailed. He had applied for the reopening of the proceedings and *Gauleiter* Murr, the brother-in-law of this *Kreisleiter*, was not at all interested in reopening the proceedings and so they were kind enough to simplify

A Monster is Born

the affair, to take him to the private concentration camp of the *Gauleiter* in Welzheim, Württemberg. Thereupon I turned to Himmler in a teletype, to the Higher SS and Police Leader, and they had enough sense of justice to intervene and fetch him out again the next day. Then I sent him to Spain.

Gottlob Berger seemed to serve as a guardian angel for Oskar Dirlewanger throughout the years of the Third Reich. Berger was born July 16, 1896 in Gerstetten, Württemberg. From 1910 to 1914 he studied to be a teacher in the town of Nürtingen. At the outset of World War I, Berger volunteered for military service and was posted initially to the 127th Infantry Regiment and shortly thereafter to the 247th Infantry Regiment. He was wounded on October 31, 1914 in the ankle – the first of four wounds he would receive during the conflict. In 1915 he fought at Ypres and was wounded in the back on March 18, 1915 and in the stomach on October 4, 1915. On November 6, 1915 he was promoted to lieutenant. In 1917 he transferred to the 476th Infantry Regiment, where he served as a battalion adjutant. In June 1918 he was wounded by grenade shrapnel. During the war Berger received numerous decorations. On November 26, 1914 he was awarded the Iron Cross 2nd Class. On May 21, 1915 he received the Württemberg Military Service Medal in Gold. On January 21, 1918 he won the Iron Cross 1st Class. Berger received the Military Service Knight's Cross on May 4, 1918 and the Wound Badge in Silver on June 18, 1918. Just as the war ended, he also received the Friedrich Order with Swords. He was retired from the service on July 13, 1919 as a first lieutenant from the 124th Infantry Regiment.[12]

Berger entered the Nazi Party for the first time in 1922. He was imprisoned in 1923 on a weapon's violation. He rejoined the party on January 1, 1931 and received a party number of 426,875. On January 30, 1936 Berger joined the SS and received membership number 275,991. He immediately received the rank of *SS-Oberführer* and became a major SS functionary for southwest Germany. Berger was married with four children. He continued his rise in the SS and was promoted to *SS-Brigadeführer* on April 20, 1939 and *SS-Gruppenführer* on April 20, 1941. He became the chief of the *SS-Hauptamt*, the SS Main Office, in 1940 and received his final promotion to *SS-Obergruppenführer* on June 21, 1943. In this position, Berger was in charge of recruiting young men for SS service; more importantly, he was widely regarded as being an inner confidant of *SS-Reichsführer* Himmler. Berger received more decorations in World War II. On July 1, 1941 he received the War Service Cross 1st Class. In 1942 he was awarded the Commander's Cross of the Order of the White Rose of Finland. On January 30, 1943 he received the Nazi Party Badge in Gold. On July 1, 1943 he acquired the German Cross in Silver.[13] He was captured by the allies at the end of the war.

The *Gauleiter* served as the highest ranking Nazi party officials below the top Reich leadership. The thirty-three *Gauleiter* supervised all political, economic, mobilization of labor and civil defense activities in their districts. Hitler directly appointed most to their position. The *Kreisleiter* were one notch below the *Gauleiter*, and were the lowest salaried officials in the party. They had similar responsibilities for their *Kreise*, or circuit. There were thirty-five *Kreis* in *Gau* (district) Württemberg-Hohenzollern.

Wilhelm Murr had been *Gauleiter* of Württemberg-Hohenzollern since 1928 and was a tough man to tangle with. By 1937 he served on the staff of *SS-Reichsführer* Himmler. He remained a high functionary in the Nazi Party throughout the war before committing suicide by biting a cyanide capsule on May 14, 1945.[14] In addition to being a *Gauleiter*, there was another problem for Dirlewanger in the presence of Murr – he was an *SS-Gruppenführer*. Murr had joined the Nazi Party on August 6, 1925 and received an early party number of 12,873. On September 9, 1934 he joined the SS as well as member 147,545 and was immediately made an *SS-Gruppenführer*. Gottlob Berger could not assist his old comrade at this time because he was still not a member of the SS. Dirlewanger would have to go it alone.[15]

Released from prison on October 11, 1936, Dirlewanger then attempted to get his case reopened and apparently raised the wrath of the *Gauleiter* as he was placed in protective custody in Welzheim from February 14th to March 19, 1937. Soon after his release from Welzheim, Dirlewanger went to Spain with the Condor Legion on the advice of Gottlob Berger.

A Monster is Born

Hitler detailed the Condor Legion, a unit of the Luftwaffe, with ground forces as well, for special duty during the Spanish Civil War. Their mission was to support *Generalissimo* Francisco Franco and his Spanish Nationalist forces. The Luftwaffe contingent was the largest element and consisted of flak troops, bomber units, fighter units and reconnaissance elements. The Army contingent was much smaller; initially composed of roughly a battalion comprised of a headquarters staff, two line companies and a field maintenance company. The Germans were armed with forty-one Mark I tanks, twenty anti-tank guns, eight 20mm cannon and ten command cars. The tank force, which deployed to Spain in September 1939, came to be code named *Drohne* (drones) and had the mission of training Spanish tank combat and maintenance crews. They were not to directly engage in battle, although this was not always the case. The actual German instructors were known as *Imker* (beekeepers). Over nineteen thousand German personnel rotated through the Condor Legion from September 1936 to May 1939. Several hundred German soldiers were killed in action or died in accidents or of illness.[16]

Dirlewanger initially served in Spain from April 1937 until November 1937. Then, the long arm of *Gauleiter* Murr learned of Dirlewanger's military activities in Spain with the Condor Legion, and apparently arranged for him to be taken prisoner in Toledo for "political unreliability" and for his transport back to Germany under the escort of a Gestapo officer. But Dirlewanger now had some allies of his own – powerful allies. The commander of panzer troops in Spain, Colonel Ritter von Thoma, worked hard for Dirlewanger's return to Spain. *SS-Standartenführer* Viktor Brack of the Chancellery of the Führer also helped. It is likely that Gottlob Berger, now in the SS and an *SS-Oberführer*, may have also assisted his old friend. Shortly thereafter, Dirlewanger returned to Spain.

Dirlewanger apparently performed well in Spain. On November 20, 1939 Colonel Ritter von Thoma wrote a statement describing Dirlewanger's performance while serving with the Condor Legion:[17]

> Dr. Oskar Dirlewanger served with me from April to October 1937 and from July 1938 to May 1939 in the training camp as a company commander, and during these seventeen months was outstanding working in training.

The Cruel Hunters

Dirlewanger received three decorations for his service in Spain. From Spain he received the Spanish Campaign Medal, as did all members of the Condor Legion, and the Spanish Military Service Cross. From Germany, he received the Spanish Cross in Silver. The German High Command awarded approximately eight thousand Spanish Crosses in Silver to German personnel who served in the Legion. Recommendations for this award had to generate from the *Oberkommando der Wehrmacht (OKW)*, with approval from Hitler. It is thus apparent that the OKW, which was not in any way controlled by the SS, chose to overlook Dirlewanger's previous offenses and submit him for this decoration.[18]

However, back in Germany, Dirlewanger was still being punished for his conviction. On May 30, 1937 a decision of the University of Frankfurt stripped Dirlewanger of his academic degree, a Ph.D.

In 1938 the *Sicherheitsdienst (SD)*, the intelligence branch of the SS, investigated Dirlewanger while he was serving in Spain. We do not know who ordered this investigation. It could have been initiated by *Gauleiter* Murr – perhaps to uncover more evidence against Dirlewanger for use in future proceedings. Or conceivably Berger wished to uncover additional information which would exonerate his friend. The following is the SD characterization of Dirlewanger's political suitability, again as shown in his SS personnel file:[19]

> Dirlewanger participated in the war from 1914 to 1918. In 1914 he was slightly injured and in 1915 he was heavily injured, became 40% disabled and was assigned to permanent office duty. He volunteered to go back into the field of battle and became leader of an machine-gun company. In 1918 he was injured again. He is the owner of the Iron Cross 1st and 2nd Class, as well as the Golden Medal for Bravery issued by Württemberg. In November 1918 he led the 2nd Battalion of the 121st Infantry Regiment back home from Southern Russia, thus saving it from impending imprisonment.
>
> During the postwar years, Dirlewanger participated in most battles against communist insurrections as

leader of an armored train and again exposed his life without any reservations. Twice (in 1920 and in 1921) Dirlewanger was imprisoned for political reasons because his participation in the removal of weapons was revealed. In 1921 Dirlewanger was again wounded, suffering a head wound, in his fight against the bandits of Hölz, in the termination of the general strike of 1919, in communist revolts in Backnang, Kornwestheim, Esslingen, Untertürkheim, Aalen, Schorndorf, Heidenheim; outside of Württemberg in Mannheim, Iserlohn, Dortmund, Sangerhausen. He was a member of the *Freikorps Epp*, *Haas* and *Sprösser*. In the year 1935 he was made Honorary Citizen of Sangerhausen as the liberator from the Red terrorists. In 1921 as a student at the Mannheim commercial college he received the "consilium abeundi" "for proven anti-Semitic instigation." In 1922 he received his doctorate – political science – at the University of Frankfurt.

In 1919 Dirlewanger became a member of the protection and defense association. On the occasion of the Munich Athletic Days in 1923, Dirlewanger joined the Party. During the Hitler-Putsch of November 9, 1923 he did not succeed in driving the armored cars of the police of Stuttgart to Munich. In 1926 he rejoined the NSDAP with a membership number 13,566. He discontinued his membership because from 1928 to 1931 he was the director of a Jewish knitting factory in Erfurt. In this capacity, he was a consistent donor of money to the SA there. In March of 1932 he went to Esslingen and immediately rejoined the Party and the SA. He became leader of the *Sturmbann* [battalion equivalent] I/122; and in July of 1932, while storming the union building in Esslingen, he was wounded and had to face the State courts in Stuttgart for civil disturbance. In 1933, in the program to find employment for old warriors, he was made Deputy Director of the Labor Office Heilbronn. In July 1934 he was taken to prison because of acts of immorality and was sentenced to two years of prison by the State Court Heilbronn. The head of Higher Court was State Judge Schliz. The sentence was sharply attacked from various sides and Justice Wild at the court in Heilbronn accused Judge Schliz of definitely bending the law, expressed in a letter to the Federal Ministry of Justice. After his release from prison on October 11, 1936, he worked on the re-opening of his case by writing to any possible official offices, and because he would not let the matter drop, he was placed in protective custody in Welzheim from February 14th to March 19, 1937. In order to make a judgment about this whole matter, it is necessary to take a look at the files. After his release, he went to the national army in Spain and again proved himself to be an extraordinary soldier.

Despite his sentence, Dirlewanger must be called absolutely reliable as far as politics are concerned. Due to his convictions and his entire past it is practically impossible for him to stand on the side of the enemies of our world philosophy. He is not bound by any religious adherence. It would be utterly desirable for Dirlewanger to be allowed to return to Spain so that he would have a chance to rehabilitate himself.

Dirlewanger returned from Spain in June 1939 with the rest of the Condor Legion. He could see that the war, which had come to a conclusion in Spain, would soon spread in Europe and wanted once again to serve Germany. One month after returning to Germany, Dirlewanger, on July 4, 1939, sent a letter to Himmler requesting admission into the Waffen-SS.[20]

Reichsführer!

In case of mobilization, I request that I be allowed to march with the SS. The following prompts my request: for the time being, I want to refer to the enclosed copy of a political evaluation of myself by the SD, at the upper region South-West of May 14, 1938, which documents my military and political career; the original can be found in my files at the Chancellery of the Führer, at the offices of Reich Chancellery Department Leader *SS-Standartenführer* Victor Brack. I would like to add the following remarks: my conviction at that time had personal and political reasons. Even though I did wrong, I never committed a crime. After I served time as my punishment, I instituted the renewal of the court case and submitted to high party administrations unquestionable documents of highly placed party functionaries from Württemberg to demonstrate the background of the trial against me and the actual reasons for my sentencing, I was then forbidden to contact the Chancellery of the Führer orally or in writing or to apply for a hearing at the regular courts regarding the slander against me. Even though I obeyed this strange order, three days later I was taken into protective custody at the prison of Welzheim. When the then *SS-Oberführer*, now *SS-Brigadeführer* Gottlob Berger who was at that time working in Stuttgart, heard about it, he immediately arranged for my release, because he, as well as many other older party members in Württemberg, knew the real reasons as well as my being sentenced and about my being taken into custody. I had lost my belief in right and justice and also my belief in the State, the foundation of which was also laid with my blood. The *SS-Oberführer* dissuaded me to reach for the pistol, but recommended that I should atone for my wrongdoing through a renewed effort for

Greater Germany and thus shame my adversaries. Through his intervention I went to Spain in March of 1937 joining the Spanish Foreign Legion at first[21]; later I succeeded in joining the Condor Legion. My commander at that time, Colonel Ritter von Thoma, as well as my battalion commander during the World War, Colonel Knörzer whom I met again in Spain, are willing to testify that I have dutifully served as a soldier.[22] When my former adversaries learned about my military activities in Spain within the Condor Legion, they arranged for my being taken prisoner in Toledo in November of 1937 because of "political unreliability" and for my transport back to the homeland under the escort of a Gestapo officer. After my arrival in Berlin, General Willberg of the Luftwaffe explained that he regretted my departure from the Condor Legion, especially since the fitness reports which had been presented by my military superiors in Spain demonstrated that I had a good record. I immediately contacted the Chancellery of the Führer, despite the existing ban, with the request for complete clearing of the whole matter after the Spanish war was over and the request for being allowed to return to the Condor Legion. Because the commander of panzer troops, Colonel von Thoma, also worked hard for my return to Spain, I was again ordered to the Condor Legion through the intervention of the Chancellery of the Führer (*SS-Standartenführer* Brack), acted again in my duties and returned to the homeland last month with the Legion.

The renewed court case which will result in my complete rehabilitation is presently worked on at the Chancellery of the Führer. However, in the opinion of professional lawyers, another two or three months may pass before the renewed court actions will exonerate me completely again. I have done my duty during the war and in fights during the revolution and also later as

A Monster is Born

SA-member and was always there where men were needed. It would be unbearable for me to just sit around while German soldiers are marching somewhere. For this reason I am requesting that I be allowed to march with the SS, even in case mobilization occurs before my court case has been heard. In conclusion I would like to add that I had the honor to meet you, *Reichsführer*, already during 1932. I was ordered by you to meet you at the Brown House in Munich and reported to you at that time that in case of interior political conflicts during the assumption of power I together with my comrades would occupy the armored train stationed in Württemberg and that it would be made available unconditionally to the party. At that time, you ordered me to ascertain the location of the remaining 11 armored trains in the country as well as the philosophical attitude of the crew and that I should report to you in writing addressing my reply to a professional engineer acting as a cover. I did this at that time.

H e i l H i t l e r !
Your devoted
Dirlewanger

Dirlewanger's request was initially denied in Berlin because of his conviction in 1934. He received this reply, dated August 19, 1939 which gave indications that the decision was perhaps not final, but could be reexamined at a later date based on the ongoing appeals process:[23]

The *Reichsführer-SS* has been presented with your letter of July 4, 1939. He is hereby informing you that he cannot grant your wish to march with the SS in case of mobilization because the results of the court proceedings for your rehabilitation, as you have requested, must be resolved. However, the *Reichsführer-SS* is of the opinion that, in view of your having been an former member of the Condor Legion, you would be allowed to volunteer in any department of the Wehrmacht in the case of serious developments.

• • •

During 1940 another action was ongoing concerning the possible formation of a new special unit. On the afternoon of March 23, 1940 *SS-Reichsführer* Heinrich Himmler's adjutant, *SS-Gruppenführer* Karl Wolff placed a telephone call to an advisor to the Reichs Minister of Justice. Wolff told the startled bureaucrat that it was Hitler's wish to grant an amnesty for selected poachers for the purpose of sending them to the front. [24] *SS-Gruppenführer* Wolff added that a letter outlining this subject in greater detail would be sent by *SS-Reichsführer* Himmler the following day. The advisor, one Herr Sommer, made a note of the call and informed the ministry's secretary of state Dr. Roland Freisler. Freisler, a hard-core Nazi and later President of the People's Court, ordered that the names of all poachers in custody should be identified immediately.[25]

The request for information on the poachers went out with typical German thoroughness to every county prosecutor for the name and sentence of offenders of Statute 292 of the German penal code or Statute 60 of the Reich hunting regulations. Violators were to be grouped into three categories; group one – those poachers convicted of their crime, sentenced to serve time in jail and who were in fact serving their sentence, group two – those sentenced to serve time but for some reason had not done so; and group three – those poachers who had received suspended sentences for minor poaching offenses. For all three groups more information was requested; family and surname, date and place of birth, terms of punishment, portion of punishment already served and so forth. When all was said and done, the German criminal system throughout the Reich identified two hundred twenty persons in group one, two hundred seventy-six in group two and seven hundred thirty-five in group three.[26]

The Ministry of Justice received *SS-Reichsführer* Himmler's letter on March 30, 1940; and the correspondence amplified Hitler's intent. The Führer wanted only those poachers who had hunted with firearms and not those who had used traps or snares. Second, Hitler was primarily interested in Bavarian or Austrian poachers as opposed to those from other areas of the Reich. The letter also stated that the former poachers would be organized into a special sharpshooter company. As the correspondence came from Himmler it could logically be inferred that this new company would fall under the SS.[27]

On April 4, 1940 representatives of the *Reichssicherheitshauptamt* (the Reich Main Security Office) and the Ministry of Justice met to work out the details of exactly which criminals were eligible to be transferred to the new unit. Supreme Court Justice Carl Westphal and assistant judge Stumpf of the ministry had many complex questions to be answered. Was there to be an upper age limit for the prisoners? What if a prisoner had also been convicted of other types of crimes? Was there a maximum limit of the sentence above which the prisoner was not eligible for release? What about the strict code of admission into the SS? Was the SS interested in obtaining only a list of offenders or did they want the prisoner's complete personal and legal file as well? Did the Ministry of Justice have any say in who was to be released? Criminal director Dr. Wiese of Department V of *SS-Oberführer* Artur Nebe's Reich Main Security Office did not have the answers but would get them.[28]

The answers were quick in coming. At 4:30 PM that afternoon Dr. Wiese telephoned Justice Westphal with the SS position. The SS would retain the right to make all final decisions concerning the prisoners. There would be no upper age limit for men accepted into the program. The SS also wanted to know if any of the convicts had attacked game wardens during the commission of their crime. Poachers who had received suspended sentences would not be accepted. The SS wanted habitual and professional offenders, not one-time "amateurs." The SS would review the files of all potential candidates.[29]

On April 10, 1940 these new guidelines went out and over the next several months the SS identified a total of eighty-four poachers as suitable for the program. In June these men transferred to the Sachsenhausen concentration camp, located twenty-five miles north of Berlin along the Hohenzollern Canal in the town of Oranienburg. There they began receiving training as members of "*Wilddiebkommando Oranienburg*" (Poacher Commando Oranienburg).[30]

Sachsenhausen was one of three concentration camps which formed the nucleus of the German penal camp system. Sachsenhausen attended to northern Germany, Buchenwald served central Germany and Dachau covered southern Germany. An *SS-Standartenführer* commanded each. Sachsenhausen held a special relationship with the *Sonderkommando* throughout the war. The Nazis established the camp in September 1936 under the initial camp commandant, the notorious Karl Koch.[31] It was intended that ten thousand prisoners would fill the camp at any given time but by war's end over sixty thousand were crammed inside its barbed wire. Unlike many other concentration camps, Sachsenhausen was a public camp. Oranienburg industry depended heavily on camp labor. Arriving prisoners marched from the central railroad station through residential and industrial areas to the lager. Sachsenhausen also held numerous notable prisoners. Dr. Martin Luther, a former Foreign Office Department chief was incarcerated here as was Dr. Kurt Schuschnigg, the former chancellor of Austria. Josef Stalin's son, who became a prisoner of war when Germany invaded the Soviet Union, was killed in the camp.

Sachsenhausen also held a large number of homosexuals. Homosexual behavior was considered a crime in Germany. In 1943 Himmler

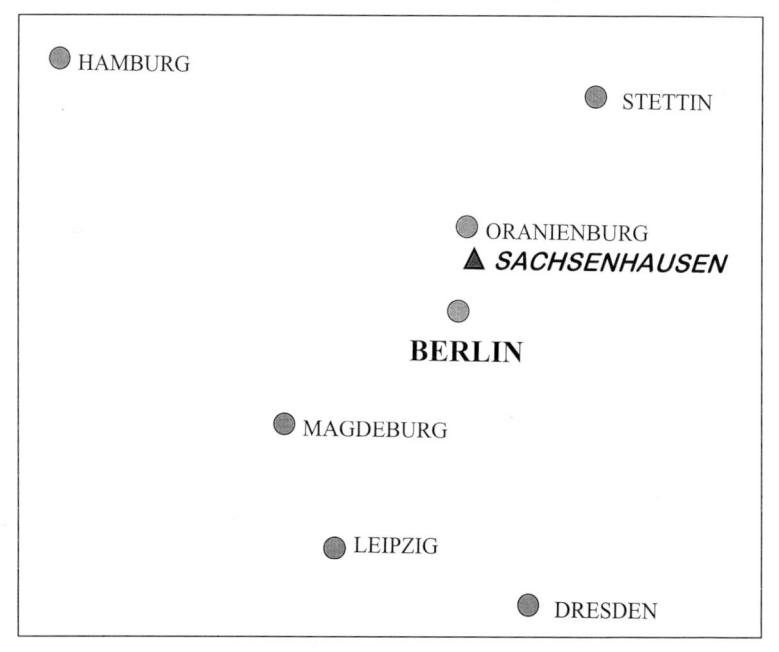

○ HAMBURG

○ STETTIN

○ ORANIENBURG
▲ *SACHSENHAUSEN*
○
BERLIN

○ MAGDEBURG

○ LEIPZIG

○ DRESDEN

A Monster is Born

published a decree that proscribed the death penalty for any member of the SS or police convicted of this offense. Sachsenhausen proved a lethal camp. Over one hundred thousand victims perished in Sachsenhausen before it was liberated by Soviet troops in 1945.[32]

At the Nürnberg Trial, Gottlob Berger gave a somewhat different view of the proceedings which led to the formation of the unit. He stated:[33]

> The Dirlewanger Brigade owes its existence to an order of Adolf Hitler, an order given in 1940 while the campaign in the West was still going on. One day Himmler called me up and told me that Hitler had ordered all men convicted of poaching with arms who were at present in prison were to be collected and formed into a special detachment. That Hitler should have such a somewhat unusual and far-fetched idea at all is due to the following reason: First of all, he himself didn't like hunting and had nothing but scorn for all hunters. Wherever he could ridicule them he did. In the second place, at this time he received a letter from a woman whose husband was a so-called 'Old Party Member.' He shot his stags in the National Forests. He was caught in the act and that's how he landed in prison for a couple of years. The woman complained that her husband was in jail and asked that he be permitted to prove himself at the front. That was the basis...Thereupon, in accordance with my orders, I got in touch with the Chief of the Reich Criminal Office, Nebe. We agreed that at the beginning of the late summer all suitable men should be sent to the barracks at Oranienburg.

Berger's testimony was flawed. Hitler's decision certainly came before March 23, not during the campaign in the West which started in May 1940. And the Nazis would not have classified the so-called "Old Party Member" as a habitual offender. Berger's tale makes more sense when we consider he undoubtedly had one eye on gaining an acquittal in his own trial – the more that could be totally blamed on a dead Führer, the better.

45

• • •

Meanwhile, Dirlewanger's case was proceeding as well. Dirlewanger successfully overturned his conviction from six years previous. On May 20 the district court for Württemberg-Hohenzollern issued its final ruling.[34]

> In the matter against Oskar Dirlewanger, Ph.D., born on September 26, 1895 in Würzburg, with earlier residence in Heilbronn, now in Esslingen, Kesselwasen 16, party membership number 1,098,716; the Third Chamber of the District Court Württemberg-Hohenzollern has declared it legal to resume the proceedings according to the application by the NSDAP received on April 30, 1940 in today's session, participated in by: H. Mühlhäuser, Dr. W. Klamm and S. Joos
>
> I. The application of the accused for resumption of the trial is admissible.
>
> II. The trial of February 26, 1936 which was legally concluded is being reopened.
>
> III. The decision of the District Court dated February 26, 1936 is being rescinded.
>
> IV. The trial will be discontinued.
>
> **JUSTIFICATION**
>
> I. On April 30,1940, the accused sent a letter with the following contents to the District Court:
>
> "Through the decision of the deputy *Gauleiter* I was expelled from the Party on August 1, 1934. After I complained, the District Court applied for keeping this de-

A Monster is Born

cision intact, and my expulsion became effective on March 27, 1936 after the State Courts in Heilbronn pronounced the sentence against me. At that time I did not voice my complaint with the Highest Party Court since it was clear to me that this would not have brought positive results while the sentence by the penal Chamber of Heilbronn was in existence. I could not consider to file a petition of grace because I was sentenced wrongfully and I only strove to have things righted by a resumption of the trial. Today I was exonerated by the Higher Court of the State Court in Stuttgart. Therefore, I apply that the party court proceedings connected with it be resumed and I request that my membership in the NSDAP be restored. In view of the fact that I have suffered great financial damage due to the wrongdoing by the State, I request that the membership dues which were payable since my expulsion are to be waived. Of course, I will gladly pay the party membership dues from May 1, 1940 on and I would be especially grateful for a swift treatment of my application."

II. The District Court, recognizing the newly emerged circumstances of this application for resumption of the trial came to the following conclusions:

The accused was born on September 26, 1895 in Esslingen. In June of 1913 he graduated from the secondary school in Esslingen and after this he served as volunteer with the Grenadier Regiment 123 in Ulm and went with this regiment to war at the outbreak of the war in August 1914. He served with this regiment and Infantry Regiment 121 until the end of the war, was wounded four times and finally released with a rating of 40% disability due to the war. Having been awarded the Iron Cross 1st and 2nd Class and the Golden Medal of Bravery from Württemberg, he was promoted to First

Lieutenant of Reserves when he was released. His studies at the commercial college in Mannheim which he started in 1919 were concluded with the diploma-exam in March 1921. In August 1922 he received his Ph.D. (political science) from the University of Frankfurt and was employed in various positions up to 1931. Until July 1933, he worked as an independent tax accountant. Then he was employed by the Labor Office of Heilbronn, where he first was a department head and later in 1934 he became deputy director.

In the postwar years the accused fought in various *Freikorps* (Epp, Haas, Sprösser) and participated in an outstanding manner in the defeat of communist rebellions in Württemberg, Thüringen and Westfalen. In the cleaning of the town of Sangerhausen (Thüringen) at Easter of 1920 he earned as leader of a armored train such awards against the bandits of Max Hölz that this town named him Honorary Citizen in 1933. In October of 1922 the accused joined the NSDAP with a membership number 12,517. But then he had to leave the party due to an imprisonment which was the result of wrongdoing in connection with the de-armament law. On March 1, 1932 he joined the NSDAP again and received membership number 1,098,716. In April of 1932 he was also admitted to the SA, in which he was promoted to *Scharführer* on August 2, 1933 and to *Truppführer* on August 4, 1933. On November 9, 1933 he became *Sturmführer*, after he had already become the leader of the *Sturmbann* I/122 on August 15, 1933.

III. On July 21, 1934, the police directors of Heilbronn were informed that the accused was going on car trips with a minor girl from the Heilbronn Girls' School, where supposedly immoral acts took place. In the course of the proceedings against him, he was booked and finally after the sentencing by the Higher Court of the

State Court in Heilbronn, he was sentenced to two years imprisonment for crimes of immorality with persons under 14 years of age. As far as other accusations were made, they were dropped. The sentencing for immoral acts had especially severe consequences for the accused. By a sentencing of the SA Special Courts in Munich he was expelled from the SA on August 30, 1934 due to crimes against morality. On August 3, 1934 he was expelled from the party by a temporary decree of the Deputy *Gauleiter* of the NSDAP of Württemberg-Hohenzollern. After the sentencing by the Penal Chamber of Heilbronn against the accused became legally binding, the District Court on February 26, 1936 applied for the adherence to the decision by the Deputy *Gauleiter* of August 1, 1934, whereby the Deputy *Gauleiter* expelled him from the Party on March 27, 1936. Besides the loss of his employment at the Labor Office of Heilbronn, he was forbidden by the respective military authorities on May 26, 1937 to wear the uniform of a reserve officer of the former 123rd Grenadier Regiment "König Karl" and he was forbidden to use the title of First Lieutenant of Reserves (retired). By decision of the University of Frankfurt on May 30, 1937, he was stripped of his Ph.D.

The accused served his sentence from January 11, 1935 in the State Penitentiary Ludwigsburg. He was released on October 12, 1936 with a parole period to October 31, 1939. From the very beginning, the accused maintained that he did not know the correct age of this girl and he insists that she told him that she was a student at the vocational technical school and was going to be 17 years old very shortly. During the time in prison, where he conducted himself well, he fought against the sentence by the Higher Court of the State Court of Heilbronn which had destroyed his life and his future, and he attempted to prepare for the resumption of the proceedings. After he was released from prison, he continued these efforts. In April 1937 he went to Spain in order to fight in the Civil War on the side of the national government. With the exception of 9 months, he was active from April 1937 to May 1939 in Spanish recruiting camps mostly as company leader and excelled at the front in an outstanding way. As a member of the Condor Legion he returned to Germany from Spain after the war was over. For his contributions, he was awarded the Spanish Cross in Silver.

Even before returning from Spain he worked again on the resumption of his trial. Also the State Courts in Heilbronn joined his application to consider the resumption of the trial as valid. After the necessary documents were obtained, the Higher Court of the State Court in Stuttgart made application on March 26, 1939 and the resumption of the trial was ordered. During the General Assembly on April 29/30, 1940 in front of this Higher Court of the State Court serving as Youth Protection Chamber of the State Courts in Stuttgart, the sentence of the Higher Court of the State Court of Heilbronn, dated September 21, 1934, by which the accused was sentenced to two years of prison due to crimes of immorality involving a child, was nullified. The accused was exonerated, and the costs of the proceedings were charged to the state treasury.

IV. In recognition of these established circumstances by the District Court through legal files, the resumption of the proceedings at the Party Court is also ordered. After the reasons were nullified, which caused the Deputy *Gauleiter* to expel the accused in August of 1934 from the NSDAP, and after the heavily burdening sentence by the Higher Court of the State Court of Heilbronn were nullified, the decision by the District Court of February 26, 1936 must also be nullified. As the accused was then also burdened with other accusations against Paragraph 4, Article 2b of the law, a resumption of party court proceeding is not necessary. With the evidence presented, the discontinuation of the trial is ordered. Only the *Gauleiter* has the right to question these decisions. Due to the fact that the political leaders did not counter-argue, the decision arrived at is legally binding.

Dirlewanger had finally won. The *Stuttgarter NW-Kurier* published the verdict on Saturday, May 25, 1940:[35]

EXONERATED AFTER SIX YEARS

The former chief of the Labor Office of Heilbronn, Dr. Oskar Dirlewanger of Esslingen was sentenced on September 22, 1934 by the Greater Judicial Authorities of Heilbronn to two years imprisonment because of indecent assault. Based on new testimony, the individual who was sentenced petitioned the reopening of the case. The Public Prosecutor agreed to have the case reopened. During the renewed hearings at the Courts in Stuttgart, another picture emerged through testimony by new witnesses which caused the representative to petition that the question of guilt be brought before the court to reexamine it. The Courts in Stuttgart struck down the sentence by the Heilbronn court of the year 1934 and, due to sufficient proof, recognized the exoneration, while also charging the cost involved to the Treasury of the State.

Events now started to steamroll. Armed with the results of these latest judicial developments, on June 4, 1940 *SS-Brigadeführer* Gottlob Berger wrote to *SS-Reichsführer* Himmler recommending Dirlewanger for admission into the SS as soon as possible, with an eye on leading the unit of poachers. Berger wrote:[36]

> Some time ago First Lieutenant Dr. Oskar Dirlewanger (of the Reserve Corps) addressed himself to the Reichs Leader with the request to be inducted into the Waffen-SS. In a purely political trial in 1935, Dr. Dirlewanger was sentenced to 2 years' imprisonment in a penitentiary on a charge of a "sexual offense." After serving his sentence he was released and attempted to reopen the case, whereupon he was taken into protective custody at Welzheim by the *Gauleiter* and Reich Governor, and only my personal intervention prevented a new breach of justice. Since Dr. Dirlewanger conducted himself well during the postwar years and in the NSDAP after 1930, and since I was acquainted with his selfless service, I made it possible for him to enter the Condor Legion. After the end of the war in Spain he returned to Germany, reopened his case and was then acquitted unconditionally. In spite of his war injuries Dirlewanger desires to be utilized at the front. I request that his wish be granted as far as possible. I should like to be permitted to suggest that the training of those persons who have been previously punished for poaching be entrusted to him, since he has received modern training in every respect. Then he is to lead these men at the front.

Himmler apparently agreed. On June 17, 1940 *SS-Sturmbannführer* Rudolf Brandt, a member of Himmler's personal staff, issued the following instructions to the Replacement Office of the Waffen-SS:[37]

> The Reichs Leader agrees to the transfer of Dr. Oskar Dirlewanger into the Waffen-SS as an *SS-Obersturmführer.* The Reichs Leader also approves of transferring to Dr. Dirlewanger the training of persons previously punished for poaching. I request you to take the necessary steps as far as these two matters are concerned.

A Monster is Born

Berger was still concerned that Dirlewanger might be taken into the army rather than the SS, which we have seen was described to him as a possibility in August 1939. On June 22, 1940 Berger wrote the following letter to the SS replacement bureau in an attempt to speed up Dirlewanger's formal admission into the SS:[38]

> I request that First Lieutenant of the Reserves, Dr. Oskar D i r l e w a n g e r be taken over by the Waffen-SS as soon as possible. His release from the Wehrmacht has already taken place. Based on the letter from the Chancellery of the Führer, the OKW intended to occupy him as Captain of Reserves. As far as I am concerned, the transfer as only an *SS-Obersturmführer* was suggested to the *Reichsführer-SS*, while a promotion can always take place after he has proven himself. Dr. Dirlewanger has a contemporary education and has especially proven himself in battle while in the Condor Legion in Spain. He should be tasked with the selection of convicted poachers for their education and service at the front.

Berger's persistence and high connections paid off. On June 24, 1940, Oskar Dirlewanger received the following letter admitting him into the Waffen-SS.[39]

> After having been presented the application for admittance into the Waffen-SS, the *Reichsführer-SS* has decided that you will be admitted to the Reserve of the Waffen-SS in the *Schutzstaffel* with the rank of *SS-Obersturmführer der Reserve* and that you will be transferred to active duty in a *SS-Totenkopfstandarte* in Oranienburg near Berlin. If you agree with this arrangement, kindly report to the SS Personnel Main Office this or next week to complete the necessary admittance documents and transfer to your unit.

Again, testifying at Nürnberg, Gottlob Berger had a somewhat different view of when Dirlewanger was selected to command the *Sonderkommando*:[40]

> ...In the middle of August [1940] I received this order to set up the brigade, and I had the somewhat foolish idea for me of suggesting Oskar Dirlewanger as leader but I told myself, "He himself is a courageous soldier. In the First World War he led his company in an outstanding manner with much personal understanding." At that time he was over 40 [actually 44], so one could assume that gradually he would become a little more sensible and to the best of my knowledge and conscience I proposed him.

At any rate, it appears that Berger suggested that Dirlewanger be named the commander of the unit, and sometime during the summer of 1940 Dirlewanger reported to his new command. In July, he received his first evaluation report which was quite glowing – considering he had been in the service only thirty days and had not yet had an opportunity to prove himself. Once again we see the powerful hand of Berger involved:[41]

PERSONNEL REPORT

of: *SS-Obersturmführer der Reserve*
Oskar Dirlewanger, Leader of a Special Command.

Party Membership Number: 1,092,492
SS Number: 357,267
Entered the service: July 1, 1940
Date of Promotion to most recent rank: July 1, 1940
Date, place of birth (district): September 26, 1895, Würzburg
Occupation by profession: Degree in economics
Current profession: SS-Leader
Residence: Oranienburg

A Monster is Born

Street: SS-Barracks
Married: No Maiden name of wife: —
Children: – Religion: –
Officially registered since: July 1, 1940
Previous convictions: none
Injuries, persecutions and penalties in the fight for the movement: shot in the head

EVALUATION

I. General evaluation:
1. Racial total picture: nordic
2. Personal bearing: very good
3. Appearance and behavior within and outside of the service: excellent
4. Financial condition: in order
5. Family relations: in order

II. Character: The rater was unable to fill out this portion of the form. However, he did state "I consider him suitable for promotion to *SS-Hauptsturmführer*."

On the report Gottlob Berger added "promote, winner of the Military Cross in Gold."

SS-Oberführer Hans Schwedler, Inspector of the *SS-Totenkopfverbände* (Death's Head Units) made this entry on the summary:

> Personally, Dirlewanger makes a very good impression. With his soldier-like appearance, he serves as a good example. Despite his short membership in the SS, I consider him suitable for promotion to *SS-Hauptsturmführer der Reserve*.

Finally, *SS-Brigadeführer* Franz Breithaupt also recommended Dirlewanger for promotion on the report. At the time Breithaupt was the leader of the 5th *Totenkopfstandarte* at Oranienburg.

The Cruel Hunters

The *SS-Totenkopfverbände* also held a special relationship with the *Sonderkommando* throughout the conflict. In 1935, sensing the need for a special branch of the armed SS to perform guard duties in the camps, Himmler charged Theodor Eicke, the Inspector of Concentration Camps and Commander of SS Guard Formations, with forming a guard unit at each camp outside the control of the *Allgemeine-SS* (the general SS). On March 29, 1936 these units were officially designated as *Totenkopfverbände*. In 1937 they underwent a reorganization and became *Totenkopfstandarten*. Originally there were three such units; *Oberbayern* stationed at Dachau, *Thuringia* at Buchenwald and *Brandenburg* at Oranienburg. The SS added more units later and gave the *Totenkopfstandarten* numerical designations.[42]

Franz Breithaupt, a key officer in the *Totenkopfverbände*, was a powerful figure in the SS. Born December 8, 1880 in Berlin, the son of a Prussian army officer, he served in World War I and won the Iron Cross 1st Class and the Black Wound Badge. He left army service as a major after the armistice. Breithaupt joined the Nazi Party and received membership number 602,663. Breithaupt joined the SS on December 1, 1932 with membership number 39,719. He was immediately made an *SS-Sturmbannführer* and became an adjutant to Heinrich Himmler. On November 9, 1938 he was promoted to *SS-Standartenführer* and in 1939 was named as leader of the 8th *Totenkopfstandarte* in Cracow. From there he transferred to Sachsenhausen. In 1941 he was promoted to *SS-Gruppenführer* and was named as the chief of the SS Legal Department (*Hauptamt SS-Gericht*). This organization applied the disciplinary and penal code to all SS and police personnel. He received his final promotion to *SS-Obergruppenführer* on April 20, 1944. Breithaupt was killed in a car accident in 1945[43] shortly before the end of the war.[44]

With these ringing endorsements it is not surprising that on August 1, 1940 Oskar Dirlewanger was promoted to *SS-Hauptsturmführer*.

• • •

On August 28, 1940 the Chief of Staff of the Headquarters of the Waffen-SS sent out a written order to the replacement battalion of the Waffen-SS Regiment "*Germania*", which at the time was a part of the SS

A Monster is Born

Verfügungs Division (later renamed SS Division "*Reich*"). The order requested that the replacement battalion transfer four junior non-commissioned officers "with good soldierly demeanor and appropriate trustworthiness" to *Sonderkommando Dr. Dirlewanger* at Oranienburg. They were to report for duty September 1, 1940 without weapons but did need to bring their gasmasks. The order also announced that on September 4, 1940 the Higher SS and Police Leader of Lublin, Poland, *SS-Oberführer* Globotznick [*sic* Globocnik] would be informed of their arrival.[45]

On September 1, 1940 the *Sonderkommando Dr. Dirlewanger* was renamed *SS-Sonderbataillon Dirlewanger* (SS-Special Battalion Dirlewanger). *SS-Obergruppenführer* Berger paid a visit to the men. He remembered there being two hundred eighty to three hundred present. Berger read Hitler's order and all the regulations concerning possible rehabilitation. The regulations provided the possibility for the men to have their status returned and their right to bear arms reinstated. He also said they could prefer to return to jail if they desired.[46] As Sachsenhausen was notoriously brutal, few men took him up on the offer to remain in confinement.

Some had no choice. Despite the infusion of some disciplined junior NCOs, several of the original poachers had not adjusted to their new way of life. On October 17, 1940 the *SS-Reichsführer's* office notified the Ministry of Justice that thirty-three of the men were unsuitable for their intended duties and would be returned to the judicial system for suitable disposition. These thirty-three transferred first back to the 5th *SS-Totenkopfstandarte* at Oranienburg and then back to the judicial districts from which they originally came.[47]

SS-Oberführer Hans Loritz served as Dirlewanger's host during this period as the commandant of Sachsenhausen. Loritz was born in Augsburg December 21, 1895. He served in World War I winning the Iron Cross 2nd Class. During the conflict Loritz transferred to the flying corps and was credited with eight bombing missions. Loritz joined the Nazi Party on August 1, 1930 and received membership number 298,668. He joined the SS one year later with SS number 4,165. Within one year of entering the SS, Loritz had risen to *SS-Sturmbannführer* and achieved his final promotion to *SS-Oberführer* on September 15, 1935. Loritz commanded the concentration camp at Dachau until 1939; he commanded at

Sachsenhausen from April 1, 1940 to September 1, 1942. Captured by the allies, Loritz committed suicide in January 1946.[48]

• • •

The SS ordered the *SS-Sonderbataillon Dirlewanger*, at this stage only a company in strength, to Poland. It initially constructed earthworks along the *Otto Line* (defensive works along the border with Russia) and then guarded a Jewish labor camp at Dzikow.

Again, Berger testified at Nürnberg to a different version of Dirlewanger's mission in Poland:[49]

> The brigade was to have a task within the area of the General Government, in particular in the very thickly wooded strip along the frontier of the German-Russian sphere of interest from Lvov to the San, that is a forested area covering about 180 kilometers long and 50 to 60 kilometers wide. In this area these men were to reinforce the German and Polish forestry personnel. There was a special reason for this. In 1939 before the Germans marched in, all prisons in Warsaw were opened. All professional criminals, many serving life sentences for robbery with murder, withdrew into this forested area. Every day we suffered losses there through snipers who picked off German and Polish forestry officials and German and Polish police officials. Far more Poles than Germans were killed...I didn't know anything about the employment of the leadership of the Jewish camp at Daikow [Dzikow]. It was not the task of that commando to supervise Jews or to supervise people for labor, or anything like that. They were to fight, man against man, in wooded areas. I don't know how long this commando stayed there.

A Monster is Born

No other testimony or historical source corroborates Berger's assertion of these events concerning released prisoners. It is far more likely that they were small units of the Polish army who had escaped the Germans in 1939 and were now forming an early resistance movement.

Later service during 1941 in Cracow netted the unit an inordinate number of convictions for looting and assault. From Cracow, Dirlewanger's unit went to Lublin, where Dirlewanger blackmailed and in general terrorized the ghetto. Dirlewanger's activities attracted the attention of a judge advocate of the SS Police Branch and an investigation was initiated.[50]

Despite the ongoing inquest, Dirlewanger's superior was pleased with his performance and wrote the following recommendation for promotion on August 5, 1941:[51]

> *SS-Hauptsturmführer der Reserve* Oskar D i r l e w a n g e r, born in Würzburg on September 26, 1895, was ordered from the 2nd SS Infantry Regiment Oranienburg as commander of the Special Commando Dirlewanger at this command post. During his activities in the construction of front-line trenches at Belzec and as commander at the Jewish camp of Dzikow, Dirlewanger has led his commando extraordinarily well. After completion of the front-line trenches at Belzec, he was made available to the SS and Police Commander at Lublin for special activities. In the fight against smuggling and illegal trade as well as against the Polish Resistance, Dirlewanger has an excellent record in all his activities and has always concluded his tasks with completely positive results. It is requested that *SS-Hauptsturmführer der Reserve* Dirlewanger be promoted to *SS-Sturmbannführer der Reserve.*
>
> *Odilo Globocnik*
> *SS-Brigadeführer*

The Cruel Hunters

On August 16, 1941 *SS-Gruppenführer* Berger sent a request endorsed by *SS-Obergruppenführer* Friedrich Krüger to the chief of the SS personnel department recommending Dirlewanger for promotion to *SS-Sturmbannführer*. On November 9, 1941 *SS-Hauptsturmführer* Dirlewanger was promoted to *SS-Sturmbannführer*.[52]

• • •

Despite the promotion, an SS investigator in Poland, Dr. Konrad Morgen, began to delve into these reports at the insistence of the Higher SS and Police Leader in Poland *SS-Obergruppenführer* Friedrich Krüger. Morgen testified after the war at Nürnberg about Dirlewanger's conduct during this period.[53]

> Dirlewanger had arrested people illegally and arbitrarily, and as for his female prisoners – young jewesses – he did the following against them: he called together a small circle of friends consisting of members of a Wehrmacht supply unit. Then he made so-called scientific experiments, which involved stripping

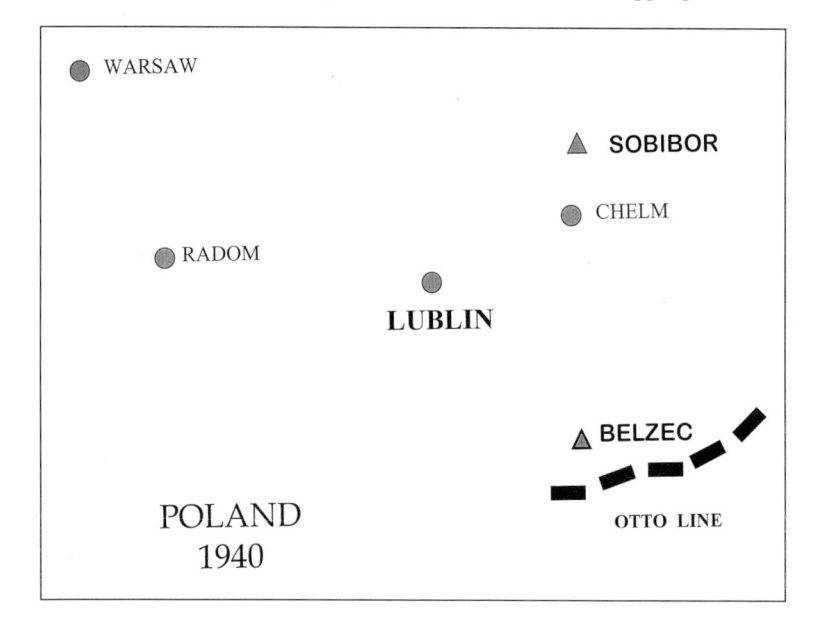

● WARSAW

▲ SOBIBOR

● CHELM

● RADOM

●
LUBLIN

▲ BELZEC

POLAND
1940

OTTO LINE

the victims of their clothes. Then they [the victims] were given an injection of strychnine. Dirlewanger looked on, smoked a cigarette, as did his friends, and they saw how these girls were dying. Immediately after that the corpses were cut into small pieces, mixed with horsemeat, and boiled into soap.

Dr. Konrad Morgen was a thorough investigator. Born in Frankfurt on June 8, 1909, he had studied law at the University of Frankfurt, at the Académie de Droit International at The Hague and at the Institute for World Economy and Ocean Traffic at Kiel. He passed his state bar examination on the first attempt and then served as a judge at the state court in Stettin. A specialist in international law, he joined the SS in 1933 while a member of the Reich Board for Youth Training. At the beginning of the war he entered the Waffen-SS, and ultimately rose to the rank of *SS-Sturmbannführer*. He was assigned to the Main Office SS Courts to the Reich Criminal Police Department in Berlin. He investigated over two hundred cases including those on five commanders of concentration camps. The SS found two of these camp commanders guilty and had them shot. Morgen specialized in prosecuting SS officials who misused their authority or conducted profiteering schemes. The SS was interested in efficient operations, not in furthering the personal gain of those involved in killing operations.[54]

The investigator appears to have been a brilliant man and a tenacious opponent. His SS personnel file states that he could speak French, German, English, Italian, Dutch and Spanish! At the time of the investigation Morgen was only an *SS-Untersturmführer*, but rank does not appear to have been an important aspect of criminal investigators in the Reich. Often Morgen got too close for comfort to senior SS leaders, who frequently responded with letters to Himmler asking for changes in Morgen's assignments.[55]

Morgen found other offenses as well. Many of Dirlewanger's soldiers had been involved in mistreating members of the civilian community and for plundering. Dirlewanger reportedly arrested numerous Jews on the charge of ritual murder; and then to have demanded up to 15,000 *zlotys* or the prisoner would be shot. He was also suspected of having sexual relations with a female Jew in Lublin. This was a violation of the Law for the Protection of German Blood and Honor, signed by Hitler in 1935. This law was designed to separate Germans and Jews and made it a crime for either marriage or sexual relations between members of these groups. Sexual intercourse was defined as *Rassenschande* or race defilement. The male partner in such a relationship could be confined in either jail or a concentration camp. To further clarify the issue the following order was issued on October 24, 1941 to all *Reichssicherheitsdienst* offices:[56]

> Lately it has repeatedly become known that, now as before, Aryans are maintaining friendly relations with Jews and that they show themselves with them conspicuously in public. In view of the fact that these Aryans still do not seem to understand the elementary basic principles of National Socialism, and because their behavior has to be regarded as disrespect toward measures of the state, I order that in such cases the Aryan party is to be taken into protective custody temporarily for educational purposes, and that in serious cases they be put into a concentration camp, grade I, for a period of up to three months. The Jewish party is in any case to be taken into protective custody until further notice and to be sent to a concentration camp.

At the Nürnberg Trial Gottlob Berger put this serious offense in perspective during his testimony:[57]

> You can see that this trial [Morgen's investigation] was started not because of cruelties, not because of robberies or spoliation, but because of race defilement, and that was just about the most dangerous thing that could happen to any SS man, being tried for race defilement...Whoever knows Globocnik...It is completely impossible that a man of such infernal sentiment would denounce one of his subordinates and start

A Monster is Born

a trial against him because he was cruel to Jews. That is impossible. That was considered as a special merit by this person [Globocnik].

SS-Brigadeführer Odilo Globocnik gathered up these and other reports of Dirlewanger's activities in Poland and flew from Lublin to Berlin on January 23, 1942 to present his case against Dirlewanger. The night before *SS-Sturmbannführer* Dirlewanger sent two teletype messages from the SS security office in Lublin to the SS Main Office in Berlin. The first was to *SS-Gruppenführer* Gottlob Berger, Chief of the Main Office. The communiqué stated that Globocnik would be flying to Berlin the following morning. Dirlewanger asked Berger:

Request that on all points of my rehabilitation, discussions of my men and the release of female Jews and their later use by my unit, you remain firm. New accusations are untrue and can be disproved if given time.

The second message went to Dr. Friedrich, an *SS-Untersturmführer* in the SS Main Office, and requested that Friedrich inform Berger of Globocnik's arrival and that the issue was not about Jewish females, but an issue of Dirlewanger's honor.[58]

Odilo Globocnik, the Higher SS and Police Leader of Lublin, Poland, was most certainly not appalled by Dirlewanger's conduct, as he had strongly endorsed his promotion, but probably simply wanted to protect his fiefdom for himself. He was born in Triest April 21, 1904. He entered the Nazi Party in 1931 and received a party number of 412,938. The following year he joined the SS. An Austrian, who had received a prison sentence in 1933 for the murder of a Viennese Jew, he served as the *Gauleiter* for Vienna from May 1938 to January 1939. However, he continued his criminal activities and in 1939 the Nazi Party stripped him of all honors for illegal speculation in foreign currency. However, Himmler pardoned his old friend and installed him as the highest SS authority in the Lublin district. Globocnik frequently circumvented the head of the General Government (formerly the bulk of Poland) Governor General Hans Frank, as he developed extensive SS economic enterprises in the

Lublin area. He later organized the *Operation Reinhard* death camps at Belzec, Sobibor and Treblinka and in 1943 went to Italy as the Higher SS and Police Leader for the Adriatic coast. He was awarded the Anti-Partisan Badge in Silver in September 1944. Odilo Globocnik committed suicide on May 31, 1945 to avoid capture by the British.[59]

Himmler created the positions of Higher SS and Police Leader (*Höhrere SS und Polizeiführer [HSSPF]*) by a decree in November 1937 for the purpose of promoting SS and police integration and to provide political direction in the various districts in Germany. In case of war, the HSSPF would take charge of all police forces. In occupied territories HSSPF forces would carry out assignments of a political nature, while remaining subordinate to army commanders in terms of supply, movement, and other logistical considerations. On May 21, 1941, Himmler defined the position further:[60]

> The Higher SS and Police Leader is placed in charge of SS and police troops and also of the operational personnel in the Security Police in order to carry out the tasks allocated to him by me personally.

The Higher SS and Police Leader for the General Government *SS-Obergruppenführer* Friedrich Krüger backed Globocnik. Morgen presented his evidence to Krüger and asked for assistance. However, Krüger informed the SS investigator that his hands were tied; he was not empowered to be the convening authority to bring Dirlewanger to trial as the *Sonderkommando* was directly subordinate to *SS-Gruppenführer* Berger and therefore did not fall under the judicial authority of an HSSPF.[61] But, he took the next best step. Krüger telephoned Berger in Berlin and denounced Dirlewanger stating:[62]

> [unless] this bunch of criminals disappears from the Government General within a week I will go myself and lock them up.

The SS was not a monolithic organization, and what followed was typical of the Byzantine power struggles within Himmler's apparatus.

A Monster is Born

Krüger and Globocnik lined up in opposition to Dirlewanger – who had Berger in support. Whatever the degree of discussions between Berger, Krüger and Globocnik, results and changes were swift in coming. On January 29, 1942 the Chief of Staff of the Headquarters of the Waffen-SS (*Kommandoamt der Waffen-SS*) within the SS Main Operational Office, *SS-Gruppenführer* Hans Jüttner immediately placed *Sonderkommando Dirlewanger* of the Waffen-SS under the control of the command staff of the *SS-Reichsführer.* Furthermore, after sufficient resupply and refitting – which would last until February 10, 1942 – the *Sonderkommando* would leave Poland and be transported to the command of the Higher SS and Police Leader of White Russia. Finally, as if to emphasize Dirlewanger's unique importance, the order stated that *SS-Sturmbannführer* Dirlewanger had been informed personally by Department Ia, SS-FHA of his departure.[63]

This was a significant order from a critical source, which belies the post-war claim that the *Sonderkommando* was not part of the Waffen-SS. The SS Main Office (*SS-Hauptamt* or *SS-HA*) controlled the entire SS establishment to include the Waffen-SS and the *Allgemeine* or General SS. This office evolved in the mid-1930s and controlled such functions as personnel, administration, medical, physical training, education, communications and so forth. As the *SS-HA* controlled all branches of the SS, it grew in both complexity and size. In 1942 it was scaled back somewhat as more and more of the SS became centered around the Waffen-SS. *SS-Gruppenführer* Kurt Wittje initially commanded the *SS-HA* until he was relieved for homosexual behavior.[64] Wittje was followed by *SS-Obergruppenführer* August Heissmeyer, who in turn was succeeded by *SS-Gruppenführer* Gottlob Berger in 1940. Berger's most important task remained the supervision of all Waffen-SS recruiting programs; recruiting for the *Sonderkommando* was obviously one of his more challenging duties. The SS Main Operational Office (*SS-Führungshauptamt* or *SS-FHA*) was essentially the headquarters of the Waffen-SS. Created in August 1940, it was designed to control the organization of field units of the SS and to monitor the training and replacement units of the Waffen-SS. It additionally looked after training schools of the Waffen-SS. The *SS-FHA* had two subordinate branches, the *Kommandoamt Allgemeine-SS*, which dealt with the general SS, and the *Kommandoamt der Waffen-SS*. The *SS-*

FHA was independent of the SS Main Office. As Dirlewanger's order came from the *SS-FHA, Kommandoamt der Waffen-SS*, it is clear that the *Sonderkommando*, at this point in time, was clearly considered a unit of the Waffen-SS proper, subject to control by the SS Main Operational Office.[65]

Berger had, at least temporarily, once again assisted his old friend. By not remaining in the General Government and also not returning to Germany, Dirlewanger and the *Sonderkommando* effectively thwarted Morgen's investigation for the time being. Instead, they would find an equally deadly and tenacious enemy in the forests of central Russia, an enemy that would neither ask for nor give quarter – the Soviet partisan.

ENDNOTES

[1] Reitlinger. *The SS: Alibi of a Nation.*, p.173.
[2] Personalakt Oskar Dirlewanger.
[3] Ibid.
[4] Ibid.
[5] Ibid.
[6] Ibid.
[7] *Trials of War Criminals before the International Military Tribunal, Volume XIII The Ministries Case, Case No. 11.* (Washington, DC: U.S. Government Printing Office, 1952), Volume XIII, p. 537.
[8] Halcomb, Jill. *The SA: A Historical Perspective.* (Columbia, S.C.: Crown/Agincourt Books, 1985), pp.71-72.
[9] Personalakt Oskar Dirlewanger.
[10] Ibid.
[11] *Trials of War Criminals before the International Military Tribunal, Volume XIII, The Ministries Case, Case No. 11,* pp. 537-538.
[12] Personalakt Gottlob Berger, Washington, D.C: National Archives Microfilm Publication A3343, Records of SS Officers from the Berlin Document Center, Roll SSO-058.
[13] Ibid.
[14] Höffkes, Karl. *Hitlers politische Generale: Die Gauleiter des Dritten Reiches.* (Tübingen, FRG: Grabert Verlag, 1986), pp. 239-240.
[15] Personalakt Wilhelm Murr, Washington, D.C: National Archives Microfilm Publication A3343, Records of SS Officers from the Berlin Document Center, Roll SSO-341A.
[16] Proctor, Raymond L. *Hitler's Luftwaffe in the Spanish Civil War.* (Westport, Connecticutt: Greenwood Press, 1983), pp. 41, 42, 253.
[17] Personalakt Oskar Dirlewanger.
[18] Angolia, John. *For Führer and Fatherland: Military Awards of the Third Reich.* (San Jose, CA: R. James Bender Publishing, 1976), pp. 31, 391, 394.
[19] Personalakt Oskar Dirlewanger.
[20] Ibid.
[21] Dirlewanger's claim of being in the Spanish Foreign Legion is undocumented in his SS personnel file.
[22] Colonel Hans Knoerzer was promoted to brigadier general in 1942 and brought back to active service. He ended the war as the military commander of the city of Freiburg.
[23] Personalakt Oskar Dirlewanger.
[24] poachers - men who hunt game illegally either without a hunting permit or without permission to hunt on a given piece of land.
[25] Seidler, Franz W. "SS-Sondereinheit Dirlewanger. Ein Sträflingsbataillon zum Einsatz im Kampf gegen Partisanen," *Damals*, 7/1977, (Giessen, Germany: Damals-Verlag), p.599.

A Monster is Born

[26] Ibid., p.600.
[27] Ibid.
[28] Ibid., p.601.
[29] Ibid., p.602.
[30] Ibid., pp. 602-605.
[31] Koch was executed during the war for graft.
[32] Feig, Konnilyn G. *Hitler's Death Camps: The Sanity of Madness.* (New York: Holmes & Meier, 1979), pp. 60-82.
[33] *Trials of War Criminals before the International Military Tribunal, Volume XIII, The Ministries Case, Case No. 11.,* pp. 534-535.
[34] Personalakt Oskar Dirlewanger.
[35] Ibid.
[36] *Trials of War Criminals before the International Military Tribunal, Volume XIII, The Ministries Case, Case No. 11.,* pp. 508-509.
[37] Ibid., pp. 509-510.
[38] Personalakt Oskar Dirlewanger.
[39] Ibid.
[40] *Trials of War Criminals before the International Military Tribunal, Volume XIII, The Ministries Case, Case No. 11.,* p. 538.
[41] Personalakt Oskar Dirlewanger.
[42] Höhne, Heinz. *The Order of the Death's Head: The Story of Hitler's SS.* (New York: Coward-McCann, Inc., 1970), pp. 454-457.
[43] One source states Breithaupt committed suicide.
[44] Personalakt Franz Breithaupt, Washington, D.C: National Archives Microfilm Publication A3343, Records of SS Officers from the Berlin Document Center, Roll SSO-104.
[45] Kommando der Waffen-SS/IIb/28.8.40 Message, Washington, D.C: National Archives Microfilm Publication T354, Roll 650.
[46] *Trials of War Criminals before the International Military Tribunal, Volume XIII, The Ministries Case, Case No. 11.* p. 535.
[47] Seidler. pp. 602-605.
[48] Personalakt Hans Loritz, Washington, D.C: National Archives Microfilm Publication A3343, Records of SS Officers from the Berlin Document Center, Roll SSO-278A.
[49] *Trials of War Criminals before the International Military Tribunal, Volume XIII, The Ministries Case, Case No. 11.,* pp. 536, 541.
[50] Reitlinger. *The SS: Alibi of a Nation,* pp. 172-173.
[51] Personalakt Oskar Dirlewanger.
[52] Ibid.
[53] Hilberg, Raul. *The Destruction of the European Jews.* (Chicago, IL: Quadrangle Paperbacks, 1967), p.623.
[54] *Trial of the Major War Criminals before the International Military Tribunal.* Nürnberg, Germany: Allied Control Authority for Germany, 1948, Volume XX, pp. 487-488.
[55] Personalakt Konrad Morgen, Washington, D.C: National Archives Microfilm Publication A3343, Records of SS Officers from the Berlin Document Center, Roll SSO-324A.
[56] Hilberg, Raul. *The Destruction of the European Jews (Revised and definitive edition).* (New York: Holmes & Meier, 1985), pp. 160-165.
[57] *Trials of War Criminals before the International Military Tribunal, Volume XIII, The Ministries Case, Case No. 11.* pp. 541-542.
[58] SS-Sonderkommando Dirlewanger, 22.1.42, Teletype Message, Washington, D.C: National Archives Microfilm Publication T354, Roll 650.
[59] Arad, Yitzhak. *Belzec, Sobibor, Treblinka: The Operation Reinhard Death Camps.* (Bloomington, IN: Indiana University Press, 1987), pp. 14-16, and Höffkes, Karl. *Hitlers politische Generale: Die Gauleiter des Dritten Reiches.* (Tübingen, FRG: Grabert Verlag), 1986.
[60] Headland, Ronald. *Messages of Murder: A Study of the Reports of the Einsatzgruppen of the Security Police and the Security Service, 1941-1943.* (London: Associated University Presses, 1992), pp. 138-139.
[61] Weingartner, James J. "Law and Justice in the Nazi SS: The Case of Konrad Morgen." *Central European History,* 16. (Atlantic Highlands, NJ: Humanities Press, 1983), p. 286.

[62] *Trials of War Criminals before the International Military Tribunal, Volume XIII, The Ministries Case, Case No. 11.*, pp. 508-509.
[63] Kommando der Waffen-SS/Ia/29.2.42 TGB Nr 524/42, Washington, D.C: National Archives Microfilm Publication T354, Roll 650.
[64] Höhne, Heinz. *The Order of the Death's Head.*, p. 145.
[65] Bender, Roger James and Taylor, Hugh Page. *Uniforms, Organization and History of the Waffen-SS, Vol. 2.* (Mountain View, CA: R. James Bender Publishing, 1971), pp. 8-15.

2

THE ANTI-PARTISAN YEARS 1942

The treatment of the civilian population and the methods of anti-partisan warfare in operational areas presented the highest political and military leaders with a welcome opportunity of carrying out their plans, namely the systematic extermination of Slavism and Jewry.
- General Adolf Heusinger, OKH[1]

White Russia stretched from former Polish territory in the west to Tver in the east. The actual territory the Wehrmacht controlled was small; the partisans controlled great tracts of land throughout the war. Within the framework of the German zones of authority (*Generalkommissariat* and the larger *Reichskommissariat*), the *Generalkommissariat White Russia* was a piece of *Reichskommissariat Ostland*. To the east lay the rear area of Army Group Center. To the south, past the Pripet Marshes, lay the *Generalkommissariat* of *Volhynia-Podolia*. To the north and west were the three *Generalkommissariat* of *Latvia, Lithuania* and *Bialystok*.[2] From January 1942 to June 1944 the Germans conducted forty-three large-scale anti-partisan operations in occupied territory in the Soviet Union, many in White Russia.[3] The Dirlewanger formation participated in over half of them.[4]

German troops generally regarded combat of partisans in forests and swamps as the most dangerous and most unpleasant of all types of warfare – favoring the hunted rather than the hunter. The partisans almost always killed captured German soldiers, frequently after inflicting horrible torture. Uniforms and boots rotted in summer and huge swarms of flies and mosquitoes made life miserable. In winter frostbite and trenchfoot were rampant. The German forces operated in an environment not con-

The Cruel Hunters

ducive to the contentment of the troops; this caused German units to resent the partisans whose activities had caused them to be there.⁵

The *SS-Sonderkommando* did not have long to wait after arriving in Russia before going into action. From March 2 to March 10, the unit encountered a strong band of partisans northeast of Osipovici. The Germans routed the partisans and captured a large amount of equipment. On the 12th the Germans struck again near Tscherwakow and defeated a group of partisans. The same day a strong group of partisans attempted to attack the community of Klicev. Through the efforts of the *Sonderkommando*, the Germans stopped the attack. Two days later Dirlewanger began an operation in the woods southwest of Mogil'ov. On March 24 the Germans further "cleansed" a segment of the Mogil'ov-Bobrujsk highway of partisans.⁶

At the beginning of April the *Sonderkommando* fell under the command of Police Regiment "*Mitte*", commanded by Colonel of Police von Braunschweig, and ordered to clear an area between the Drut and Beresina Rivers, destroying all partisans found there. German intelligence believed the area, north of the Mogil'ov-Bobrujsk highway to be infested with about six hundred partisans armed with heavy and light machine-guns,

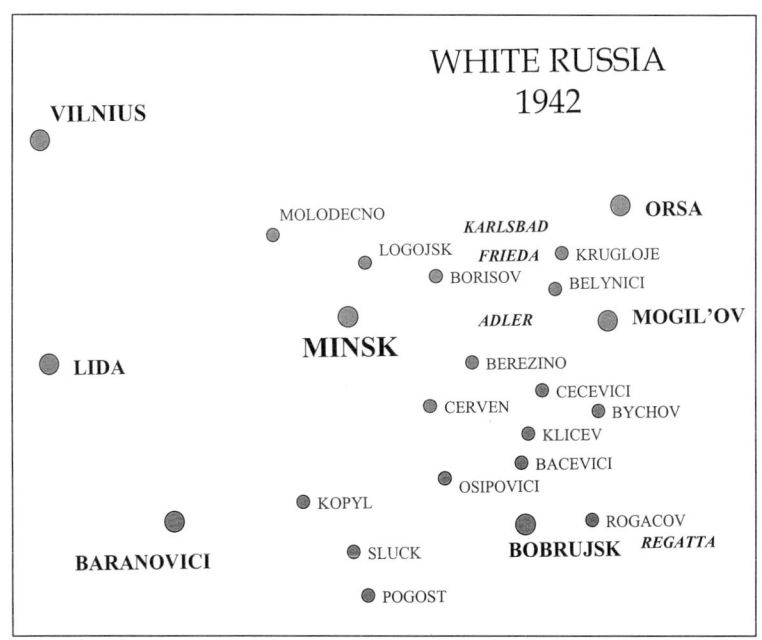

WHITE RUSSIA 1942

VILNIUS

MOLODECNO
KARLSBAD
LOGOJSK *FRIEDA* KRUGLOJE
BORISOV BELYNICI
ORSA
ADLER **MOGIL'OV**
MINSK BEREZINO
CERVEN CECEVICI
BYCHOV
KLICEV
BACEVICI
OSIPOVICI
KOPYL
ROGACOV
BARANOVICI SLUCK **BOBRUJSK** *REGATTA*
POGOST

LIDA

70

some anti-tank cannons, light mortars and various automatic weapons. The mission commenced April 2, 1942 and the units were instructed to take five days worth of supplies with them. In addition to *SS-Sonderkommando Dirlewanger*, Police Battalions 32 and 307 took part.[7]

During the operation, Dirlewanger rescued an army unit which had been encircled by attacking partisans near Illisowa. He stormed the heavily occupied villages of Selleri and Lushiza and pursued the enemy, who had not been killed, into a treacherous swamp area north to Bacevici. During ensuing fighting near Cecevici, from April 8 to April 15, 1942, the *Sonderkommando* encircled and destroyed several more strong groups of bandits.[8]

Dirlewanger's superior apparently was highly pleased with the performance of the unit on its first anti-partisan mission. On April 23, 1942 he wrote to the SS Main Office stating that it was best demonstrated in White Russia that *Sonderkommando Dirlewanger* was better suited than any other organization for combating partisans in difficult terrain. He also requested that the strength of the unit be increased to 250 men.[9]

• • •

The SS Main Office was busy during this time, as well, reviewing the ongoing case against Dirlewanger from activities in Poland. On April 13, representatives of *SS-Gruppenführer* Gottlob Berger sent the following letter to *SS-Sturmbannführer* Dr. Rudolf Brandt on Himmler's personal staff:[10]

Dear *SS-Sturmbannführer,*

As referred to earlier, I am sending you enclosed the available proceedings concerning *SS-Sturmbannführer* Dr. Dirlewanger, as requested by the *SS-Gruppenführer*. Kindly note and return.

With best greetings and
Heil Hitler

Brandt, in turn, sent these results on April 18, to *SS-Obersturmführer* Dr. Ralf Wehser, who at the time was on Himmler's special train *Heinrich*.[11] The following is Brandt's letter forwarding the proceedings, and indicates that *SS-Gruppenführer* Gottlob Berger had controlled the dossier for at least a time:

> Dear Comrade Wehser,
> Enclosed I am sending you the proceedings in the matter concerning Dirlewanger which were sent to me today by *SS-Gruppenführer* Berger. Perhaps you will be able to evaluate these examinations for the trial which is now taking place. They had already been used earlier. At the given time, I kindly request that the files be returned to me so that I can pass them on to *SS-Gruppenführer* Berger.
>
> Heil Hitler

SS-Obersturmführer Dr. Ralf Wehser was assigned at this time to the SS Main Legal Office. Born April 15, 1905 in Halle, he had joined the Nazi Party on March 1, 1933 with a membership number of 1,777,253. Previously a self-employed lawyer, Wehser became a member of the SS in August of that year and received membership number 221,244. On April 25, 1942 he was reassigned to the Waffen-SS staff detachment on Himmler's personal staff. On September 1, 1942 he joined the prestigious personal staff of the *SS-Reichsführer*. Wehser was promoted to *SS-Hauptsturmführer* on December 1, 1942 and finally to *SS-Sturmbannführer* on January 30, 1944.[12]

But Konrad Morgen was not part of the investigation. In 1942, Morgen wrote a letter to *SS-Obersturmbannführer* Hinderfeld of the SS Legal Department requesting he be relieved of his duties in Poland. Morgen's enemies took advantage of the situation. While the details of the incident remain unclear to this day, the SS reduced Morgen to the rank of *SS-Sturmann*, ordered him to a punishment unit at Stralsund, and transferred him subsequently to the SS Division *"Wiking"* on the eastern front. For the time being, Dirlewanger was safe from his most tenacious foe.[13]

The Anti-Partisan Years - 1942

• • •

The ruthless tactics employed by the *Sonderkommando* contributed to the effectiveness of the unit. During these anti-partisan operations, Dirlewanger frequently rounded up women and children, who had been left behind in the partisan villages, and marched them through minefields which protected guerrilla positions. Needless to say, this technique killed and maimed many innocent people.[14] In another tactic, Dirlewanger would fly in a light observation aircraft over suspected Russian villages. If he received gunfire from in or near a village he would annotate the location on a map. Later, he would return in a ground action, set fire to the entire hamlet and kill all the inhabitants. On these punitive operations there were no prisoners.[15]

When prisoners were taken, they fared poorly as well. On May 5, 1942 the Germans publicly hanged twenty-eight captured partisans in Minsk.[16]

During the first ten days of May 1942, Dirlewanger and his men searched for additional partisan activity with little success. On May 12, they burned the village of Sucha to the ground because they suspected the inhabitants to be assisting the partisans. On May 25 a group of about thirty partisans armed with at least one machine-gun ambushed a *Sonderkommando* command car (a Ford, license SS 202419) at 5:00 AM about ten kilometers from Cecevici. *SS-Scharführer* Oswald Egger, *SS-Unterscharführer* Werner Schmalkoke and *SS-Sturmmann* Peter Gaertner were killed and *SS-Rottenführer* Wilhelm Voigt was seriously wounded. Three army troops from another unit were killed as well. On May 29 Dirlewanger's men captured one partisan and shot five near the village of Dolgoje; the same day they killed another near Raswada. The following day they burned the village to the ground and did the same to a group of twenty-one houses near Podgorje on May 31.[17]

Dirlewanger was personally rewarded for the good start demonstrated by the *Sonderkommando*. On May 24, 1942 Oskar Dirlewanger was awarded the Bar to the Iron Cross 2nd Class.

At the beginning of June the *Sonderkommando* defeated a large group of partisans in the wooded area between Orsa and Bastocholi. From there on June 10, Dirlewanger advanced northwest of Orsa and once again engaged a band of irregulars. On the 16th, after partisans ambushed and killed seventeen German police officials, Dirlewanger set out on a "punishment expedition." Three days later the Germans found an enemy camp and destroyed it near Stochowtschina. A few days later they struck the partisans again near Nowy Gorodek. On June 26 Dirlewanger seized the fortified area of Stary Bichow-Lubianka, and ended the month by defeating another group of freedom fighters northwest of Orsa.[18]

Dirlewanger needed more men and if he couldn't get German poachers from prison, he would recruit Ukrainian turncoats. A message dated May 28, 1942 from the *Ukrainer Schützmannschafts – Ausbildungs Bataillon* (Ukrainian Self-defense Training Battalion) stated that three sergeants, eight corporals and forty-nine privates would shortly be reporting to Dirlewanger's command.[19]

Dirlewanger also needed a translator, both to interrogate captured partisans and to coordinate with local officials. On June 23, Captain of Police Dietrich, from the headquarters of the Higher SS and Police Leader for White Russia sent a letter to Dirlewanger stating that a translator, an ethnic German from the Volga region, Robert Iskam would be assigned. Dirlewanger would pay Iskam as a private for his services.[20]

In June 1942 Gottlob Berger wrote a letter to Himmler expressing regret over the way Dirlewanger had been treated during the investigation of his conduct in Poland. Berger noted that surprise attacks by Polish partisans in the Cracow area had commenced as soon as Dirlewanger's commando had left the area. Berger believed Dirlewanger's actions had been correct and stated "better shoot two Poles too many than two too few. A savage country cannot be governed in a decent manner." Berger went on to ask the *SS-Reichsführer* if he might be able to comb the prisons again for more poachers. Himmler and Hitler gave an enthusiastic "yes" to the idea.[21]

Himmler further decided to not only search the prisons but also to scour the concentration camps for suitable men for the *Sonderkommando*. Three of the first concentration camp inmates sent to Dirlewanger came from Dachau where they had worked at Dr. Sigmund Rascher's notorious research experiment at the camp on freezing human beings.[22]

Discipline was harsh in the *Sonderkommando* but Dirlewanger declared some soldiers to be rehabilitated. On July 11, 1942 for instance,

Dirlewanger sent a teletype message to the military staff judge advocate to the army's 137th Infantry Division that a Sergeant Walter Pfeiffer – who had been sent from the division to Dirlewanger – was performing well. Dirlewanger went on to state that as Pfeiffer was an old National Socialist and a former *Freikorps* soldier, it would be a shame to continue to hold his one bad incident against him.[23]

At the beginning of July the *Sonderkommando* took part in an operation with Wehrmacht forces in the district of Klicev. At a battle near Wojenitschi, they destroyed a partisan group; but on July 9 Dirlewanger was wounded in the arm. On July 12, 1942 Dirlewanger sent a message to Berger announcing that among other things, Dirlewanger would be in Berlin the following Friday [July 19]. Finally, without giving any details of the event, Dirlewanger relayed to Berger that in the *Sonderkommando's* last action in July, they had lost one man killed and six wounded.[24]

Before he left, Dirlewanger received the Wound Badge in Gold on July 12. This award had a long history in the German military. Kaiser Wilhelm II instituted the Wound Badge on March 3, 1918, to measure wounds received in combat. The Germans awarded different grades based on the cumulative number of incidents in which wounds were received. The wound badge in black designated one or two wounds, the badge in silver for three to four wounds, and the badge in gold for five or more wounds. Hitler reinstituted the award at the beginning of World War II – the number of wounds was a cumulative total and covered both world wars. Dirlewanger had been wounded six times in World War I, once during *Freikorps* service, and once again to this point in World War II.

While Dirlewanger was back in Germany, the *Sonderkommando* was involved in a particularly nasty incident. A German plane had crashed in their area, and the unit received the mission to locate the plane and recover the dead, any important papers and airplane parts. On July 19 a party of one officer, four NCOs, thirty-nine German soldiers and forty Ukrainian troops, all under the command of the *Sonderkommando*, began the search. They immediately ran into a force of twelve partisans and promptly killed three but the rest, including one wounded, escaped. The Germans finally found the wreckage near the village of Wetrenka along with the bodies of the four passengers. However, while attempting to recover the remains, they inadvertently triggered a large explosive device which the partisans had placed under the dead crew members as a booby trap. Two Ukrainians were killed and two more were seriously wounded, while *SS-Unterscharführer* Hunke received light wounds. On the way back to camp the Germans came across three suspicious persons who they later turned over to the *Sicherheitsdienst* (Security Service).[25] Dirlewanger would be cited in a recommendation for the German Cross in Gold as having displayed special bravery in the operation, but as the record shows he was in Germany at the time of the incident.

July was a bloody month for the attached Ukrainians who began the month with eleven NCOs and fifty soldiers but by month's end had lost eight soldiers (13%). One soldier had been the victim of an accidental shooting, four had been killed in the booby trap at the aircraft (the two wounded died in hospital), two troops had been wounded in a later incident (one by an "exploding" round) and one very sick soldier had been evacuated. Perhaps as a harsh repayment for their losses, on July 26 the Ukrainian detachment found a partisan camp in the woods near Michalewka and executed nine partisans, including two women and a Jew. They then burned the area and its six houses to the ground.[26]

The *Sonderkommando* actions in July were part of a larger undertaking, *Operation Adler* (Operation Eagle), an anti-partisan sweep against two thousand to five thousand irregulars in partisan groups Nitschipurowitsch and Kulik in the Bobrujsk, Rogacov, Osipovici, Berezino, Bykhov, Belynici, Svisloc and the Berezina and Drut River areas July 1 to August 12, 1942. During the operation the *Sonderkommando* operated under the Higher SS and Police Leader White Russia, which at the time was commanded by *SS-Obergruppenführer* Erich von dem Bach-Zelewski, with Police Regiment 2 and some *Sicherheitsdienst* commandos as part of Battle Group Buchmann. The units of the army's 286th Security Division and the 203rd Security Division participated as well.[27] Fighting was heavy; the *Sonderkommando* participated in assaults at Ussakino, on August 8 and Kutschino on August 11.[28] An after action report from the 286th reported friendly losses at twenty-five killed, two missing and sixty-four wounded while 1381 were killed and 428 were taken prisoner. Additionally, the Germans captured eight howitzers, four field cannon, five anti-aircraft guns, nine anti-tank guns, thirteen mortars, twenty-two machine-guns, three hundred seventy-seven rifles and twelve pistols.[29]

Brigadier General Johann-Georg Richert commanded the army's 286th Security Division during this time. Richert had previously commanded the 23rd Infantry Regiment and would later command the 35th Infantry Division. Highly decorated – he won the Knight's Cross with Oak Leaves, Richert was later captured by the Soviets, tried for war crimes after the war and hanged at Minsk on January 30, 1946. German rear area anti-partisan operations were not limited to the Minsk area – and many army generals later paid a high price for their participation in these fights. The Soviets executed other army generals for rear area war crimes including Major General Friedrich Bernhard, commander of Rear Army Area 532 (2nd Army) – hanged December 30, 1945 and Major General Karl Burckhardt, commander of Army Rear Area 593 (6th Army) – hanged January 30, 1946.

After visiting Berlin, Dirlewanger went to his home in Esslingen, Germany to rest – it had been a busy two years. On July 27, 1942 he again wrote *SS-Gruppenführer* Berger asking for necessary supplies, trucks and cars. He reiterated that the *Sonderkommando* were specialists in sniper and partisan warfare with a great degree of battle experience, and added the rhetorical question, "wasn't it pointless to make a unit designed to be partisan fighters undergo long and bloody months of activity because of a lack of transport?"[30]

Difficulties in the fight against the partisans were not limited to the *Sonderkommando*. On July 28, 1942 Himmler appointed *SS-Gruppenführer* Kurt Knoblauch to the position of Chief of the *Reichsführer-SS* Command Staff and gave him the special responsibility for the partisan war. Knoblauch was to coordinate support of the *Oberkommando des Heeres* (OKH) and the *Oberkommando des Wehrmacht* with the SS and to provide all Higher SS and Police Leaders in the East with SS units as needed. He additionally was to begin operations for the removal of families of known partisans to concentration camps. Two weeks later German agencies were instructed to cease using the word "partisan" and substitute instead the term "bandit."[31] This was followed on August 18, 1942 by *Hitler's Directive Number 46 – Instructions for intensified action against banditry in the East*. In this order Hitler stated:[32]

The Cruel Hunters

In recent months banditry in the East has assumed intolerable proportions, and threatens to become a serious danger to supplies for the front and to the economic exploitation of the country. By the beginning of winter these bandit gangs must be substantially exterminated, so that order may be restored behind the Eastern Front and severe disadvantages to our winter operations avoided. The following measures are necessary:

1. Rapid, drastic and active operations against the bandits by the coordination of all available forces of the Armed Forces, the SS and Police which are suitable for the purpose.

2. The concentration of all propaganda, economic and political measures on the necessity of combating banditry.

Hitler went on to state that although the most rigorous measures should be taken against all members of the gangs and those who supported them, the local population should be handled strictly but justly. The Führer named the *SS-Reichsführer* as the central authority for the collection and evaluation of all intelligence concerning the bandits and stated that Himmler would have the sole responsibility for combating banditry in the Reich Commissioners' territories. This included White Russia.

Dirlewanger sent a message from Germany to the *Sonderkommando* on July 30 telling them he would fly back to Russia on August 5. He instructed them not to make any purchases of market wares until his return. On a far more ominous note, he instructed *SS-Obersturmführer* Narnischmacher not to conduct any additional Jewish actions (most certainly killing) until he returned as well.[33]

August was a month for promotions in the unit, indicative that not all personnel had been assigned to the *Sonderkommando* as punishment. On the 13th *SS-Obergruppenführer* Eric von dem Bach-Zelewski promoted a Ukrainian officer in the *Sonderkommando* to platoon leader. Dirlewanger

The Anti-Partisan Years - 1942

promoted *SS-Unterscharführer* Schneidt and Schwippe, *SS-Rottenführer* Mammitsch, Selzer, Vieregge and Gottlieb Zalsky, *SS-Sturmmann* Illing, Hellkamp, H. Kraus, Weinert and W. Winkelbauer and *SS-Schützen* Hesener, Lowitz and Scheungraber each one grade.[34]

Dirlewanger had the authority, according to Gottlob Berger, to authorize promotions through the rank of *SS-Hauptscharführer*. He could not promote enlisted personnel into the officer grades without special permission.[35] SS officers were only commissioned after completing training in the SS officer school at either Braunschweig or Bad Tolz. These schools were called *SS-Junkerschulen*. In some instances an SS man who had joined the organization in the early 1920s and therefore had a very low SS number could receive a commission.[36] Several soldiers in the *Sonderkommando* were early members of the SS, but there are no records of the unit promoting them in this manner.

Anti-partisan operations continued. On August 19, 21, 22 and 23 the *Sonderkommando* engaged partisan bands but had no reported results. In that same month, the *Sonderkommando* notified the SS Main Office that *SS-Oberscharführer* Heinz Feiertag had transferred to his home in Berlin to recuperate from his wounds.[37]

• • •

Back in the Reich, the investigators continued reviewing Dirlewanger's conduct in Poland. On August 21, 1942 *SS-Obersturmführer* Meine of the *SS-Reichsführer's* personal staff sent a letter to *SS-Obersturmführer* Wehser at the SS court. The letter read:[38]

> Dear Comrade Wehser,
> On April 18, 1942, *SS-Obersturmbannführer* Dr. Brandt forwarded to you some details in the matter concerning Dirlewanger. Could you please advise *SS-Obersturmbannführer* Brandt what has happened to the proceedings in the meantime?

> Heil Hitler
> Meine

Wehser responded almost immediately with a letter back to Meine.[39]

> Dear Comrade Meine,
> As ordered by the *Reichsführer-SS*, in the case of Dirlewanger, the proceedings were handed over to the SS Legal Department which is to conduct an SS and police court investigation against Dirlewanger. Obviously this investigation procedure has not been concluded because if it had, the *Reichsführer-SS* would have been asked to confirm the sentence. I will inform you as to the conclusion of the case against Dirlewanger without further reminder.
>
> Heil Hitler!
> Wehser

• • •

On September 7, 1942 the *Sonderkommando* engaged ten partisans killing four and captured a partisan camp. Inside the camp they captured two machine-guns, nine rifles, five hundred hand grenades, one thousand mines and many uniforms. They also found three women who were wives of partisans – and executed them as well.[40] Two days later, they assaulted partisans in a forest near Smoliza.[41] On September 14, the *Sonderkommando*, reinforced with a platoon of armored cars, deployed as part of Police Regiment 14 against partisans along the Drut River. Two days later Dirlewanger went out again on an operation.[42] On September 16, 1942 Oskar Dirlewanger was awarded the Bar to the Iron Cross 1st Class. On October 9, 1942 he was awarded the Eastern People's Medal for Bravery 2nd Class in Silver with Swords. He received the same medal in 1st Class status on November 10, 1942.[43]

Dirlewanger gained still another ally back in Germany during the month. On September 24, *Reichsmarschall* Hermann Göring sent an in-

The Anti-Partisan Years - 1942

quiry to the Ministry of Justice asking whether the *Sonderkommando* could possibly be reinforced by conscripting armed gangs of smugglers and other types of criminals into the unit.[44]

At the beginning of October 1942 the *Sonderkommando* participated in *Operation Regatta*, an anti-partisan operation in the Rekota, Moshkovo, Dobraya and Ryabki areas October 4-7, 1942. For this operation the *Sonderkommando* deployed a battle strength of three hundred and fifty-two men and were under control of Security Regiment 36. Listed in the regimental order as Police Battalion South (*Polizei Bataillon Süd*), their mission was to move from Mogil'ov through Ssuchari, Mabje Buschkowo, Shanowitschi and Korowtschino, and take up a sector some ten kilometers wide between Nowy Pribush and Schathewa. Dirlewanger would set up this blocking position on October 4. Early the following morning, the *Sonderkommando* was to attack north and achieve successive daily objectives which they were to report by radio. Dirlewanger was further instructed not to burn down villages as long as the villagers themselves were not directly involved in the fighting. The regimental headquarters would be located at Jermaki.[45]

The Germans issued the following warning to the citizens of Moschlow, Rekotka and Dobraja through an interpreter:[46]

> The German Wehrmacht has occupied the villages and has searched the surrounding woods because during the last few months the German troops were consistently attacked by bandits in the surrounding areas of the woods. During these attacks, German motor cars and convoys were shot at, telephone lines and bridges were destroyed, and railroad lines were destroyed.
>
> The German Reich is conducting the war with its troops against the Army of the Soviets. Whoever is found behind the German front with armed fighters, is a thief and a bandit and will be removed without mercy. Whoever helps these bandits and their leaders and commissioners is just as guilty and this blame concerns the village which is now occupied.

It was proven that bandits were given food and were taken care of by this village. The cattle of this village were made available to the bandits. The bandits could come and go in this village. It was found that only two days ago they were partying in Moschkowa. Very close to the villages, as in Rekotka, camps were established where inhabitants of the villages helped in their construction, and the existence of these camps must definitely have been known in the village.

Despite the demand by the German authorities, the village has not made one single contribution of cattle or wheat, in contrast to other villages which were occupied by the German Wehrmacht. It is necessary that the inhabitants realize just as sensibly that the Soviets have lost the war and that they have to deliver cattle and wheat.

Therefore, at first all cattle will be taken from the village and gathered in Gorki. As soon as the amount of wheat demanded has been collected, the cattle will be returned to their owners.

The men who were participating in the activities of the bandits will be executed according to martial law. Suspicious persons will first be taken to a prisoner of war camp. Women who were active in service to the bandits in a secondary role will also be executed.

Whoever stays away from the bandits and reports to the German commanders about activities by the bandits in the surrounding villages outside of the forests as soon as they appear will remain unharmed; in addition, the German Wehrmacht and police as well as the administration and rural authorities will do everything to assure a peaceful existence for the village population.

The news smuggled in occasionally by commissioners, Jews and agents in Moscow is wrong. It is nonsense to maintain that the German front has been broken somewhere or would be in danger. Whoever believes this should just take a trip to Leningrad, to Rzev, to Stalingrad or to Maikop to reassure themselves there where the German army stands. The war is lost for the Soviets and here – many hundred kilometers behind the front nothing war-connected should occur any longer. The only disturbing forces in your farming activities are the members of the bandits and it is in your best interest to contribute to their removal.

To conclude, we will leave you in peace, but we are making this announcement:

If in your village once again the attempt is shown to act with weapons against the German troops if the German troops are not notified immediately as soon as members of the bandits appear, then this village will be burnt down and the total population will be executed.

The *Sonderkommando* after action report, prepared October 8, detailed the conduct of the operation:

October 4, 1942 – departed Mogil'ov at 7:00 AM. set up blocking position by 1:00 PM. Reconnaissance to the north found nothing.
October 5, 1942 – began attack north at 5:30 AM. Reached day's objective at 11:00 AM with no contact. At 4:50 PM discovered a partisan camp near Abraimowka which was seized and burned. Killed seven partisans and wounded two; captured one machine-gun and five rifles. One *Sonderkommando* soldier lightly wounded. At 8:00 PM killed two more partisans.
October 6, 1942 – continued the attack, burned six unoccupied partisan camps.
October 7, 1942 – returned to Mogil'ov.

Dirlewanger offered several observations in his report. First he stated, reconnaissance from the air failed to find partisans in thick woods. Second, the *Sonderkommando* had an attack zone ten kilometers wide in this difficult terrain. This was too large a zone to adequately cover with just three hundred fifty men. Finally, at the start of the attack the woods were free of smoke and fog. However, once the attack began, thick smoke blanketed much of the area thus limiting sight to only ten meters in many places. This further complicated Dirlewanger's task of finding well camouflaged partisans.[47]

Later in October the *Sonderkommando* participated in *Operation Karlsbad*, an anti-partisan operation north of the Beresino-Cerven' highway against a partisan force believed to be six thousand strong under a Colonel Nitschipuronitsche. Dirlewanger was subordinated to the 1st SS Infantry Brigade (motorized), commanded by *SS-Brigadeführer* Karl von Treuenfeld. The brigade's mission was to clear the area of partisans commencing October 14. Von Treuenfeld commanded a wide variety of units for the operation including SS Infantry Regiment 8 (motorized), SS Infantry Regiment 10 (motorized), the 255th Lithuanian *Schuma* Battalion, the 1st Battalion, 638th French Infantry Regiment (a part of the French Volunteer Legion under Major LaCroix), Police Regiment 14 and Cossack Detachment 102. Dirlewanger, initially ordered to move from Mogil'ov through Krugloje to Denisovici and then to clear an area north to Selischtsche, Pyschatschje and Kupienka, would advance to the Mosha River and establish a bridgehead there. The *Sonderkommando* reached this objective and received further instructions to set up a blocking position facing south in the Brusjeta salient to prevent the enemy from passing through this sector. Meanwhile, SS Infantry Regiments 8 and 10 would close the noose around the partisans. After destroying any enemy attempting to break through, the *Sonderkommando* would then form the brigade reserve.[48]

The Germans formed the *Schützmannschaft* or *Schuma* battalions as self defense forces. Russian, Ukrainian, Latvian, Lithuanian or Estonian volunteers manned these units which the Germans organized along regular military lines. The officers of a *Schuma* unit were often ethnic German nationals or in some cases former Soviet Army NCOs. The fighting capabilities of these units varied tremendously from rabid anti-Stalinists to far less stable organizations.

The Germans also employed police (*polizei*) units in the fight against the partisans. In June 1942 the Germans organized the many separate police battalions into motorized police regiments. In February 1943 the Germans redesignated these units as SS-Police Regiments. There were a total of fourteen regiments: the 2nd, 6th, 9th, 10th, 11th, 13th, 14th, 15th, 16th, 17th, 22nd, 24th, 26th and 38th. Additionally, there were seven mixed German-Russian units called Police Rifle Regiments – the 31st, 33rd, 34th, 35th, 36th, 37th and 38th.[49]

SS-Brigadeführer von Treuenfeld congratulated all soldiers in the brigade on October 24 for a successful operation. He thanked them for cleaning a large area free from partisans and destroying the partisan operational center of Borisov – a large grouping of partisans between Borisov and Orsa. He also paid homage to those soldiers who had fallen in combat.[50]

The 1st SS Infantry Brigade (motorized) had previously been involved in the murders of many Jews and had served as an auxiliary force to the *Einsatzgruppen*. During the fall of 1941 the unit reported killing 1358, 1018, and 437 Jews in different operations.[51] *Einsatzgruppe A* Operational Situation Report Number 59, dated August 21, 1941 and Number 86, dated September 17, 1941 singled out the brigade for its performance.[52]

The *einsatzgruppen* were special mobile formations charged with carrying out liquidations in occupied countries (primarily the Soviet Union) and of supervising various aspects of the final solution. The *einsatzgruppen* were formed in the spring of 1941 after Hitler issued an order that the Security Police and Security Service would assist the army in combating resistance behind the front. Shortly thereafter, Reinhard Heydrich met with the Quartermaster General of the Army, Brigadier General Eduard Wagner to reach an agreement concerning the activation, command and jurisdiction of the units of the SD which would operate in the rear operational areas of the field armies. They would carry out tasks specifically designated by Heydrich and Himmler; their respective army commander would provide much logistical support. The Germans formed four *einsatzgruppen*. *Einsatzgruppe A* was attached to Army Group North, *Einsatzgruppe B* was attached to Army Group Center, *Einsatzgruppe C* was attached to Army Group South and *Einsatzgruppe D* was assigned to the German 11th Army.[53]

The Cruel Hunters

Each *einsatzgruppe* had a strength of five hundred to eight hundred men. The officers generally came from the SD, SS, Criminal Police (*Kripo*) and *Gestapo*. Enlisted personnel were drawn from the Waffen-SS, Gestapo, Order Police (*Orpo*), and locally-recruited police. *Einsatzgruppen* were further divided into subordinate units called *einsatzkommando*. The *einsatzgruppen* generally accomplished their mission either by deceiving victims to report to a central location for the purposes of relocation, and then killing them instead, or by conducting manhunts through a district. Although carbon monoxide gas vans were sometimes used, the preferred method of execution was by shooting. The following description by a German civilian testifying before the Nürnberg Military Tribunal is typical of an *einsatzgruppe* operation:[54]

> I walked around the mound and found myself confronted by a tremendous grave. People were closely wedged together and lying on top of each other so that their heads were visible. Nearly all had blood running over their shoulders from their heads. Some of the people shot were still moving. Some were lifting their arms and turning their heads to show that they were still alive. The pit was already two thirds full. I estimated that it contained about 1,000 people. I looked for the man who did the shooting. He was an SS man, who sat at the edge of the narrow end of the pit, his feet dangling into the pit. He had a tommy gun on his knees and was smoking a cigarette. The people, completely naked, went down some steps which were cut in the clay wall of the pit and clambered over the heads of the people lying there, to the place to which the SS man directed them. They lay down in front of the dead or injured people; some caressed those who were still alive and spoke to them in a low voice. Then I heard a series of shots. I looked into the pit and saw that the bodies were twitching or the heads lying already motionless on top of the bodies that lay before them. Blood was running from their necks. I was surprised that I was not

The Anti-Partisan Years - 1942

> ordered away, but saw that there were two or three postmen in uniform nearby. The next batch was approaching already. They went down into the pit, lined themselves up against the previous victims and were shot.
>
> When I walked around the mound, I noticed another truckload of people which had just arrived. This time it included sick and infirm persons. An old, very thin women with terribly thin legs was undressed by others who were already naked, while two people held her up. The woman appeared to be paralyzed. The naked people carried the woman around the mound.

Other methods were even more hideous. Former *SS-Hauptscharführer* Adolf Ruebe testified after the war that there were SS executioners who invented novel ways to kill their victims.[55]

> On the occasion of an exhumation in Minsk, in November 1943, *SS-Obersturmführer* Heuser arrived with a Kommando of Latvians. They brought eight Jews, men and women, with them. The Latvians guarded the Jews while Harter [another SS man] and Heuser erected a funeral pyre with their own hands. The Jews were bound, put on the pile alive, drenched with gasoline and burned.

The exact number of people killed by the *einsatzgruppen* will never be known. Many historians believe the figure to be approximately 1,300,000. An analysis of reports of *Einsatzgruppe B* – within whose area of responsibility Dirlewanger operated, indicate that from June 1941 to December 1942, the group slaughtered 134,000 men, women and children.[56]

Einsatzgruppe B, headquartered at Smolensk, operated in White Russia and consisted of *Einsatzkommandos 8* and *9*, *Sonderkommando 7a* and *7b* and *Vorkommando Moskau*. *Einsatzkommando 8* had subordinate *teilkommandos* (squads) at Vitebsk, Gomel, Orsa and Krichev. *SS-Brigadeführer* Artur Nebe, the same individual who had helped organize

The Cruel Hunters

the *Sonderkommando* back in 1940, initially commanded *Einsatzgruppe B*; *SS-Oberführer* Erich Naumann commanded the unit during operations with Dirlewanger. *SS-Sturmbannführer* Bradfisch, *SS-Sturmbannführer* Heinz Richter and *SS-Sturmbannführer* Hans-Gerhard Schindhelm in turn led *Einsatzkommando 8*, headquartered at Mogil'ov.[57]

As *Einsatzgruppe B* and *Einsatzkommando 8* worked frequently with the *Sonderkommando*, it is appropriate to examine their commanders. *SS-Brigadeführer* Erich Naumann was born in Meissen on April 29, 1905. He entered the Nazi Party July 1, 1935 and received party number 107,496. He entered the SS on November 1, 1929 with an SS number of 170,257. He was married with one son. Naumann commanded an *einsatzkommando* unit in the Polish campaign and assumed command of *Einsatzgruppe B* on November 1, 1941. He received the Iron Cross 1st and 2nd Class, the Eastern Front Medal and the War Service Cross 1st Class. Naumann later served as the commander of security police in The Hague, Netherlands and then became the security commander of Nürnberg.[58]

The allies tried Naumann after the war at Nürnberg in the *United States of America vs. Otto Ohlendorf, et al.* (Case No. 9), which came to be known as the "Einsatzgruppen Case." He made the following statement at the beginning of the proceedings:

> My position as chief of *Einsatzgruppe B*, my conduct in Russia, and my inner attitude have given me the confidence so that I was able to answer the question of the president of this Tribunal which he put to me on 15 September 1947 [how do you plead?], with a clear conscience and deep conviction by "Not Guilty."

The court did not agree. It convicted him on April 9, 1948, sentenced him to death by hanging and executed him in 1951.

SS-Sturmbannführer Otto Bradfisch occupies a unique place in the history of SS officers and executors of the Final Solution – he may have been of Jewish ancestry. Born May 10, 1903 in Zweibrücken, he was a lawyer, married with three children. He joined the Nazi Party January 1, 1931 with party number 405,869 and entered the SS on September 26, 1938 with SS number 310,180. An efficiency report on Bradfisch lists his

The Anti-Partisan Years - 1942

racial makeup as *"Guter Mischling."* A *Mischling* was defined as a non-Aryan – not a Jew but of mixed Jewish blood. A *Mischling* of the first degree was a person with two Jewish grandparents who himself did not adhere to the Jewish religion and who was not married to a Jewish person. A *Mischling* of the second degree was a person who had one Jewish grandparent. Applications for service in the SS as an officer required proof on non-Jewish descent from 1750 forward; it is not known how Bradfisch complied with this requirement. The report does not further classify as to the degree of *Mischling* for Bradfisch. Although it is possible that in this context *Mischling* may have been used to describe a mixture of nordic, Aryan traits, it is not likely that one SS officer would use this meaning in describing the racial makeup of another SS officer. Bradfisch was awarded the Iron Cross 2nd Class and War Service Cross 1st Class. He commanded *Einsatzkommando 8* from June 1941 to January 1942. He then was assigned to the police bureau at Lódz and was promoted to *SS-Obersturmbannführer* on April 20, 1943.[59]

Bradfisch personally demonstrated his craft to Heinrich Himmler in August 1941. Near Minsk, members of *Einsatzkommando 8* and Police Battalion 9 conducted a mass shooting of Jews and partisans. During the proceeding, Himmler observed that one of the victims was still alive. Bradfisch agreed, removed his pistol, handed it to a reserve police officer and ordered him to finish the man off – which the officer did.[60]

The allies brought Bradfisch to trial after the war. In 1961 he was sentenced in a German court at Straubing to ten years for his *einsatzkommando* activities, and in 1963 was sentenced in Hannover to thirteen years for his crimes in Lódz.[61]

SS-Sturmbannführer Heinz Richter was born in the city of Güben on February 13, 1903. He originally entered the Nazi Party in 1926 with a party number of 48,512. He received SS number 280,049 when he joined this organization on October 1, 1936. In 1938 Richter was assigned to the Gestapo. He assumed command of *Einsatzkommando 8* in January 1942. His superior *SS-Oberführer* Erich Naumann, stated that Richter was the type of person that was not suited to be a commander of an *einsatzkommando*, but under the right circumstances could be a good worker. Richter was awarded the War Service Cross 2nd Class and the Eastern Front Medal, and was reassigned to Paris as an SS court official in November 1942.[62]

SS-Sturmbannführer Hans-Gerhard Schindhelm was born July 5, 1908 in Dresden. He entered the Nazi Party in May 1933 with a party number of 2,452,706. On June 27, 1938 he joined the SS and received an SS number of 353,427. A lawyer by training, he was married and had one child. Schindhelm took command of *Einsatzkommando 8* on November 13, 1942 and was awarded the War Service Cross 2nd Class and the Eastern Front Medal. He received the following efficiency rating from *SS-Standartenführer* Erich Ehrlinger describing his performance:[63]

> On November 13, 1942 Schindhelm took over the *Einsatzkommando 8* in the *Einsatzgruppe B*, located at Mogil'ov. The area of the *Einsatzkommando 8* was marked by heavy activity by bandits who maintained their contacts up to the communities within the sphere of the *Einsatzkommando* and who were continuously active in heavy sabotage acts on public installations, railroads and roads. At the same time there was heavy spy activity by the enemy in the area of Army Group Center in preparation of offensive intentions. Recognizing the fact that additional help by other units was necessary, *SS-Sturmbannführer* Schindhelm started in a timely way to build up a criminal police service (*Hilfskriminalpolizei*), which he further expanded during the course of the year 1943 and which at the end was molded into an instrument for spy and sabotage defense that proved itself many times to be very valuable. With his troops, which were spread all over the are of endeavor, he destroyed numerous terrorist and sabotage troops of the enemy. He was also able to continuously supply to the leaders of the *Einsatzgruppe B* with confidential reports as well as the Commander of the Army District valuable information about movements of the bandits. *SS-Sturmbannführer* Schindhelm was a just superior to his men. He always watched out that they were not occupied with security police and non-SD tasks and that they continued their professional

The Anti-Partisan Years - 1942

education. During the period of his leadership as commander of the *Einsatzkommando 8* he accomplished extremely good work in the sector of security policy and in addition he took on with great interest and energy the professional security tasks. In his personal demeanor and in private contact, Schindhelm was always a good example for his men. His character and philosophical attitude are without criticism.

The *einsatzgruppen* generally had a good working relationship with the army, freeing up army security forces for front-line action. Army commanders were often aware of the activities of these SS units. In a group of assembled army commanders at Orsa in December 1941, Colonel General Franz Halder, the Chief of Staff of the Army said:[64]

> These people [the *einsatzgruppen*] are worth their weight in gold to us. They guarantee the security of our rear communications and so save us calling upon [army] troops for this purpose.

Army headquarters frequently approved awards and decorations to *einsatzgruppe* personnel in their area. For example, on August 26, 1943, Colonel Paul Herrmann, the chief of staff for the 16th Army signed an order for an Infantry Assault Badge to Vice-corporal Leonid Waldowski of *Einsatzkommando 2* part of *Einsatzgruppe A*.[65]

On October 23, 1942 *SS-Reichsführer* Himmler appointed the Higher SS and Police Leader for Central Russia *SS-Obergruppenführer* Erich von dem Bach-Zelewski to the post of *Bevollmächtigte für die Bandenbekampfung im Osten* – the Plenipotentiary for Combating Partisans in the East. Von dem Bach would have no authority in this position to issue commands to SS troops remaining with the *SS-Reichsführer's* Command Staff, but could issue reports, propose courses of action, and liaise between the OKH, OKW and SS.[66]

SS-Obergruppenführer Erich von dem Bach-Zelewski's wartime career touched on the *Sonderkommando* time and time again. He was born March 1, 1899 in Lauenburg, Pomerania. He served in World War I as a

The Cruel Hunters

lieutenant, winning the Iron Cross 2nd Class on August 5, 1915 with the 3rd West Prussian Infantry Regiment Number 129, and the Iron Cross 1st Class on September 25, 1918 while serving with the 1st Silesian Infantry Regiment "Kaiser Friedrich Wilhelm II." During this period his name was Erich Julius Eberhard von Zelewski. After the war he served in various police units, in part because his fellow army officers found him socially unacceptable as his two sisters had both married Jews.[67] Von dem Bach was married and had six children. In the late 1930s he went through legal proceedings to add "von dem Bach" to his family name perhaps in an attempt to make his name sound less Slavic and more German. On this formal change, his name was listed differently being "von Zelewsky." Von dem Bach joined the Nazi Party in 1930 with party number 489,101. He joined the SS on February 15, 1931 and received an SS membership number of 9,831. His rise through the SS was meteoric. He was promoted to *SS-Untersturmführer* July 20, 1931 and then skipped the next two ranks – being directly promoted to *SS-Sturmbannführer* on December 6, 1931. He then skipped another rank and made *SS-Standartenführer* on September 10, 1932, *SS-Oberführer* only twenty-six days later and *SS-Brigadeführer* on December 15, 1933. On July 11, 1934 he was promoted to *SS-Gruppenführer*, and on November 9, 1941 he was selected as an *SS-Obergruppenführer*.[68]

Von dem Bach was awarded the Golden Party Badge in 1939. He received the Bar to the Iron Cross 2nd Class on August 31, 1941 and the Bar to the Iron Cross 1st Class on May 20, 1942. On February 23, 1943 he received the German Cross in Gold for services rendered as the Higher SS and Police Leader for Central and White Russia. During the Warsaw Uprising Lieutenant General Nikolaus von Vormann, the commander of the German 9th Army, recommended him for the Knight's Cross; Colonel General Georg-Hans Reinhardt, the Commander of Army Group Center, seconded the recommendation. Von dem Bach received this award on September 30, 1944. A post-war German court convicted von dem Bach of several wartime crimes but issued a lenient sentence.[69]

In October 1942, a macabre incident occurred involving von dem Bach-Zelewski. As the Higher SS and Police Leader for Central and White Russia, Bach sent a several crates of items to Himmler for distribution as Christmas gifts to children of SS families. This gift included ten thousand pairs of children's socks and two thousand pairs of children's gloves. We do not know where Bach procured these items. Did they come from unused stocks of clothes found in Russian warehouses, or confiscated from the small victims of the ongoing anti-partisan operations?[70]

Battle Group von Gottberg reported the following enemy losses for the operation: 798 partisans killed, 353 suspects executed, 1826 Jews shot and 7 gypsies killed.[71] The commander of all security forces for Army Group Center, Lieutenant General Max von Schenckendorff, sent a message on October 25 to the Higher SS and Police Leader for White Russia and to the 1st SS Infantry Brigade praising the units for their numerous successful battles along the railroad between Borisov and Orsa and giving them his personal thanks. Von Schenckendorff, a senior army officer, had formerly been the commander of the XXXVth Army Corps and served as the rear area commander for the army group from 1941 to his death in July 1943. It would not be the last time the Wehrmacht praised Dirlewanger.[72]

Discipline problems continued though. On October 26 the staff physician at the Higher SS and Police hospital in Mogil'ov sent Dirlewanger a letter stating that a member of the *Sonderkommando*, who had been in the hospital since October 10, had fallen ill due to not using a condom. The doctor recommended that the *SS-Schütze* be punished by having no leave for a six month period. Dirlewanger agreed.[73]

On November 1, 1942 the *Sonderkommando* was instructed to accompany *Einsatzkommando 8* on an "action" west of the Berezina River in the district of Cerven'. The action was to commence on November 4, and Dirlewanger was to report daily progress to the headquarters of *Einsatzkommando 8*. *Einsatzgruppe B* received a copy of the order as well.[74] The action with *Einsatzkommando 8* was just a warm-up for November. The 1st SS Infantry Brigade (motorized) was to commence another anti-partisan undertaking, *Operation Frieda*, beginning on November 6. The *Sonderkommando* was to headquarter at Sloboda and clear a large wooded area north of the Sakowschtschina-Makon road. SS Infantry Regiment 8 would furnish the *Sonderkommando* with two 37mm anti-tank guns for the operation, presumably for use against fortified houses or bunkers. On November 8 the operation came to an end and the *Sonderkommando* returned to base.[75]

On November 13, 1942 Dirlewanger was ordered to provide security for the transportation of livestock, captured during *Operation Frieda*, out of the area to Cerven'. The Germans habitually rounded up livestock and foodstuffs from a partisan area to deny these supplies to any partisans who may have survived. Unfortunately, the removal of these food sources also devastated local populations through starvation. The battalion operation's order showed the unit was then organized into the 1st and 2nd Russian Companies, commanded by *SS-Obersturmführer* Waldemar Wilhelm, a German company, commanded by *SS-Untersturmführer* Waldemar Bodammer, and a reconnaissance platoon. During the mission the *Sonderkommando* was headquartered at Rowanitschi.[76]

SS-Obersturmführer Waldemar Wilhelm was born January 30, 1896 in Oberweissberg. He served in World War I and won the Honor Badge for Front-line Service. Wilhelm joined the Nazi Party January 1, 1927, receiving party number 49,242. A machinist by trade, he also served as an automobile salesman. Married with three children, he entered the SS in the early 1930s and received SS number 28,346. During the war he was awarded the Iron Cross 2nd Class, Eastern People's Bravery Medal 2nd Class, War Service Cross 2nd Class, Infantry Assault Badge and both the 10 and 15 Year NSDAP Long Service Medals. He ended the war with the 4th Panzer Grenadier Training and Replacement Battalion.[77]

SS-Untersturmführer Waldemar Bodammer was born in Stuttgart on October 4, 1903. He served in *Freikorps Oberland* after World War I. He entered the Nazi Party in 1931 with party number 717,530. His SS number was 31,159. Assigned to the *Sonderkommando* in September 1942, he remained in the unit until February 23, 1943 when he was transferred to Waffen-SS Replacement Command Southwest in Stuttgart because of a chronic illness. There is no evidence in his personnel record of any disciplinary incidents which caused him to be assigned to the *Sonderkommando*. He was promoted to *SS-Obersturmführer* June 21, 1943 and to *SS-Hauptsturmführer* one year later. He received the Iron Cross 2nd Class, Infantry Assault Badge, Eastern People's Bravery Medal 2nd Class, and the War Service Cross 2nd Class with Swords.[78]

On November 22, 1942 *SS-Obergruppenführer* Erich von dem Bach-Zelewski departed command of the Higher SS and Police Leader for Central Russia. *SS-Brigadeführer* Georg Henning von Bassewitz-Behr replaced him and served in the position until March 24, 1943. He, in turn, was succeeded by *SS-Gruppenführer* Gerret Korsemann who held the position until July 5, 1943. The last HSSPF for Central Russia was *SS-Gruppenführer* Curt von Gottberg who served in the position until June 21, 1944 when the Soviet offensive to liberate the area began and made the position unnecessary.[79]

While operations in Russia continued to proceed, Dirlewanger's investigation was still apparently on the back burner. On November 25, *SS-Obersturmführer* Meine again inquired as to the status on behalf of Himmler.[80]

> Dear Comrade Wehser,
> On August 22, 1942, you sent me a short interim report regarding *SS-Sturmbannführer* Dirlewanger. Has a decision been made in this matter in the meantime?
>
> Heil Hitler!
> Meine

Wehser sent a reply back one week later on December 2, 1942.

> Dear Comrade Meine,
>
> In the case of Dirlewanger, a final report about the proceedings has not yet been received by the SS Main Legal Office. I have already inquired about it recently at the Legal Office.
>
> Heil Hitler!
> Wehser

The *Sonderkommando* went through still another name change on November 2. On that date the unit changed titles from *SS-Sonderkommando* Dirlewanger to *SS-Sonderbataillon* Dirlewanger (SS Special Battalion Dirlewanger).

On December 22 and 23, the *Sonderkommando* conducted an opera-

The Cruel Hunters

tion under control of Battle Group Kutschera. The battalion killed sixteen partisans, executed fourteen suspected persons and captured eight rifles and four hand grenades. German losses were one killed and one lightly wounded.[81]

SS-Brigadeführer Franz Kutschera commanded Battle Group Kutschera. Kutschera was born February 22, 1904 in Oberwaltersdorf, Austria. He had been the *Gauleiter* of the Kärnten district of Austria. He had entered the Nazi Party in 1930 with party number 363,031 and the SS in 1931 with SS number 19,659. Selected as a *SS-Brigadeführer* in 1942, he served in numerous anti-partisan operations prior to being named the SS and Police Leader for Warsaw on September 25, 1943. He was killed under mysterious circumstances on February 1, 1944 in Warsaw – most likely assassinated by the Polish underground.[82]

On Christmas Eve 1942 *SS-Sturmbannführer* Dirlewanger sent a teletype message to the armed forces reserve hospital at Nassau a.d. Lahn in Germany. The communiqué announced that an Iron Cross 2nd Class was hereby awarded to *SS-Rottenführer* Rudolf Nickel of the *Sonderkommando* who was recovering from his wounds in the hospital. During the course of the war many more medals were given to soldiers in the *Sonderkommando*, not indicative of a unit held in low esteem.

On December 25 the *Sonderkommando* was ordered to conduct an operation to open the Berezino-Cerven' road which had been closed by partisan bands. Dirlewanger would operate under the command of the 286th Security Division; the operation was scheduled to last ten or eleven days. The operation was named *Berezino-Mogil'ov*. Dirlewanger deployed the German company both Russian companies, a reconnaissance platoon and two armored cars and would be led by *SS-Sturmbannführer* Magill. The unit would engage any enemy roadblocks with strong frontal fire, while sending elements to flank the enemy. The Germans expected partisan strong points at Kolbtscha, Golynka and Shabowka.[83]

SS-Sturmbannführer Franz Magill was born August 22, 1900 at Kleist near Köslin. He entered the SS April 4, 1933 and had an outstanding record prior to his service in the *Sonderkommando*. In 1935, while serving as a riding instructor at the SS Leader School at Braunschweig he received a recommendation for promotion from *SS-Standartenführer* Paul Hausser. Hausser, who later commanded a division, a corps and an army, had this to say:[84]

The Anti-Partisan Years - 1942

SS-Untersturmführer Magill has been a soldier for twelve years, is very quiet and reserved, comradely and a good riding teacher. He is especially qualified for promotion.

From the school he went to command a squadron of cavalry in the *SS-Totenkopfverbände* (Death's Head unit). In September 1939, Magill was assigned to SS Cavalry Regiment 1. There, he commanded the 1st Squadron and led this unit to Posen, Poland. There, his unit enforced the laws of the new German General Government of Poland and also helped capture criminals who had escaped Polish prisons during the attack. He then assumed command of the 11th Squadron at Lublin. On June 14, 1940 Magill assumed command of the 2nd *SS-Totenkopf-Reiterstandarte* – which later became SS Cavalry Regiment 2. He commanded this unit until April 10, 1941, when he assumed command of the Mounted Detachment of the regiment.[85] On October 28, 1941 the commander of the SS Cavalry Brigade *SS-Standartenführer* Hermann Fegelein wrote the following efficiency report on Magill:[86]

SS-Cavalry Brigade Berlin, October 28, 1941

RATING

of *SS-Sturmbannführer* Franz M a g i l l, SS-Cavalry Regiment 2, Party Member No. 4,137 171, SS-Nr. 132,620, promoted to *SS-Sturmbannführer* on April 20, 1938

Predominantly Nordic appearance, good military carriage, strong appearance. He served with the SS-Cavalry Regiment 1 from September 16, 1939 and from time to time was leading the SS-Cavalry Regiment 2.

He was to stay with the regiment longer. He discharged the purely organizational tasks to absolute satisfaction. It is especially noteworthy that he got along with all authorities and offices due to his friendliness. Unfortunately he did not succeed in getting the SS-

> Cavalry Regiment 2 under control so that his personality could flourish. As soon as he was put under pressure by his superiors, all was in order again. Because of this moment of weakness in the education of his leadership, he was not able to give the example which is demanded from a regimental commander.
>
> He is a straight, sincere soldier and he is convincing and enthusiastic in accomplishing his tasks. It is recommended that he watch his enjoyment of alcohol because it would be regrettable, considering his age, to neglect himself in this regard. As *SS-Sturmbannführer* in a cavalry regiment, he can only be used as squadron commander. He is not capable of higher duties. Due to his talent for organizing and his former occupation as a farmer, as well as his desire to stay on the Eastern Front, he is especially capable to be on the staff of a Higher SS and Police Leader. His two years of experience in the East vouch for his success. His family situation is of a very happy nature.

At least one source states that while Magill was with the unit, the SS Cavalry Brigade conducted *Final Solution* operations in Russia. From July 29 through August 12, 1941 the brigade conducted operations in the Pripjet marshes area. *SS-Standartenführer* Hermann Fegelein reported that 14,178 looters, 1001 partisans and 699 Red Army soldiers were executed. On August 2, Magill sent his First and Fourth Companies to Pinsk. A reported eight thousand Jewish males were killed; the women and children were to be driven into the marshes. During the entire Pinsk operation at least eleven thousand Jews were executed.[87]

On November 15, 1941 Magill was reassigned to the Higher SS and Police Leader White Russia staff and from there went to the *Sonderkommando*. He would serve as acting commander of the *Sonderkommando* from December 28, 1942 to February 20, 1943. In March 1943, *SS-Obergruppenführer* Erich von dem Bach-Zelewski, the commander of all SS anti-partisan forces, recommended Magill for promotion with this endorsement:[88]

Justification for promotion to the recommended grade is proven by: the exemplary fulfillment of all tasks required of him. As leader of the *SS-Sonderbataillon* Dirlewanger he especially proved his leadership qualities and led the battalion to considerable successes in the fight against bandits. For these deeds in leading the troops and for his personal engagements Magill was recommended to receive the Iron Cross 1st Class. Leading this battalion in a Russian area far away from other units of the Army and the police was especially difficult because the battalion consisted of 50% of Germans with heavy criminal records and of 50% of assistance groups (Russians and Ukrainians).

Since November 15, 1941, *SS-Sturmbannführer* Magill has been with me on the Eastern Front and belongs to my personal staff in dispensing the tasks of the Waffen-SS. He was took part repeatedly in leading operations against bandits. From December 28, 1942 to February 20, 1943, he was involved in fights against bandits more extensively as leader of the *SS-Sonderbataillon* Dirlewanger. He executed all tasks demanded from him in an exemplary manner, whereby he demonstrated strength and decisiveness, paired with thoughtfulness and a talent for organizing. To sum it up, he is an SS leader who proves himself in every situation and shows leadership qualities. *SS-Sturmbannführer* Magill possesses a decent, quiet character. He is well liked among his comrades and is respected as a strong and just leader by the men under him. His bearing is military, his behavior positive and immaculate. He has always fought for the National Socialistic philosophy and the National Socialist state.

Participation in battles: Cleansing of the swamps of Pripet, during which there was heavy fighting near Tourow. February/March 1942 fighting against bandits in the area of Klicev and Cerven' and several further engagements. From December 28, 1942 to February 1943 as leader of the *SS-Sonderbataillon* Dirlewanger, took part in the following missions and battles: On December 29, 1942 fighting against bandits south of Berezino. January and February 1943 *Operation Franz, Erntefest I, Erntefest II* and *Hornung*.

After service with Dirlewanger, Magill later was assigned to the 14th Waffen-SS Division *"Galician"* as the commander of the division supply troops. In this position he received the following report from Fritz Freitag, his division commander:[89]

> Magill has been engaged with the 14th Waffen-SS Volunteer Division *"Galician"* as commander of the division supply troops from March 2, 1944. His character is open and truthful, clean decent attitude, modest behavior. Slender, sporty figure, fully ready for action. Magill has a quiet but definite demeanor, gets results.
>
> Due to his knowledge and life experience he completely accomplishes his tasks at the level of his rank. His behavior towards superiors is correct in a military way, he is well liked and respected among his peers. For the men he is in charge of, he is a caring leader. His world philosophy is immaculate, and he is able to educate his men in a clear and definite manner. He is capable of being the commander of the division supply troops.

Magill was awarded the War Service Cross 2nd Class with Swords in 1940, the Iron Cross 2nd Class in 1941, the Eastern Front Medal in 1942. He appears to have had some alcohol related incidents in his career, but there is no evidence of criminal conduct in his file which would warrant his assignment to the *Sonderkommando* for disciplinary reasons.[90]

On December 29 the *Sonderkommando*, along with two battalions of *Osttruppen* (eastern troops), attacked a strong partisan camp. *SS-Schütze* Karl Hörath, Waldemar Appold and Karl Benkert were killed in the ac-

The Anti-Partisan Years - 1942

tion while *SS-Schütze* Wilhelm Ruch and Fridolin Wiesshaupt were seriously wounded. Four other Germans were lightly wounded; two soldiers from one of the Russian companies were killed as well.[91]

Departing the *Sonderkommando* in December was *SS-Obersturmführer* Hans Georg Weber. Weber had served in the unit since July 24, 1942 having previously served with the SS Main Office. He was born in Hannover September 4, 1901 and was an old SS fighter, having joined the organization on April 1, 1930 with an SS number of 2,752. He joined the Nazi Party the same year with membership number 265,118. Weber was an *SS-Obersturmbannführer* in the *Allgemeine-SS*, and received a commission as an *SS-Obersturmführer* in the Waffen-SS so he could perform front-line service. Gottlob Berger thought highly of Weber and probably sent him to the *Sonderkommando* so he could see combat and win some decorations – both of which would further his career. He received the War Service Cross 2nd Class, the Iron Cross 2nd Class, the Eastern Peoples Bravery Medal and several other decorations. Dirlewanger had this to say in an efficiency report about Weber's performance in the unit:[92]

> According to an order by the *SS-Führungshauptamt, Kommandoamt* of the Waffen-SS, *SS-Obersturmführer* Hans-Georg Weber, SS-No.2,732, was transferred to military duty with the battalion here.
>
> *SS-Obersturmführer* Weber commenced his service here on August 1, 1942, and by means of a telegram dated December 15, 1942 from the Main Office, Replacement Office of the Waffen-SS-Berlin was called back to Berlin.
>
> He served here as a company commander and at times as deputy battalion commander. He participated in all missions fighting the bandits during his time here. During the missions, he has always demonstrated courage and decisiveness. Because of his exemplary courageous behavior during these missions, he was awarded the Iron Cross 2nd Class on January 8, 1943. In his capacity as an SS-leader, he undertook to establish au-

thority. He was respected and appreciated by his troops. As far as his philosophical outlook is concerned, he is thoroughly convinced and serves as an example.

His attitude during duty hours and after can only be declared as very good.

Dirlewanger
SS-Sturmbannführer

In 1943 Weber returned to Germany and moved to the SS Replacement Department for southeastern Germany. He finished the war as an *SS-Standartenführer*.[93] As with many other officers who served with Dirlewanger, Weber went to the *Sonderkommando* not as punishment but for career advancement.

The year ended with the *Sonderkommando* having made significant contributions to German anti-partisan operations in White Russia. Dirlewanger was in Germany, but he would quickly be needed back in Russia.

ENDNOTES

[1] Lukas, Richard C. *The Forgotten Holocaust: The Poles under German Occupation, 1939-1944.* (Lexington, KY: The University Press of Kentucky, 1986), p.5.

[2] Reitlinger, Gerald. *The House Built on Sand: The Conflicts of German Policy in Russia, 1939-1945.* (New York: The Viking Press, 1960), p.397.

[3] Shown on maps at each chapter; name of operation in *italics*.

[4] Seidler. "SS-Sondereinheit Dirlewanger", p.616.

[5] Cooper. *The Nazi War.*, p.89.

[6] Personalakt Oskar Dirlewanger.

[7] Polizeiregiment Mitte/Ia/31.3.42 Regimentsbefehl 4, Washington, D.C: National Archives Microfilm Publication T354, Roll 650.

[8] Personalakt Oskar Dirlewanger.

[9] Seidler. "SS-Sondereinheit Dirlewanger", p.609.

[10] Personalakt Oskar Dirlewanger.

[11] The German Armed Forces made extensive use of Europe's railway systems during the war; the Reichsbahn (State Railways) could create special trains, composed of a specified kind and combination of Pullman cars, for Hitler, visiting heads of state, and high ranking German officials. Hitler's special train was initially codenamed *Amerika* which was later renamed *Brandenburg*. Goering had a train *Asien* later named *Pommern*, GFM Keitel had a special train *Afrika*, later known as *Braunschweig*, and the OKW staff had two Specials — *Atlas*, later renamed *Franken I*, and *Franken II*. Himmler's train was named *Heinrich*. One of Hitler's trains, for example, had the following composition of cars: locomotive, armored anti-aircraft car with 20mm cannon, baggage and power-engine car, Hitler's private Pullman, conference car with communications center, escort car for Hitler's SS escort detachment, dining car, two sleeping cars for guests, bath car, dining car, two cars for secretaries and aides, press chief's car, baggage and power-engine car, and anti-aircraft car.

[12] Personalakt Ralf Wehser, Washington, D.C: National Archives Microfilm Publication A3343, Records of SS Officers from the Berlin Document Center, Roll SSO-225B.

[13] Weingartner. "Law and Justice in the Nazi SS.", pp. 286-287.
[14] Reitlinger. *The House Built on Sand.*, p.235.
[15] Michaelis, Rolf. *Die Grenadier Divisionen der Waffen SS*, Band III. (Erlangen, Germany: Michaelis Verlag, 1995), p. 157.
[16] Arad, Yitzak, Shmuel Krakowski and Shmuel Spector. *The Einsatzgruppen Reports.* (New York: Holocaust Library, 1989), p. 346.
[17] Tätigskeitsbericht des SS Sonderkommandos Dirlewanger, Mai 1942, Washington, D.C: National Archives Microfilm Publication T354, Roll 650.
[18] Personalakt Oskar Dirlewanger.
[19] Ukrainer-Schützmannschafts-Ausbildungs Bataillon, 28.5.1942, Message, Washington, D.C: National Archives Microfilm Publication T354, Roll 650.
[20] Höhere SS-und Polizeiführer Russland-Mitte, Schutzmannschaften, 23.6.42, Letter, Washington, D.C: National Archives Microfilm Publication T354, Roll 650.
[21] Reitlinger. *The SS: Alibi of a Nation.*, p.173.
[22] Meyer. *Nacht über Hamburg.*, p.214.
[23] Fernschreiben an das Kriegsgericht der 137 I.D., 11.7.42, Washington, D.C: National Archives Microfilm Publication T354, Roll 650.
[24] Fernschreiben an SS-Gruppenführer Berger, SS Hauptamt, 12.7.42, Washington, D.C: National Archives Microfilm Publication T354, Roll 650.
[25] Einsatzbericht vom 19.7.42, Washington, D.C: National Archives Microfilm Publication T354, Roll 649.
[26] Bericht über die zugeteilte Ukrainer-Schutzmannschaft, Monat Juli 42, Washington, D.C: National Archives Microfilm Publication T354, Roll 650.
[27] Sicherungs Division 286 "Kampfgruppe Adler" Abschlussbericht Unternehmen "Adler", 8.8.42, Washington, D.C: National Archives Microfilm Publication T354, Roll 649.
[28] Personalakt Hans Georg Weber, Washington, D.C: National Archives Microfilm Publication A3343, Records of SS Officers from the Berlin Document Center, Roll SSO-222B.
[29] Sicherungs Division 286 "Kampfgruppe Adler" Abschlussbericht Unternehmen "Adler", 8.8.42, Washington, D.C: National Archives Microfilm Publication T354, Roll 649.
[30] Seidler. "SS-Sondereinheit Dirlewanger", p.609.
[31] Cooper. *The Nazi War.*, pp. 86-87.
[32] Trevor-Roper, H. R. ed. *Blitzkrieg to Defeat: Hitler's War Directives 1939-1945.* (New York: Holt, Rinehart and Winston, 1964), p. 132.
[33] Fernschreiben an Sonderkommando Dirlewanger, 30.7.42, Washington, D.C: National Archives Microfilm Publication T354, Roll 650.
[34] Sonderkommando Dirlewanger Beförderungsurkunde, 13.8.42, Washington, D.C: National Archives Microfilm Publication T354, Roll 650.
[35] *Trials of War Criminals before the International Military Tribunal, The Ministries Case, Case No. 11.*, p. 543.
[36] Gutman Yisrael and Berenbaum, Michael. *Anatomy of the Auschwitz Death Camp.* (Bloomington, IN: Indiana University Press, in association with the United States Holocaust Memorial Museum, 1994), p.282.
[37] Fernschreiben an das SS Hauptamt, Berlin 29.8.42, Washington, D.C: National Archives Microfilm Publication T354, Roll 650.
[38] Personalakt Oskar Dirlewanger.
[39] Ibid.
[40] Höheren SS-und Polizeiführer Russland-Mitte, 9.9.42, Written Report, Washington, D.C: National Archives Microfilm Publication T354, Roll 650.
[41] Personalakt Hans Georg Weber.
[42] Höheren SS-und Polizeiführer Russland-Mitte, 9.9.42, Written Report, Washington, D.C: National Archives Microfilm Publication T354, Roll 650.
[43] Personalakt Oskar Dirlewanger.
[44] Reitlinger. *The House Built on Sand*, p.237.
[45] Regimentsbefehl, Sicherungs regiment 36, 3.10.42, 5.10.42, Washington, D.C: National Archives Microfilm Publication T354, Roll 649.
[46] Sicherungs Regiment 36, 7.10.42, Instructions, Washington, D.C: National Archives Microfilm Publication T354, Roll 650.

[47] Einsatzbericht Unternehmen "Regatta" vom 4. bis 7.10.42, Washington, D.C: National Archives Microfilm Publication T354, Roll 649.

[48] 1. SS Infanterie Brigade (mot) Einsatzbefehl 1 (Unternehmens "Karlsbad") 6.10.42, 15.10.42, Washington, D.C: National Archives Microfilm Publication T354, Roll 649.

[49] Thomas, Nigel and Peter Abbott. *Partisan Warfare 1941-45*, Osprey Men at Arms Series 34, (London: Osprey Publishing Ltd, 1983), p.10.

[50] 1. SS Infanterie Brigade (mot) Tagesbefehl, 24.10.42, Washington, D.C: National Archives Microfilm Publication T354, Roll 649.

[51] Büchler, Yehoshua, "Kommandostab Reichsführer-SS: Himmler's Personal Murder Brigades in 1941." *Holocaust and Genocide Studies*, (Oxford, Great Britain: Pergamon Press, 1986), Volume 1 Number 1, pp. 16-18.

[52] Arad, Yitzak, Shmuel Krakowski and Shmuel Spector. *The Einsatzgruppen Reports,* pp. 100, 134.

[53] International Military Tribunal Nürnberg. *Trials of War Criminals before the International Military Tribunal, Volume IV, United States of America vs. Otto Ohlendorf, et al., Case No. 9.* (Washington, DC: U.S. Government Printing Office, 1949), pp. 36-37.

[54] Ibid., p.40.

[55] Ibid., p.448.

[56] Headland. *Messages of Murder.,* p.105.

[57] Hilberg. *The Destruction of the European Jews.*, pp. 190-195.

[58] Personalakt Erich Naumann, Washington, D.C: National Archives Microfilm Publication A3343, Records of SS Officers from the Berlin Document Center, Roll SSO-344A.

[59] Personalakt Otto Bradfisch, Washington, D.C: National Archives Microfilm Publication A3343, Records of SS Officers from the Berlin Document Center, Roll SSO-096. Author note: I have examined several thousand SS officer personnel records for this and two subsequent works and Bradfisch is the only one with annotations of Mischling. I believe this further supports the contention that it was not a word commonly used to simply indicate a mixture of non-Jewish characteristics — but that its use in the Bradfisch report was intentional.

[60] Breitman, Richard. *The Architect of Genocide: Himmler and the Final Solution.* (New York: Alfred A. Knopf, 1991), p. 196.

[61] Hilberg. *The Destruction of the European Jews (Revised and definitive edition).,* p.1092.

[62] Personalakt Heinz Richter, Washington, D.C: National Archives Microfilm Publication A3343, Records of SS Officers from the Berlin Document Center, Roll SSO-027B.

[63] Personalakt Hans-Gerhard Schindhelm, Washington, D.C: National Archives Microfilm Publication A3343, Records of SS Officers from the Berlin Document Center, Roll SSO-078B.

[64] Höhne. *The Order of the Death's Head.*, p.369.

[65] Hartung, Lothar. *Verleihungs-Urkunden des 3. Reiches*, (Fürstentum, Liechtenstein: Infora Research Est., 1982), p.71.

[66] Cooper. *The Nazi War.*, pp. 94-95.

[67] Breitman. *The Architect of Genocide.*, p. 191.

[68] Personalakt Erich von dem Bach-Zelewski, Washington, D.C: National Archives Microfilm Publication A3343, Records of SS Officers from the Berlin Document Center, Roll SSO-023.

[69] Schneider, Jost. *Their Honor was Loyalty!* (San Jose, CA: R. James Bender Publishing, 1977), pp. 21-22.

[70] Funkspruch HSSUPF Russland Mitte, 18.10.42, Washington, D.C: National Archives Microfilm Publication T175, Roll 18.

[71] Personalakt Curt von Gottberg, Washington, D.C: National Archives Microfilm Publication A3343, Records of SS Officers from the Berlin Document Center, Roll SSO-024A.

[72] Der Kommandierende General der Sicherungstruppen und Befehlshaber im Heeresgruppe Mitte, Abschrift, 25.10.42, Washington, D.C: National Archives Microfilm Publication T354, Roll 649.

[73] Erweiteres Krankenrevier bei Höherer SS und Polizei Führer Russland-Mitte, 26.10.42, Washington, D.C: National Archives Microfilm Publication T354, Roll 649.

The Anti-Partisan Years - 1942

[74] Sicherheitspolizei und SD Einsatzkommando 8, Einsatzbefehl, 1.11.42, Washington, D.C: National Archives Microfilm Publication T354, Roll 649.

[75] 1.SS Infanterie Brigade (mot) Tagesbefehl, 5.11.42, Washington, D.C: National Archives Microfilm Publication T354, Roll 649.

[76] SS-Sonderbataillon Dirlewanger Tagesbefehl, 13.11.42, Washington, D.C: National Archives Microfilm Publication T354, Roll 650.

[77] Personalakt Waldemar Wilhelm, Washington, D.C: National Archives Microfilm Publication A3343, Records of SS Officers from the Berlin Document Center, Roll SSO-246.

[78] Personalakt Waldemar Bodammer, Washington, D.C: National Archives Microfilm Publication A3343, Records of SS Officers from the Berlin Document Center, Roll SSO-081.

[79] Mehner, Kurt. *Die Geheimen Tagesberichte der Deutschen Wehrmachtführung im Zweiten Weltkrieg 1939-1945*. (Osnabrück, FRG: Biblio Verlag, 1988), Volume 6, p.553.

[80] Personalakt Oskar Dirlewanger.

[81] Funkspruch, Fernspruch, Fernschrift, 23.12.42, 8:20 AM, Washington, D.C: National Archives Microfilm Publication T354, Roll 649.

[82] Höffkes. *Hitlers politische Generale*., pp. 202-203.

[83] Höherer SS und Polizei Führer Russland-Mitte, Ia, Befehl, 25.12.42, Washington, D.C: National Archives Microfilm Publication T354, Roll 650.

[84] Personalakt Franz Magill, Washington, D.C: National Archives Microfilm Publication A3343, Records of SS Officers from the Berlin Document Center, Roll SSO-288A.

[85] Yerger, Mark C. *Riding East: The SS Cavalry Brigade in Poland and Russia 1939-1942*. (Atglen, PA: Schiffer Publishing, 1996), pp. 40-42, 51, 78. It is quite likely that Magill met Dirlewanger at Lublin in 1940 when both were operating in the area, although no documentation exists to support this assumption. Magill's replacement in SS Cavalry Regiment 2 was SS-Standartenführer Heino Hierthes, but Fegelein replaced him in early September 1941 due to Hierthes' lack of aggressiveness.

[86] Personalakt Franz Magill.

[87] Büchler. "Kommandostab Reichsführer-SS", pp. 16-17. This is not the same characterization of the operation as given by Mark Yerger in *Riding East: The SS Cavalry Brigade in Poland and Russia 1939-1942*. Yerger characterizes the fight as one of the SS cavalry against partisans and bypassed Red Army troops. Given the large disparity between reported German losses and enemy killed, I believe that many of the Russian casualties must have been civilian noncombatants.

[88] Personalakt Franz Magill.

[89] Ibid. Fritz Freitag ended the war as an SS-Brigadeführer. He committed suicide on May 20, 1945 in Austria.

[90] Ibid.

[91] SS-Sonderbataillon Dirlewanger, Bericht, 30.12.42, Washington, D.C: National Archives Microfilm Publication T354, Roll 650.

[92] Personalakt Hans Georg Weber.

[93] Ibid.

3

THE ANTI-PARTISAN YEARS 1943

Only villages which are judenrein do not become partisan bases.[1]
- Hermann Fegelein[2]

Oskar Dirlewanger began the year on leave in Germany and other soldiers in the *Sonderkommando* were permitted to depart as well. At the beginning of January 1943 the battalion prepared a plan for allowing leaves for deserving soldiers. Five troopers would begin their leave on January 7, five more would start on January 11, nine more, including *SS-Obersturmführer* Wilhelm, on January 18, and ten more on January 27.

Meanwhile, another anti-partisan operation was brewing. *Operation Franz*, scheduled to run from December 28 to January 14, was an attempt to eliminate some two thousand five hundred partisans in the Berezino, Cerven', Khutor, Novaya Niva, Novyye Lyady, Petrovka and Bogushevichi. Intelligence reports stated that the partisans operated in groups of one hundred to two hundred, were armed with machine-guns and artillery, had many Jews among them with many partisans probably clad in captured German uniforms. The overall plan for the operation called for an attack by Battle Group Kutschera from the north and Battle Group von Gottberg from the south to converge on the partisans and in the German vernacular "clean the area." *SS-Brigadeführer* Kutschera would command the northern group of forces.[3]

SS-Brigadeführer Kutschera reinforced the *Sonderkommando* with four tanks and an artillery battery of 76.2mm Russian cannon from the 56th *Schuma* Artillery Battalion. *SS-Sturmbannführer* Franz Magill formed the unit in column on January 6 one kilometer south of Berezino. The battalion advance guard, under *SS-Obersturmführer* Egyd Ingruber had one tank, the reconnaissance platoon and some wheeled vehicles with machine-guns. Ingruber would prevent the battalion from being ambushed. The rest of the battalion formed up behind him. The key aspect of the operation, from Magill's standpoint, was to reach each day's objective while maintaining contact with flank units, so no partisans could slip through. Then the battalion would quickly surround and destroy any groups of partisans they discovered.[4]

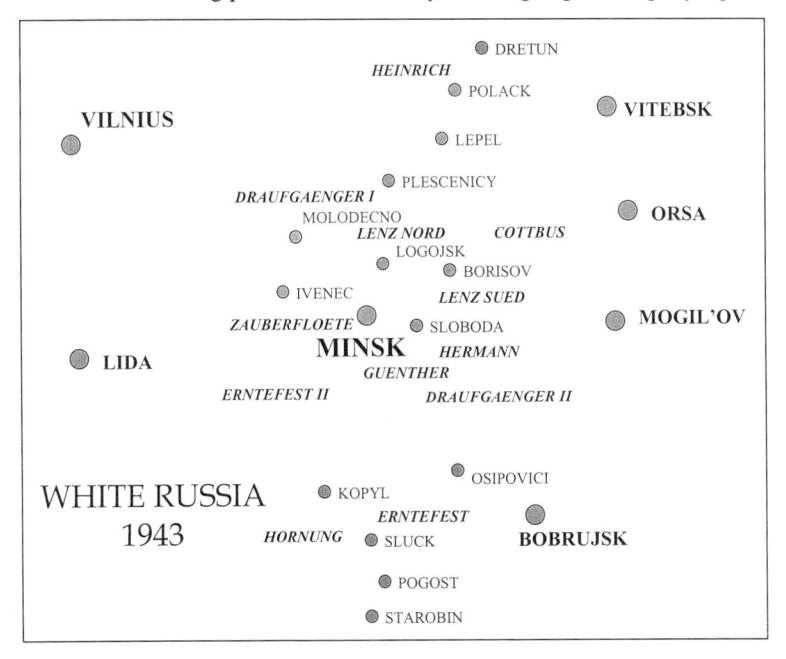

Magill made steady progress; on January 7 the battalion headquarters reached Krasnaja Sloboda and later Kopsewitschi. On January 9 Magill attacked southwest from the village. The partisans tried to flee to the northeast and the battalion received fresh instructions to set up a defense one kilometer north of Wesseloff near Jaswenski, and defend facing south. On January 10, *SS-Sturmbannführer* Magill ordered the battalion to round up all persons in the area between the ages of sixteen and fifty who were fit for work – they would be shipped off to Germany as slave labor. As usual, the *Sonderkommando* also confiscated livestock. The battalion continued attacking partisans on January 12. Magill gave amplifying instructions on capturing persons fit for work. Men could be between the ages of sixteen and forty-five, while unmarried women should be between sixteen and thirty. The SS would take these persons to a collection camp at Berezino. On January 14, *Operation Franz* came to an end, and the battalion prepared to move to Osipovici for a new action. Overall casualties for the operation are unknown. However, Battle Group von Gottberg, the southern group of German forces, reported killing 1,349 partisans and capturing 280 rifles, one 76.2mm howitzer, two anti-tank guns and two heavy mortars.[5]

SS-Obersturmführer Egyd Ingruber, commander of the battalion advance guard on the operation, was born at Mittersill near Salzburg, Austria on April 14, 1920. Entering the SS on April 4, 1938, he received SS number 317,056. Promoted to *SS-Untersturmführer* on November 9, 1940, he was then assigned to SS Regiment "*Nordland*." On August 22, 1941 he was promoted to *SS-Obersturmführer*. He was later assigned to the Higher SS and Police Leader Ostland and on November 29, 1942 was again reassigned, this time to the Higher SS and Police Leader for White Russia. For most of his tenure in the *Sonderkommando*, he served as the administration officer. He won the Iron Cross 1st and 2nd Class, the Eastern Front Medal, the War Service Cross 2nd Class with Swords, the Infantry Assault Badge, the Eastern People's Bravery Medal and the Anti-Partisan Badge. He later served in the *SS-Verwaltungs Hauptamt* (the Main SS Economic Office) and the Higher SS and Police Leader *Alpenland* staff. The following is an efficiency report Dirlewanger wrote on *SS-Obersturmführer* Ingruber:[6]

EVALUATION

SS-Obersturmführer
I n g r u b e r Egyd, SS-Nr. 317 056
born on April 14, 1920
in Mittersill/Salzburg.

Since November 28, 1942, *SS-Obersturmführer* I n g r u b e r has been a member of the *SS-Sonderbataillon* Dirlewanger as procurement leader [supply officer].

The Anti-Partisan Years - 1943

These tasks which were not easy, especially because of units of foreigners among them, were accomplished by him to my fullest satisfaction due to his diligence and prudence. As a young SS leader, convinced of the ideas of the Führer, he did not shy back and participated in the battles of the unit, despite his difficult duties as administrative leader. First as leader of the reconnaissance unit, he has proven his military abilities and through his exemplary bravery he has inspired his men to be decisive.

After the company commander *SS-Hauptsturmführer* Gramatke was wounded, he took over the leadership of this company. He was able to lead his company to significant successes. With that he proved that he could master the most difficult tasks at a field unit, not only as administrative officer, but by fulfilling the tasks of the field troop as a soldier and military leader.

He was awarded the Iron Cross 2nd Class for the courage which was proven often and his demonstrated bravery as well as the Eastern People's Bravery Medal in Silver on June 2, 1943. The Infantry Assault Badge in Silver was awarded to him on June 21, 1943 for participation in storm attacks.

On July 20, 1943, *SS-Obersturmführer* Ingruber was badly wounded in a mine explosion. He lost his left eye, and his left leg was broken in two places. Because of this incident, the unit lost a proven leader once again – a leader who had earned the respect of everyone by his attitude.

Politically speaking, *SS-Obersturmführer* Ingruber has a sound foundation. When he was the leader of the Hitler Youth, he was transferred to the Waffen-SS and has always translated the aims of our Führer into action. His character is of the type of an SS Leader who is highly respected and regarded by leaders, officers of lower grade and enlisted due to his steadiness.

The Dirlewanger battalion was then ordered to participate in *Operation Erntefest* (Operation Harvest), an anti-partisan operation, scheduled to begin on January 19, in the Minsk, Ivenets, Nagornoye, Krugloye, Osipovici, Sluck, Rakov, Osovo, Omgovichi and Kopyl' areas to confiscate agricultural products and livestock and to secure local personnel for the labor force in Germany. For the operation, the battalion would be assigned to *Einsatzgruppe* Griep. The area to be searched was divided in half – *Einsatzgruppe* Griep would secure the southern half of the zone and *Einsatzgruppe* Worm would secure the northern half.[7] On January 16, the battalion cleaned weapons and performed other refitting tasks, and on the 17th *SS-Obersturmführer* Ingruber traveled to Bobrujsk to get winter uniforms and camouflage clothing. On January 19, the *Sonderkommando* entrained to travel to Sluck; it conducted the operation as planned until January 26 when it was ordered to attack suspected partisan camps near Krugloje. Magill found an abandoned camp that day but made no contact with the enemy.[8]

Numerous soldiers deserted the unit and its harsh conditions. During the month the military commander in the city of Gera back in Germany reported holding *SS-Schütze* Stübner in detention. Likewise, the SS and police authorities in Kiev apprehended *SS-Rottenführer* Mössner. It is not known what finally happened to these two soldiers.

SS-Sturmbannführer Magill completed an after action report on January 28 for the operation. The *Sonderkommando* reported killing forty-eight partisans and executing thirty-four suspicious persons. Additionally, the Germans captured twenty-six partisans. The enemy killed three *Sonderkommando* soldiers (including a translator) and wounded four. The battalion detained seventy-seven work-capable civilians, seized 164 large livestock and eighty five tons of foodstuffs.[9] Overall in the operation, the Germans reported killing 805 partisans and executing 1,165 suspects. Additionally, they reported capturing thirty-four partisans.[10]

Back in Germany, other actions were occurring which would directly affect the *Sonderkommando*. In January 1943 Hitler decreed that German soldiers could not be brought to trial for atrocities committed during anti-partisan operations. He further declared that the Geneva Convention and the traditional rules of chivalry had no place in anti-partisan warfare.[11] Additionally, Dirlewanger's unit would receive a distinctive collar insignia. The *SS-Reichsführer* Himmler chose a model, featuring a German style hand-grenade with two crossed rifles, from four possible designs.[12]

At the end of January the *Sonderkommando* was assigned to Battle Group Binz for further anti-partisan operations. On January 30 the battalion established its headquarters at Makawczyce and killing two partisans. The next day they arrested forty-four suspicious individuals, killed three partisans and moved to Rudnia. On February 2, the *Sonderkommando* executed seventy-eight people and burned eighteen houses to the ground. One day later they killed eleven partisans and shot forty-three other people. On February 4, the unit killed one partisan and executed six other persons, moving to Kopyl' in the process. The battalion strength during this operation was listed at 320 hundred twenty soldiers, two anti-tank guns, eleven trucks, twenty-two machine-guns and five mortars.[13]

The *Sonderkommando's* next operation was *Operation Hornung* (Operation February) – an anti-partisan operation to secure agricultural products and executing the civilian population in the Ratkovo, Povarchitsky, Milevichi, Moroc', Staryye Velichkovichi and Starobin areas of the Pripet Marshes February 11 to 17, 1943. The Germans estimated the partisan strength in the area at between three and four thousand, and therefore formed five battle groups: Battle Group East, led by Police Regiment 2, Battle Group North, led by 1st Battalion, Police Regiment 23, Battle Group West, led by Police Regiment 13, Battle Group South, led by Police Regiment 10, and Battle Group Southeast, led by the 101st Slovakian Infantry Regiment. The overall commander of the operation was *SS-Brigadeführer* Curt von Gottberg; he gave the *Sonderkommando* the mission to destroy partisan groups and secure agricultural products.[14]

Born February 11, 1896 in Preussisch-Wilten, East Prussia, Curt von Gottberg entered the party on February 1, 1932 with a party number of 948,753. Five months later he entered the SS with a number of 45,923. Von Gottberg quickly moved through the ranks to *SS-Oberführer* before the war broke out. In Poland he commanded three *einsatzgruppe*; later he assumed the position of SS and Police Leader White Russia on November 4, 1942. Von Gottberg received the German Cross in Gold August 7, 1943 and the Knight's Cross on June 30, 1944. Ending the war as an *SS-Gruppenführer*, he committed suicide May 9, 1945 near Leutzhöft by Flensburg.

The battalion's axis of advance was generally east to west with three companies on line. The 2nd Russian Company pushed forward in the north was – they were to maintain contact with the flank unit of Battle Group West. The German company advanced in the middle, while in the south, the 1st Russian Company attempted to maintain contact with *Schuma* Battalion 57. Dirlewanger made three personnel switches for the operation. *SS-Schütze* Mittelhäuser was assigned to the 1st Russian Company and *SS-Unterscharführer* Schall and *SS-Schütze* Lehmann went to the 2nd Russian Company. Before the operation began, *SS-Oberscharführer* Böhme took the kitchen wagon to Sluck. *SS-Unterscharführer* Vogl would control the motor vehicles at Sluck. However, discipline problems continued; Dirlewanger shipped *SS-Mann* Strasdun back to a concentration camp for stealing. The operation commenced on the 11th. The next day the battalion reported killing two partisans and capturing two automatic weapons, some hand grenades and a horse and sleigh. The battalion headquarters moved to Wieliczkowicze Stare, but there was no contact with *Schuma* Battalion 57 to the south. On February 13, the Germans killed three partisans and captured one rifle, one pistol and a horse drawn cart. The headquarters, meanwhile, moved to Dobre Strazn. On February 15 fire from the *Schuma* Battalion killed a Ukrainian in the 1st Russian Company.[15]

From February 15 to 17 the *Sonderkommando* conducted one of its most infamous operations of the entire war. The unit was to move north for a two day period and destroy everything that could be used later by the partisans; the Germans would seize animals along with hay to feed them. Leftover hay would be burned. All persons captured would be shot. The *Sonderkommando* would turn the area into a no-man's land – *"Das Gebiet wird Niemandsland."* Dobre Strazn, Wejna, Wieliczkowicze Nowe and Wieliczkowicze would cease to exist.[16]

The Germans decided that security in Mogil'ov should be improved after numerous partisan incidents. The chief of staff for the Higher SS and Police Leader put out a three-page order in February 1943 on security measures for all German units in and around Mogil'ov. All soldiers would carry firearms at all times. At night, Germans soldiers would not travel alone. Each organization would maintain an "alarm detachment" who would sleep with their weapons. And finally, the first floor windows of all buildings would be fitted with anti-handgrenade shields – occupants would sleep on upper floors only.[17]

Operation Hornung ended on February 26. Von Gottberg claimed to have killed 9,662 partisans during the operation.[18] However, the operation, like many others, served not only an anti-partisan campaign but also a killing operation against Jews in the area. On March 8, 1943 von Gottberg sent a message to *SS-Gruppenführer* Maximilian von Herff stating that 3,300 Jews were killed in the operation.[19]

Shortly after the end of the operation, Dirlewanger reorganized the battalion as follows: battalion adjutant – *SS-Obersturmführer* Walser, administration officer – *SS-Obersturmführer* Ingruber, rations officer – *SS-Oberscharführer* Böhme, armorer – *SS-Unterscharführer* Mammitsch, finance officer – *SS-Unterscharführer* Selzer, clerk – *SS-Unterscharführer* Strumpf and translator – Dawid. The commander for the German company was *SS-Sturmbannführer* Praefke, the commander of the 1st Russian company was *SS-Hauptsturmführer* Gramatke, while the commander of the 2nd Russian company was *SS-Obersturmführer* Wilhelm. Dirlewanger ordered that in the future battalion staff personnel would come from those soldiers who had served in the battalion for two years. Additionally, he would personally assign all wounded soldiers when they finally returned to the battalion.

Dirlewanger was constantly looking for more soldiers but did not like to be dictated to. In March 1943, the commander of the Order Police in Minsk wanted to send the *Sonderkommando* a Latvian engineer soldier who had recently been convicted. Dirlewanger refused to take the soldier, stating that none of the foreign troops in the battalion were convicts. Dirlewanger also wrote to Berlin reporting that Adolf Schulz, Walter Stübner, Johann Wallner, Otto Ruppert and Wilhelm Wicky would all be sent back to the concentration camp at Oranienburg.[20]

On March 13, 1943 the *Sonderkommando* seized and "cleansed" three villages near the Borisov-Minsk rail line. The German company moved on the village of Prilepy, the 1st Russian Company did the same to Ljada and the 2nd Russian Company finished with Dubrovo. All three companies took livestock to the battalion headquarters at Ostroschitzy. Each company had a section of SD men with them to assist in the operation.[21]

The German company of the *Sonderkommando* went on a joint operation with the 118th Battalion on March 22, in the area of Molodecno. They killed thirty partisans and "cleansed" the village of Kossino. German language in the Dirlewanger battle reports, as well as those for many other Waffen-SS and Army units, avoided criminal terms in describing orders and actions, preferring to use more antiseptic terminology. There is no doubt that murder and killing is what actually transpired based on the "body counts" tallied in these reports.[22]

During March and April 1943, the battalion participated in *Operation Lenz Süd* (Operation Spring South) against partisan groups Rossgrom, Bolschevik and Burya in the Borisov, Cerven', Sloboda, Smolevici, Dubniki, Zhodino, Zabashevichi areas. Commencing March 31, the *Sonderkommando* operated with Police Regiment 13, the 1st Battalion Police Regiment 23 and several *Schuma* battalions, under overall control of *Einsatzstab* Schimana – which was commanded by General of Police Walter Schimana. Dirlewanger was augmented with *Schuma* Battalion 202 and Police Panzer Company 12, which possessed several armored cars.[23]

The Germans had excellent intelligence about the three thousand partisans in the area, who were organized in three groups. Group Rosgram was five hundred men strong and led by a former colonel in the Red Army, Vladimir Panow. The unit chief of staff was Sergei Orlov, with the group located in the Smolevici area, northeast of Minsk. The Germans believed the group possessed ten machine-guns in addition to other small arms. A partisan named Derbun commanded the second group, Group Bolschevik. Six hundred men strong, it was located in the Cerven', Osipovici and Borisov districts east of Minsk, and was even better armed with two light tanks, two anti-tank guns and twelve machine-guns. Group Burja was the last and largest group at about two thousand men. German intelligence said it was commanded by a man called "Uncle" Koller and was believed to be armed with eighty to ninety machine-guns, four 76.2mm howitzers and twelve tanks – a force that could have easily mauled the *Sonderkommando* in a fight.[24] Many of the partisans were known to wear German uniforms, so for the operation each *Sonderkommando* soldier wore a wide band of white cloth on his left shoulder strap.

On April 3, 1943 the battalion received orders to finish *Operation Lenz Süd* and to prepare to commence *Operation Lenz Nord* (Operation

Spring North), a continuation of the original operation against partisan group Dowgalenok, a force of two thousand, in the Borisov, Molodecno, Smolevici, Logojsk, Antonopol, Zembin and the Tsna, Vsyazha and Gavja River areas. *Einsatzstab* Schimana controlled would again control the *Sonderkommando*; they initially detached *Schuma* Battalion 202 from the battalion. Other German forces consisted of SS-Police Regiment 2, SS-Police Regiment 13, 1st Battalion SS-Police Regiment 23, the *Sonderkommando*, two *Schuma* battalions and Police Panzer Company 12.[25] Dirlewanger was to commence his attack at 8:00 AM on April 8 by seizing the partisan village of Chutenowe, shooting a partisan there named Schmanaj, destroying the village bakery and taking livestock. Next, the battalion advanced to and destroyed the partisan villages of Sagerje Ost and Antonopol before moving to Logojsk to await further orders. There they continued to hunt partisans until April 13 when the operation terminated.[26]

With so many convicts in the unit, there were many incidents of looting and thievery. On April 3, 1943, for example, *SS-Grenadier* Neustedt was caught looting and was given four weeks of hard labor in the battalion.

Winter was turning to spring and on April 5, 1943 all battalion personnel returned their winter uniforms to the battalion supply section. Soldiers who had lost this winter suit were to be held accountable – as partisans frequently used captured German camouflage clothing to help infiltrate German positions, and an annotation was made in their soldier's book.

• • •

SS-Hauptsturmführer Wehser of the SS Legal Office finally replied to Himmler's personal staff on the conduct of the continuing investigation against Dirlewanger on April 7. Had Berger been involved in stalling the investigation or had *SS-Gruppenführer* Breithaupt, the chief of the entire SS Legal Department – and who had recommended Dirlewanger for promotion in 1940, somehow delayed the proceedings? Or perhaps, regardless of the good intentions of the SS investigators, there were simply not enough eyewitnesses alive to cement the case?[27]

Dear Comrade Meine,

Referring to a reminder by the SS Legal Department of March 31, I have learned in the matter of *SS-Sturmbannführer* Dirlewanger that the investigations have not yet been concluded. The respective SS- and Police Court XV Breslau were ordered to conduct the pending investigations as soon as possible and to report on them. In our files it is noted that your office will be notified without further reminder as soon as the results of the suit are clearly stated.

Heil Hitler!
Wehser

• • •

On April 11, 1943 Dirlewanger sent a letter to the chief physician of the Higher SS and Police Leader in Minsk requesting that two doctors be assigned to the battalion. He complained that the forty kilometer trip to the nearest SS hospital at Minsk caused the condition of many of the wounded and sick to deteriorate.[28]

The next mission for the *Sonderkommando* was *Operation Zauberflöte* (Operation Magic Flute), a large scale anti-partisan operation against hostile elements and to secure slave laborers for the Reich in the city of Minsk, April 17 to 22, 1943. The capital of White Russia, Minsk, was not free of its own partisan activity. A city of 130,000 inhabitants, it had many houses, buildings and ruins, not to mention the Minsk ghetto, considered hiding places for saboteurs, agents, deserters and propaganda writers. The commander of the security police and SD would be the commander on the ground.[29]

The Germans assembled a large number of forces to conduct the operation and included: the 141st Reserve Division from the Army, all security police and SD units for White Russia, SS-Police Regiment 2, SS-Police Regiment 13, 1st Battalion SS-Police Regiment 23 and *Sonderkommando* Dirlewanger. The plan called for the 141st Reserve

Division and other Wehrmacht units to surround the city by April 17. The Germans then divided Minsk into six parts which were to be cleared in six days. SS-Police Regiment 2 would clear section one on April 17. A total of five hundred fifty eight men would cordon off the section, which had a circumference of 6.7 km, man two checkpoints which controlled access into this part of the city (and shoot anyone who failed to follow instructions), search this part of Minsk, and operate collection points to assemble and transport persons who would be shipped to Germany. SS-Police Regiment 13 would do the same for section 2 on April 18. With a circumference of 4.5 km, it was thought that four hundred seventy men could accomplish this mission – given two men per 50 meters on the cordon line.[30]

SS-Police Regiment 2, with six hundred forty men, would clear section five on April 19. The following day SS-Police Regiment 13 would clear section four with five hundred forty men. On April 21, it was SS-Police Regiment 2's turn again; this time to use four hundred seventy men to clear section three. Finally, on April 22, over eleven hundred men of the Army and SS-Police Regiment 2 would clear section six the largest section of the city. Additionally, six hundred SS and SD men under the command of the SD would roam through the city in search operations. The *Sonderkommando* cordoned off the Minsk Ghetto for the entire operation and also escorted SD men in and out of the ghetto. SS officials reminded Dirlewanger that no looting or plundering of the area would be permitted and violators would face the sharpest of penalties.[31]

On April 30, 1943 *SS-Sturmbannführer* Dirlewanger prepared a status report covering the last thirty days for the battalion. With its headquarters at Logojsk, northeast of Minsk, the battalion strength was five hundred sixty-nine – seven officers, seventy-one non-commissioned officers and four hundred eighty-one men; of which one officer, forty-four NCOs and three hundred twenty-two men were not German. *SS-Sturmbannführer* Dirlewanger was the battalion commander, *SS-Sturmbannführer* Karl Praefke and *SS-Obersturmführer* Egyd Ingruber were assigned to the battalion headquarters as well, but the unit had no doctor or dentist. *SS-Hauptsturmführer* Gramatke commanded the 1st Russian Company while *SS-Hauptsturmführer* Schreier commanded the 2nd Russian Company. The German company had no officers. As for awards, five soldiers won the Wound Badge in Black, one the Wound Badge in Silver and thirty-four the Eastern Front Medal. Thirty-five men had been killed in action during the preceding month, forty-eight had been wounded, six were missing and three had died of other causes.

SS-Sturmbannführer Karl-Joachim Praefke was born July 7, 1898 in Neustrelitz, Mecklenburg. With a Nazi Party number of 2,817,216 he joined the SS in 1934 and received an SS number of 234,960. During World War I, he entered service in March 29, 1916 with Fusilier Regiment 73. Praefke fought at the Somme in 1916 and Flanders in 1917. He was promoted from corporal through lance corporal on July 31, 1917. On that day British soldiers captured him near Langemark; he was repatriated on October 11, 1919. Praefke was promoted to lieutenant on March 3, 1920. He was married between the wars and fathered seven children; during World War II his family lived on Antonienstrasse in Munich. Praefke served in SS-Regiment *"Deutschland"* from 1937 to 1940; in 1941 he was assigned to *SS-Leibstandarte Adolf Hitler*, where he served as the commander of the replacement and training battalion. He then served with the Higher SS and Police Leader White Russia before joining the *Sonderkommando*. There is no indication in his personnel file that indicate that he was sent to the *Sonderkommando* for disciplinary reasons. From May 1, 1943 to December 15, 1943 he served with Dirlewanger as the German company commander. After leaving the *Sonderkommando*, he was assigned to various replacement units before his transfer to the panzer grenadier school at Kienschlag.[32]

The Higher SS and Police Leader for White Russia frequently distributed lists of code names to be used by the Germans to make intelligence gathering by the partisans more difficult. On April 28, 1943 the following code names went into effect and show the large number of units under the control of the Higher SS and Police Leader: Higher SS and Police Leader White Russia – *Panther*, SS Police Leader Mogil'ov – *Earth*, Police Commander Minsk – *Bird*, Police Commander Mogil'ov – *Cat*, Police Commander Bobrujsk – *Lion*, Police Commander Vitebsk – *Flower*, SS-Police Regiment 2 – *Winter*, SS-Police Regiment 13 – *Saxony*, *SS-Sonderbataillon* Dirlewanger – *Magpie*, Police Panzer Company 9 – *Highway*, Police Panzer Company 12 – *Devil*.[33]

This was just a partial listing. The code name list also showed the

118

strength of German forces in the area; there are ten SS-police battalions, two police panzer companies, eleven *Schuma* battalions, two Latvian *Schuma* battalions, five Lithuanian *Schuma* battalions, a Polish *Schuma* battalion, eleven motorized gendarme platoons, the *SS-Sonderbataillon* Dirlewanger, and an SS-Group Drushina – an aggregate of thirty battalions of troops available for anti-partisan operations.[34]

Dirlewanger next participated in *Operation Draufgänger I and II* (Daredevil I and II). *Operation Draufgänger I* was an anti-partisan operation to secure agricultural products and slave laborers in the Molodecno, Plescenicy and Logojsk areas from April 28 to 30, 1943. *Operation Draufgänger II* was a continuation of the anti-partisan mission and included the execution of suspicious villagers and confiscation of agricultural products in the Molodecno, Borisov and Starinki areas during the first ten days of May. Lieutenant Colonel of Police Griep commanded both operations. *Operation Draufgänger II* started for the *Sonderkommando* on May 1 as the 1st Russian Company moved to Korytnica and then captured Starzynki. The 2nd Russian Company, meanwhile, moved forward to Dworzez while the German company and battalion headquarters initially remained in Kapuscina. The plan called for transporting all work-capable persons and livestock to Ilja. On May 2, at 10:30 PM Soviet night attack aircraft bombed the battalion area but no one was injured. On May 4, the German company seized the pro-partisan village of Brygidovo. On the 5th, the battalion reported shooting one hundred fifteen partisans and killing a further sixty-five women and children. The *Sonderkommando* additionally captured twenty rifles and appropriated seventy-five head of cattle and twenty horses.[35]

On May 6 the battalion reported attacking a large camp, killing thirty partisans and destroying seventeen bunkers, as the battalion headquarters moved to Rudnia. On the 7th, the Germans burned the village of Krzemieniec and shot ten partisans. The next day the 2nd Russian Company killed six partisans and executed fifteen civilians, while the 1st Russian Company killed eight partisans and shot one civilian. On May 10 the battalion submitted an after action report for *Draufgänger II*. In the report 386 partisans were reported killed and 294 civilians executed; while the *Sonderkommando* suffered only three wounded. Additionally, the Germans reported capturing one machine-gun, 110 rifles, 117 horses, 248

The Cruel Hunters

head of cattle and thirty-three persons for slave labor. The villages of Starzynki, Brygidovo, Lubca, Baturyn, Krzeminiec and Januszkowicze were reported destroyed.[36]

The disparity of partisan losses to German, combined with the few number of captured weapons, indicate that this was more a killing operation than a pitched battle between partisan and anti-partisan forces. This was a war against civilians – women and children were fair game.

The battalion status report for May showed an increased strength for the *Sonderkommando* to 612; ten officers, seventy-one NCOs and 531 men. Dirlewanger also received a physician during the month, and an additional officer, *SS-Hauptsturmführer* Erwin Walser reported to the battalion staff. One soldier had been killed during the month, three wounded and twenty reported sick. Among the seriously wounded was *SS-Untersturmführer* Wilhelm Reiner. And the month was profitable personally as well; Dirlewanger was promoted to *SS-Obersturmbannführer* on May 12.

SS-Hauptsturmführer Erwin Walser was born August 1, 1910 in the district of Matzingen. A member of the Nazi Party, he carried party number 568,963. He joined the SS in 1931 and received SS number 28,478 after having previously trained to be a salesman. Walser was married and had three children. He was promoted to *SS-Untersturmführer* September 13, 1936 and during this period served in several SS cavalry assignments. On April 20, 1938 he was promoted to *SS-Obersturmführer* and joined the staff of the *Reichsführer-SS*. Exactly two years later he was promoted to *SS-Hauptsturmführer*. In 1942 he was reduced to the rank of *SS-Mann* for an unnamed offense and was assigned to the *Sonderkommando* on instructions from Gottlob Berger, where he served as the battalion adjutant until April 1944. His official record reinstated his previous officer rank on November 26, 1943. By German standards, Walser had an outstanding military record. He won the Iron Cross 2nd Class, was awarded the Iron Cross 1st Class and Close Combat Bar in Bronze in December 1943 and received the Infantry Assault Badge. After leaving the battalion, he received the Anti-Partisan Badge in Silver in May 1944, the War Service Cross 2nd Class and on September 21, 1944 the War Service Cross 1st Class. After serving with the *Sonderkommando*, Walser returned to the SS Main Office, and was promoted to *SS-Sturmbannführer* on June 21, 1944.[37] He would survive the war.

The Anti-Partisan Years - 1943

SS-Untersturmführer Wilhelm Reiner was born March 7, 1895. He was assigned to the *Sonderkommando* on March 1, 1942. A teacher by profession, he had taught in the high school in Württemberg in 1914 before entering World War I. Reiner received the Iron Cross 2nd Class on April 18, 1915 and the Iron Cross 1st Class on January 28, 1918. On August 4, 1918 he received the Wound Badge in Silver. After the war he rejoined the teaching profession first as a teacher and then senior teacher and rector of the *Horst Wessel* School in Friedrichshafen. He joined the Nazi Party on September 6, 1930 with a party number of 333,808. In 1932 he assumed command of an SA detachment at Munsingen and in 1934 assumed command of SA Standard 49 as an *SA-Sturmhauptführer* (somewhat equivalent to a military captain.) In 1937 Reiner held the rank of lieutenant of reserves in the army's Infantry Regiment 14. On January 6, 1938 he was jailed for having sex with underage girls at a finishing school and kicked out of the army, party and his job. He served two and one half years in prison for the offense; on his release he was employed by a glider manufacturing company. Reiner applied to the Ministry of Justice and *SS-Hauptamt* to atone for his record; he joined the *Sonderkommando* shortly thereafter. He was assigned to the Higher SS and Police Leader for White Russia after his convalescence; later he was assigned to the *SS-Hauptamt* and at the end of the war to the XIIth SS Corps.[38]

• • •

Had Dirlewanger been aware of events in Germany, he may have tempered his promotion celebration. In May 1943 Himmler recalled Konrad Morgen from the Russian Front, restored him to his former officer rank, appointed him to the Reich Criminal Police Office (*Reichskriminalpolizeiamt*) and elevated him to the position of SS Judge.[39]

At the beginning of June 1943 *SS-Obersturmbannführer* Dirlewanger, now back in Berlin, spoke with *SS-Brigadeführer* Richard Glücks – the head of all concentration camps. Glücks announced that over the next several weeks he would assemble an additional 350 prisoners and 150 poachers at Oranienburg for later shipment to the *Sonderkommando*. On June 8, Dirlewanger informed *SS-Gruppenführer* Berger[40] that the battalion currently consisted of a German company with one hundred fifty men, a German reconnaissance platoon of forty men, three Russian companies of 150 men each, a platoon of forty Ukrainians and an artillery battery with forty Germans and forty Russians – a total strength of 760 men. With the additional "recruits" promised by Glücks, Dirlewanger planned to form an additional two companies. For this increase, Dirlewanger stated, he would need an additional 600 rifles, 120 twenty sniper rifles, fifty pistols, six motorized field kitchens, sixty-two machine-guns, twelve mortars and forty-six vehicles. He also asked for twenty trained vehicle drivers and sixteen radio operators.[41]

Richard Glücks knew how to get things done. Born April 22, 1889 in Odenkirchen near Mönchen-Gladbach, he entered the Nazi Party on March 1, 1930 with membership number 214,855. A master improviser, he found himself at the beginning of World War I in South America. He obtained Swiss papers and joined the crew of a Norwegian ship, avoided Allied internment and made his way back to Germany. Glücks joined the SS on November 16, 1932 and received SS number 58,706. By the end of 1934 Glücks had risen to *SS-Obersturmbannführer*. Most of his assignments in the SS were related to the concentration camp system. He became the inspector of the concentration camp system in 1939 before assuming command of the entire system in 1942. Glücks was promoted to *SS-Gruppenführer* on November 9, 1943. In 1945 he received the German Cross in Silver for his long-time work in the camps. The certificate read:[42]

> *SS-Gruppenführer* Glücks has been the chief of Department D in the SS Economics and Administration Head Office for the past two years. In this capacity, he is responsible for all matters which are connected with the concentration camp system. He does not only have to supervise the military leadership of 40,000 men who are in the camp guard system, but he is also responsible for military order and SS-like leadership of presently 15 concentration camps and 500 sub-camps with a total number of prisoners of around 750,000. In this capacity, which *SS-Gruppenführer* Glücks already had as inspector of concentration camps before becom-

The Anti-Partisan Years - 1943

ing department chief, he has earned significant awards for the war armament because of the consistent use of prisoners in the weapons industry.

That there were no difficulties during all the years of the war and that the war industry was supplied with the demanded work force, then it was because of the efforts of *SS-Gruppenführer* Glücks. Through his accomplishments, he contributed considerably to the war supplies and with that for the conduct of the war. The amount of these contributions warrant awarding him the German Cross in Silver.

The *Sonderkommando* was having difficulties with drivers using military vehicles for their own personal use and in general "joyriding." Dirlewanger threatened future punishment if the practice continued and made all battalion drivers sign the order stating they had read it. The following soldiers acknowledged receipt of these instructions: *SS-Oberscharführer* Koschka, *SS-Rottenführer* Stollwerk, Westphal and Klak, *SS-Sturmmann* Drabek, *SS-Grenadier* Heyn, Barainsky, Rentmeister, Hagen, Waldmann, Kapferer, Keiper, Eiding, Busch, Thielecke and Bock.

Sometimes, due to outstanding sustained performance in the *Sonderkommando*, an individual would have his record cleared. Such was the case with *SS-Oberscharführer* Heinz Feiertag. On June 17 Dirlewanger received a letter from the SS Main Office stating that the Ministry of Justice had approved the SS court's request to have Feiertag's record of conviction wiped clean.[43]

The Wehrmacht occasionally pulled soldiers out of front-line service if they qualified as the last surviving son in a family (i.e. when all other sons had been killed in action). Such was the case on June 24, 1943 when inquiries revealed that *SS-Unterscharführer* Willy Meyer qualified for this program. That the *Sonderkommando* complied with these regulations is indicative that it was considered more of a regular unit than testimony later at the Nürnberg War Crimes Trial would have us believe.

Dirlewanger from time to time received requests from high ranking Nazi bureaucrats for him to procure foreign laborers for them. These letters usually began "Dear Comrade Dirlewanger!" On June 24 the chief of

The Cruel Hunters

department A-I of the SS Main Office in Berlin-Wilmersdorf wrote Dirlewanger asking if the *Sonderkommando* could procure and transport fifty Russian men and ten women to the SS Main Office as laborers.[44]

On June 28, 1943 the *Sonderkommando* received orders to participate in *Operation Günther*, an anti-partisan mission against partisan groups Djadja Wasja, Fuer's Vaterland, Kowtow and Raykow in the Molodecno, Besyady, Rudnya and Manyly forest areas. For the operation the Germans fielded SS-Police Regiment 2, known as Regiment Griep, Regiment von der Golz from the Army and the *Sonderkommando*. *SS-Gruppenführer* Gerret Korsemann served as the overall commander of the operation. The three major German units were to close in on the partisan groups from three sides and destroy them. The *Sonderkommando* initially positioned itself east of the Manyly Forest. On July 4, the German company captured seventy-eight persons for emigration as slave labor as well as seventeen head of cattle. The next day the company collected 758 persons, 130 cattle and eighty-six horses. On July 6, the 1st Russian Company rounded up 465 persons, fifty-four horses and eighty-seven head of cattle. The same day the German company killed two partisans and executed 176 suspects. On that day *SS-Gruppenführer* Korsemann sent a message to all units thanking them for their efforts.[45]

In an after action report compiled on July 9, Dirlewanger reported that for the entire operation the *Sonderkommando* had killed twenty-five partisans, executed two hundred sixty-six suspects and taken three prisoners. One German had been wounded, two foreign troops had been killed and one foreign trooper had been wounded.[46]

On July 10, 1943 Dirlewanger conducted another major reorganization of the battalion. There were now six companies. The 1st Company, formerly the German company, was commanded by *SS-Hauptsturmführer* Kurt Weisse. The 2nd Company, consisting of new recruits, was commanded by *SS-Hauptsturmführer* Rudolf Stöweno. The 3rd Company, also consisting of new recruits, was led by *SS-Oberscharführer* Böhme. The 4th Company, formerly the 1st Russian Company, was commanded by *SS-Hauptsturmführer* Josef Grohmann. The 5th Company, formerly the 2nd Russian Company, was commanded by *SS-Obersturmführer* Wilhelm. The final unit was the Staff Company under *SS-Hauptscharführer* Beller.[47] As part of the reorganization some key personnel

The Anti-Partisan Years - 1943

were reassigned. To the 1st Company went *SS-Oberscharführer* Binder; to 2nd Company went *SS-Hauptscharführer* Weyand, *SS-Oberscharführer* Schall, *SS-Scharführer* Dinkgräfe, *SS-Unterscharführer* Credner and Sörnitz and *SS-Rottenführer* Hesener. *SS-Oberscharführer* Engelniederhammer, *SS-Unterscharführer* Selzer, Brusberg and Rett and *SS-Rottenführer* Seiliez and Doll-Wimmer. Finally, *SS-Rottenführer* Illing went to the 5th Company and *SS-Oberscharführer* Lirs was assigned to the staff.[48]

SS-Hauptsturmführer Kurt Weisse was born October 11, 1909 in Ehrenfriedersdorf of the Erzgebirge region of Germany. Not an early member of the Nazi Party due to his age, he joined in 1931 and received party number 563,159. He joined the General SS in 1932 and was issued SS number 129,822; he transferred to the Waffen-SS in 1933. Able to speak English and French, he was promoted to *SS-Untersturmführer* February 16, 1935 and *SS-Obersturmführer* on January 30, 1936. He was promoted to *SS-Hauptsturmführer* on September 13, 1936 and was then assigned to command the 2nd Battalion of the Death's Head unit in Saxony. Weisse was married but had no children; during the war, his wife lived at Taucha near Leipzig. In 1941 he was assigned to the *"Deutschland"* Regiment of the SS Division *"Das Reich."* He received the Iron Cross 2nd Class on August 12, 1941 and the Eastern Front Medal July 29, 1942. In September of 1941 he was wounded by a shell fragment in the ankle. He was then assigned to the SS *"Totenkopf"* Division with duty at the Sennelager Training Area. While there he got into serious trouble. On January 23, 1943 a field court martial headed by *SS-Obersturmbannführer* Heinz Lammerding, convicted him of negligent homicide involving the death of a subordinate and also for striking a junior soldier who had been caught stealing. His original sentence was life imprisonment. He was assigned to the *Sonderkommando* on July 1, 1943. His combat career blossomed in the unit; he won the Infantry Assault Badge November 20, 1943, the Close Combat Bar in Bronze December 7, 1943, the Iron Cross 1st Class December 13, 1943 and the Wound Badge in Silver in January 1944. He additionally won the Eastern People's Bravery Medal 1st and 2nd Class, the 8 and 10 Year NSDAP Service Medal, the Sudentenland Medal, the Austria Anschluss Medal, the War Service Cross, and the Anti-Partisan Badge in Bronze. On September 9, 1944 he was awarded the German Cross in Gold. His citation for this award follows:[49]

Since June of 1943, *SS-Sturmbannführer* Weisse has been a member of the *SS-Sonderregiment* Dirlewanger. After he first served as leader of the 1st Company, he was made the leader of a battalion due to his superior military capabilities. *SS-Sturmbannführer* Weisse participated in all battles of the unit and led his battalion to great success through his personal courage, bravery and circumspection. Because of his engagement at the front southwest of Newel he was awarded the Iron Cross 1st Class for his outstanding bravery. Next to his personal bravery and courage in every situation, the following outstanding displays of courage are especially noteworthy:

On December 23, 1943, a reinforced reconnaissance troop under the leadership of *SS-Sturmbannführer* Weisse was employed for the purpose of a forceful search of enemy positions south of Malt-Puschtscha/ Dretun. Despite most severe enemy resistance, Weisse, in the front line of his men, pushed through to the enemy positions and caused considerable damages to the enemy in hand-to-hand fighting. With this forceful act, it was possible to take prisoners and also to clean out and destroy important positions in the enemy system. The ensuing interrogation of the prisoners revealed the intentions of the enemy, which could be thwarted by their own counter measures.

On January 3, 1944 at the Beresno Lake, the foremost German position was under fire from snipers from the trees. Scouts which were sent out could not verify the position of the shooters, while our own losses mounted. Weisse made the quick decision to gather a few courageous men and led them to flank the enemy and get to his rear. After hard fighting, he was successful in destroying the enemy positions and to establish his own battle front station which brought important observation results for the continuation of the attack.

The Anti-Partisan Years - 1943

On March 22, 1944, a heavily secured convoy was attacked by bandits during which our own forces were more and more pushed together by the superior enemy forces. A messenger brought this message to the station whereupon *SS-Sturmbannführer* Weisse went marching with a pioneer group to the area of attack. He was able to relieve the troops which were pushed together in a very small area while they were constantly shot at and could only attack the enemy with simple weapons by a skillfully conducted attack, causing the enemy heavy losses and saving our own forces from destruction.

During *Operation Frühlingsfest* on April 19, 1944, the village of Tscherniza in the area of Polock was extremely defended by Bolschevik bandits. In mostly difficult forested and swampy areas, the attack went very slow and the danger existed that a stop would result due to strong anti-tank and grenade fire from the enemy. Here again, *SS-Sturmbannführer* Weisse motivated his men to gather all their strengths so that the commanded destination could be reached. In front of his men, he stormed over a narrow bridge over the Tscherniza, encouraging his men with this act to come along and then to destroy and occupy strong fortified enemy bunkers along the outskirts of the village. By succeeding in occupying the outskirts of the village, the condition was created for occupying the village which had been heavily armed by the bandits in their defense.

On April 25, 1944, *SS-Sturmbannführer* Weisse demonstrated again extraordinary courage and unconditional personal commitment in the attack of Height 184.9 near Lessiny in the area of Polock. He led his men in storming the height, destroyed bunkers which were erected there and smoked them out including the enemy forces in this position. Through his decisive act a corner position of the defense system of the enemy was broken, many losses to be caused from the enemy positions were spared and the condition for a successful continuation of the attack was created.

In the early morning hours of May 26, 1944, the base of the unit in Usda was attacked by heavy bandit forces. Immediately *SS-Sturmbannführer* Weisse had all necessary preparations made which were necessary for the defense of the base. Personally in front of a strong pioneer group he went on the attack, caught the enemy in the flank, destroyed a large part and caused the rest to flee. A Pak, horses and other military supplies could be garnered. According to statements made by prisoners afterwards, it was the intention of the bandits to conquer the base. Only because of the decisiveness of *SS-Sturmbannführer* Weisse to go on a counter-attack, did the enemy not realize their plans.

On July 7, 1944, during the general withdrawal movements in Army Group Center, *SS-Sturmbannführer* Weisse could register considerable success. When the enemy with heavy infantry forces attacked the newly established position near Lida, *SS-Sturmbannführer* Weisse, realizing the danger, made the decision to attack the flank with a company. With his courageous handling of the situation, he became an example of willingness to fight for his men. Through his ruthless personal engagement and decisiveness his men were motivated and it was possible to force the enemy to retreat under heavy losses by a well led push to the flank. Through the beating back of the enemy, the conditions were created that large parts of the equipment of several units could be transported on the highway which otherwise would have been cut off and would not be able to escape destruction.

On August 5, 1944, the SS-Regiment Dirlewanger under the leadership of *SS-Sturmbannführer* Weisse was ordered to attack along the Litzmannstadt-Strasse towards Warsaw. Most severe street fighting with heavy losses developed. After only a few hundred meters, the attack threatened to come to a standstill. Heavy barricades and bunker-like fortified houses forced our own men to fight for every foot-length of space. Towards the evening of the first day of battle, enemy resistance was severely fortified. *SS-Sturmbannführer* Weisse made the decision to attack and destroy the enemy barricades and minefields during the night. By the morning of August 6, 1944, some hundred meters of ground was again regained and the barricades were destroyed. During the course of the day the remaining enemy nests along the battle route were cleaned up and the attack under the constant personal engagement of *SS-Sturmbannführer* Weisse in the front line was continued. In burning house ruins, the attack during the late afternoon hours of August 7, 1944 threatened to come to a standstill once again. Collapsing houses caused debris to be an obstacle for the men fighting under the leadership of Weisse from step to step. Despite the heavy engagement of the troops called to battle, *SS-Sturmbannführer* Weisse ordered in the evening hours of August 7, 1944 to advance further during the night under merciless re-igniting of the buildings so that during the course of August 8, 1944 the ordered destination (Markthallengelände – market hall area) could be reached. The battle group, personally led by Weisse in front position, reached the destination around noon of August 8, 1944, even though heavy losses were incurred. Several hundred meters east of the Markthallengelände the German War flag of the Army City Commander was waving. Weisse made the decision to push through the heavily occupied area in-between as a last endeavor of all forces, so that a connection to the army units there could be established. It was only through his decisiveness, his personal courage and the consistent readiness for battle that the link-up from the western border of Warsaw to the Vistula, and with that to the east towards the front, could be established. This bold deed was accomplished after a short battle during which *SS-Sturmbannführer* Weisse, standing on a tank while encouraging his men, came rolling in as the first one in the courtyard of the Army Commander.

Dirlewanger
SS-Oberführer

—

The recommendation is endorsed.

von dem Bach
SS-Obergruppenführer

The German Cross in Gold was a prestigious award and was presented to distinguished Luftwaffe aces, U-boat commanders and Army officers and enlisted personnel just to name a few. The award to a member of the *Sonderkommando* certainly was an indicator that this unit was far from being a pariah organization.

On July 7, 1943 the battalion received an operations order from Battle Group von Gottberg for *Operation Hermann*, an anti-partisan operation to destroy partisans and confiscate agricultural products and livestock and to secure a labor force in the Rakov, Radoshkovichi, Zaslavl', Grodek, Ivenec, Volozhyn and Niemen River areas. Other units in the operation included the 1st SS Infantry Brigade, SS-Police Regiment 2, *Schuma* Battalions 115, 118 and 15 and Police Regiment 31.[50]

For combat on July 10, 1943 at Molodsi, the battalion was credited with an infantry assault day. *SS-Unterscharführer* Otto Brune, Gustav Brusberg and Josef Doll-Wimmer were particularly singled out as having performed well.

On July 19 the 1st Company reported capturing three hundred fifty-

The Anti-Partisan Years - 1943

five persons fit for work and sent them to a collection area at Jarszewicze. On July 20 *SS-Obersturmführer* Ingruber was seriously wounded when his motor vehicle ran over a mine 12 kilometers from Lahoisk at 7:00 AM. Ingruber and three soldiers were taken to the SS hospital in Minsk; he would lose his left eye and had his leg broken in two places. Later that day one of the soldiers, *SS-Grenadier* Kuhles died of his wounds. The 1st Company recorded executing five persons and seizing two hundred fifty-four people and forty-two horses. The battalion reported that near Dobrinewo, *SS-Grenadier* Geiselbacher had been killed, *SS-Grenadier* Keiper seriously wounded and *SS-Unterscharführer* Stollewerk lightly wounded. On July 21 the 1st Company noted burning the village of Dubowce, killing one partisan, executing two hundred eighty-seven suspects, rounding up three hundred forty-seven work-capable persons and seizing fifteen horses while losing only one man lightly wounded.

On July 22 the 1st Company liquidated the village of Popki killing nine suspects and seizing four hundred twenty-four work-capable persons. On July 27 the battalion reported seizing three hundred fourteen work-capable persons and sixty-two head of cattle. The next day was a light one with the unit reporting killing only one partisan. On the 28th the *Sonderkommando* reported killing twenty-five partisans but lost *SS-Grenadier* Putz and Busse killed in action. On August 1, the battalion reported killing seventeen partisans and twenty Jews. On August 5, the Germans killed two partisans and captured three more. The next day they reported killing one partisan and capturing one more, while seizing eight men, ten women and eight children. On August 7 the battalion reported one man killed and eighteen wounded in an accident with a hand grenade in addition to rounding up 394 people and destroying eleven villages. One of the wounded was the battalion adjutant *SS-Obersturmführer* Werner Blessau.

On July 29, *SS-Obergruppenführer* Friedrich Jeckeln, The Higher SS and Police Leader for *Ostland* and North Russia, awarded the Iron Cross 2nd Class to *SS-Hauptsturmführer* Erwin Walser, *SS-Hauptsturmführer* Kurt Gramatke, *SS-Obersturmführer* Egyd Ingruber, *SS-Untersturmführer* Heinrich Amann, *SS-Oberscharführer* Friedrich Böhme, *SS-Unterscharführer* Hans-Friedrich Lühr, Captain of Police Thido Mehlen and First Lieutenant of Police Joseph Steinhauer.

SS-Obergruppenführer Friedrich Jeckeln was born February 2, 1895 in Hornberg, Baden. He served in the field artillery in World War I, winning the Iron Cross 2nd Class. After the war he served in the police and joined the Nazi Party in 1930 with party number 163,348. He was also an early member of the SS and held SS number 4367. He won the Iron Cross 1st Class on May 12, 1942, the German Cross in Gold on December 19, 1943, the Knight's Cross on August 27, 1944 and the Oak Leaves to the Knight's Cross on March 23, 1945. He ended the war as the commander of the Vth SS Mountain Corps. For his reign as the Higher SS and Police Leader for *Ostland* and Northern Russia he was tried by the Soviets after the war and was hanged in Riga on February 3, 1946.

Alarmed perhaps by situation reports indicating prisoners were being killed, *SS-Gruppenführer* von Gottberg ordered on August 11 that henceforth no captured partisans or partisans who had deserted to the Germans would be shot. Instead, he ordered, they should be turned over to the SD.[51]

However, about the same time, Himmler ordered more draconian measures in the fight against partisans:[52]

> The Führer has decided that the partisan-infested areas of the north Ukraine and Central Russia are to be evacuated of their entire population. The entire able-bodied male population will be assigned to the Reich Commissioner for Allocation of Labor, in accordance with arrangements yet to be decided upon – under conditions applicable to prisoners of war, however. The female population will be assigned to the Reich Commissioner for Allocation of Labor for employment in the Reich. A part of the female population and all orphaned children will enter our reception camps. In an accordance with an agreement yet to be reached with the Reich Minister for Food and the Minister for Occupied Eastern Territories, the Higher SS and Police Leaders are to arrange, as far as practicable, for the farming of the areas evacuated of their population; to have them planted, in part, with Kok-Sagys and to utilize them for agricultural purposes, as far as possible. The children's

camps are to be located at the border of these areas, so that the children will be available as manpower for the cultivation of Kok-Sagys and for agriculture.

The effect was the destruction of almost every family caught in the German web. With fathers taken almost anywhere, mothers transported to Germany, and children moved to a different area in Russia, it became problematic that these families would never be reunited again, even after the war.

Some civilians faced even worse fates. In a post-war deposition, a former member of the command recounted one of the worst excesses:[53]

> During a march – and we had driven 200 km close to Smolensk – the villages were encircled. Nobody was allowed to leave or enter. The fields were searched and the people were sent back to the village. The next morning around 6:00 AM. all these people – it was a larger village with approximately 2,500 people – children, women, the elderly were pushed into four or five barns. Then Dirlewanger appeared with 10 men, officers, etc. and said: "Shoot them all immediately." In front of the barn, he positioned four SD-men with machine pistols. The barn was opened and Dirlewanger said, "Fire freely." Then there was indiscriminate shooting into the crowd of humans with the machine pistols, without distinction whether children, women, etc. were hit. It was a most horrendous action. The magazines were taken out, new ones were inserted. Then new aiming started. After that, the barn was closed again. The SD-men removed straw from the roofs and set the barns on fire. This was the most horrible spectacle which I have ever seen in my life. The barns were burning brightly. Nobody could escape until the barns fell down. Meanwhile, Dirlewanger and his staff positioned themselves with the Russian rapid fire guns about 50 meters away from the barn. Then from the barns some lightly wounded,

some heavily wounded and others who had not yet been hit stormed out, burning all over their bodies. Now these bastards shot these people who tried to escape, with Dirlewanger in front, until there was nobody left. I have witnessed this example which I have described in at least four or five other cases. Each of these villages was leveled down to the ground.

On August 14 *SS-Obergruppenführer* Jeckeln awarded the Bar to the Iron Cross 2nd Class to *SS-Untersturmführer* Wilhelm Rainer and *SS-Hauptscharführer* Paul Zimmermann. He additionally awarded the Iron Cross 2nd Class to *SS-Sturmbannführer* Joachim Praefke, *SS-Obersturmführer* Waldemar Wilhelm, *SS-Oberscharführer* Willi Meyer, *SS-Oberscharführer* Helmut Pfaffenrodt, *SS-Oberscharführer* Wilhelm Schall, *SS-Unterscharführer* Bruno Kostelnik, *SS-Rottenführer* Paul Illing, *SS-Rottenführer* Rudolf Lowitz, *SS-Rottenführer* Wilhelm Wächter, *SS-Rottenführer* Friedrich Walter, *SS-Sturmmann* Peter Gossens, *SS-Sturmmann* Gerhard Henze and *SS-Sturmmann* Georg Scheppach.

On August 15, 1943 *SS-Gruppenführer* von Gottberg and *SS-Obergruppenführer* von dem Bach-Zelewski recommended Dirlewanger receive the German Cross in Gold. The following is the recommendation for the award:[54]

On July 1, 1940 he took over the *Wilddieb-kommando Oranienburg* under which he was engaged from September 1, 1940 to the end of February 1942 as *SS-Sonder-Bataillon-Dirlewanger* in the struggle against the bandits in the General Government. Here he was active anywhere when the situation demanded an especially sharp dare-devil who was not afraid of any danger. Already in the General Government, his engagements brought noteworthy results. From end of February 1942 on, *SS-Obersturmbannführer* Dirlewanger with his SS-Special Battalion were active in the fight against bandits in areas behind the front lines, i.e. in White Russia. During more extensive and inde-

The Anti-Partisan Years - 1943

pendently run less extensive tasks, *SS-Obersturmbannführer* Dirlewanger has won everlasting rewards as a leader and exemplary fighter.

March 2 – March 10, 1942: Mission against a strong group of bandits northeasterly of Osipovici. Under his leadership, and while being personally engaged in the battle, a strong fortified bandit camp was stormed near Lawitsche. The group was destroyed and a rich booty was taken.

On March 12, 1942, a strong group of bandits attempted to attack the community of Klitschow. Through the engagement of his battalion, the attack was stopped. In the battle near Tscherwakow, the enemy was beaten bitterly by Dirlewanger.

On March 14, 1942, Dirlewanger stormed the heavily fortified village of Usochi in pursuit of the enemy. Also here, Dirlewanger stood out for his bravery as a tactical leader and individual fighter.

From March 16 to March 22, 1942, a considerable number of bandits were killed during active pioneer activities of the Battalion Dirlewanger in the woods southwest of Mogil'ov, in which also Dirlewanger fought personally during the most important phases and was an example for everyone.

From March 24 to March 28, 1942, Dirlewanger cleaned the road from Mogil'ov to Bobrujsk which had been occupied by the bandits, whereby in several larger fights he could again destroy a large number of bandits.

From April 2 to April 5, 1942, Dirlewanger rescued an army unit which had been encircled near Illisowa. At this occasion, the heavily occupied villages of Selleri and Lushiza were stormed by Dirlewanger and the enemy soldiers who had not been killed were pursued into the most treacherous swamp area up to Bacevici. During ensuing fighting near Cecevici from

April 8 to April 15, 1942, further strong groups of bandits were encircled and destroyed.

On April 26, 1942, Dirlewanger conducted a forceful reconnaissance against "The Bandit Republic of Usakino," which led to extensive fights during which Dirlewanger demonstrated once again what an outstanding tactical leader and fighter he was, despite the superiority of the enemy.

From May 8 to May 13, 1942, the battalion again proved itself within the Battle Group Schimana near Usakimo and Sucha. Under the courageous leadership of Dirlewanger, the heavily fortified railway station of Sucha was taken by storm, resulting in considerable weakening of the fighting power of the enemy.

During the forceful reconnaissance activities in the area of Dolgoje from May 24 to May 29, 1942, strong enemy forces were destroyed in heavy fighting near the village of Roswada under the calm dare-devil behavior of Dirlewanger.

During June 2 to June 6, 1942, Dirlewanger again destroyed a sizable group of bandits in a single attack in the forest between Orsa and Bastocholi under most difficult circumstances as to the location and fighting.

From June 10 to June 16, 1942, Dirlewanger took part in massive undertakings by the Wehrmacht and Police units. Also here, Dirlewanger excelled due to his personal bravery.

During a penalizing expedition on June 16, 1941 because of 17 murdered police men at the highway between Mogil'ov and Bobrujsk, Dirlewanger was able to annihilate a sizable group of bandits after lengthy fighting.

On June 19, 1942, Dirlewanger stormed a bandit camp in the forest near Stochowtschina which was very successful. On June 22, 1942, with the additional forces of the Police, Dirlewanger could disband a large group of bandits. On June 26, 1942, Dirlewanger occupied the heavily fortified towns of Stary Bichow and Lubiana after preparations by the Luftwaffe and heavy fighting. On June 28, 1942, another group of bandits were encircled by his battalion northwesterly of Orsa and subsequently destroyed.

From July 3 to July 11, 1942, the Battalion Dirlewanger, together with other army forces, took part in missions against a strong group of bandits in the area of Klicev. Stationed at the focal point, Dirlewanger and his battalion were outstanding during the fights near Wojenitschi.

On July 17, 1942, Dirlewanger was able to again encircle and destroy a group of bandits in a battle near Titakowoitsche.

On July 19, 1942, Dirlewanger demonstrated special bravery during a sudden encounter with bandits near Krasnica.

During July 20 to August 7, 1942, the Special Battalion Dirlewanger was engaged in a mammoth *Operation Adler* near Tschetschiwiltschi, and from August 14 to August 20, 1942, they were engaged in the *Operation Greif* west and east of the roads Orsa-Vitebsk.

Dirlewanger was placed at the focal points of the above and the missions below due to his extreme reliability:

August 23, 1942 mission in the area of Usakino. From August 25 to August 28, 1942 missions at the runway near Rogacov. From September 2 to September 5, 1942, *Operation Nordsee* east of the T.K.-street Stary-Byrkow. From September 10 to 14, 1942, engagements southeast of Mogil'ov, together with SS-Police Regiment 14 near Stary Bykrkow – Cecevici. From September 17 to 24, 1942, engaged in clean-up of he runway south of Cecevici.

October 3 to 8, 1942, *Operation Regatta* south of

Gorki and Rakotka. October 14 to 26, 1942, *Operation Karlsbad* north of the road Beresino-Cerven'. October 28 to December 16, 1942, engaged in normalizing the area around Cerven, reconnaissance for the *Operation Franz* and leading a group during *Operation Franz* up to January 8, 1943.

January 18 to 27, 1943, *Operation Erntefest I* in the area northwest of Sluck. From January 30 to February 15, 1943, *Operation Erntefest II* in the area west of the Minsk-Sluck highway. From February 16 to 26, 1943, *Operation Hornung* in the swamps of Pripjet. From February 27 to April 16, 1943, independent activities in clean-up of the area around Logojsk. From April 17 to 24, 1943, *Operation Zauberflöte* for clean-up of the town of Minsk. From April 26 to May 10, 1943, *Operation Draufgänger I and II* as participant in the mammoth *Operation Kottbus*, in the area of Borisov-Lepel up to June 21, 1943.

July 2 to 7, 1943, *Operation Günther* in the area of Manila-Waldes, and during July 15 to August 5, 1943, *Operation Hermann* in the area of the Nalibeki forest.

During all these large and small undertakings, the *SS-Sonderbataillon* Dirlewanger which was in part composed of foreigners and which was called to duty mostly at the crucial points, could register extraordinary results. For instance, the battalion alone destroyed approximately 15,000 bandits, 20 cannons, 8 anti-tank guns, 2 tanks, 62 heavy machine-guns, 112 light machine-guns, 70 automatic pistols,, 82 machine pistols, 1,100 guns, several telephone relay stations, parachutes, a large amount of ammunition, mines, dynamite and other enemy material were captured or destroyed.

When such great successes could be achieved, then it is the exclusive merit of *SS-Obersturmbannführer* Dirlewanger who always had his battalion under control due to his exceptional leadership and good tactical know-how and who engages them at the spot where the enemy can be beaten decidedly due to his correct judgment of the situation. His success was achieved with the least losses in the own ranks, i.e. there were only 92 dead, 218 wounded and 8 missing in action. Besides the merit which Dirlewanger earned as leader of his battalion and as leader of one to four battalions and with units which were reinforced with heavy weapons, he also – as previously mentioned – excelled in nearly all undertakings because of his special personal bravery and exemplary dare-devil behavior. He can be found everywhere where the situation is the most difficult. Through his personal initiative, the situation could be mastered even in situations when the enemy was far superior and their own attacks came to a slow-down.

Some of his especially brave activities should be mentioned:

During the *Operation Erntefest I*, a strong group of bandits tried on January 26, 1943 to break out of the encirclement 2 km north of Schantarowschischinia towards the east. Dirlewanger who recognized the situation immediately threw himself in front of a few men of his battalion against the enemy, and he succeeded in beating back the repeated attacks by the enemy, until reinforcement arrived. During these fights, the enemy lost 230 men. The fact that this break-through could be aborted was the exclusive merit by *SS-Obersturmbannführer* Dirlewanger who challenged his men to the utmost resistance with his example.

On February 11, 1943, during the *Operation Hornung* Dirlewanger was encircled by strong enemy forces about 2 km southwest of Starobin. The situation for Dirlewanger and his men was very dangerous, especially since there was the threat that ammunition would run out and no replenishing was thinkable. In this situation, Dirlewanger himself took over the distribution of the ammunition and only through his coldbloodedness and calm he was the soul of the resistance until he and his company could be replaced.

Operation Kottbus:

On May 28, 1943, Dirlewanger arrived at the extremely heavily fortified height 199.1 some 5 km west of the Paliksee. With a pioneer group which consisted of foreigners, Dirlewanger was the first to force himself into the field fortification and, under heavy enemy fire he cleared several ditches. This action was the preparation for a quick conquest of this height.

On June 1, 1943, Dirlewanger was with his staff on the road from fighting stand to the front lines. Suddenly Dirlewanger saw himself confronted by a strong group of bandits who had hidden in paths in the swamps despite heavy combing of the area. It was unavoidable that Dirlewanger and his men were temporarily encircled. *SS-Obersturmbannführer* Dirlewanger placed himself at the front of his group, and in close range fighting he was able to break the ring of the encirclement. The bandits who tried to retreat to the swampy paths were all destroyed and at the same time, some weapons and ammunition were captured.

Operation Hermann:

During the clean-up of the remaining encirclement, the enemy succeeded on August 1, 1943 to break through the seam between Battalion Dirlewanger and the Commando Kreikenboom. *SS-Obersturmbannführer* Dirlewanger was the one who with the help of some brave men brought the bandits to a standstill and the previously existing ring could be closed. During this action, a shot went through his sleeve and he sustained a grazing shot on his breast, while a third one threw the cigarette out of his mouth.

The Anti-Partisan Years - 1943

• • •

Not everyone was pleased with Dirlewanger's results. A civilian propaganda officer toured the area encompassed by *Operation Kottbus* shortly after its conclusion. He reported that some of the partisans had been burnt alive and their half-roasted bodies had been eaten by pigs. The *Reichskommisar* (governor general) for White Russia, Wilhelm Kube protested the action through Alfred Rosenberg to *SS-Reichsführer* Himmler. Berger responded that it was all nonsense and that the Dirlewanger Brigade was really quite decent.[55]

On August 15, 1943 Dirlewanger promoted the following individuals: *SS-Oberscharführer* Max Schreiner to *SS-Hauptscharführer*, *SS-Unterscharführer* Erich Selzer and Gustav Strumpf to *SS-Oberscharführer* and *SS-Rottenführer* Saillies to *SS-Unterscharführer*.[56]

Many of the men in the *Sonderkommando* continued to break rules and regulations and were punished by Dirlewanger. *SS-Unterscharführer* Klak received fourteen days arrest for going into a Russian female's house while *SS-Grenadier* Esser received five days for allowing a female to ride in his truck. *SS-Grenadier* Franz Ernst stole rations from the kitchen of 1st Company, and for this offense he was sent back to a concentration camp.[57]

Not all personnel actions for the month were adverse. On August 26, 1943 *SS-Obergruppenführer* Jeckeln awarded the Iron Cross 1st Class to *SS-Oberscharführer* Heinz Feiertag of the *Sonderkommando*.

In late August 1943 the battalion, with *Schuma* Battalion 57, took part in a small operation to secure the Plescenicy-Okolowo area. On the 30th the battalion reported killing thirty-eight partisans and capturing four, although only one machine-gun and five rifles were taken. One German was killed and one missing, while four foreign soldiers were wounded. On September 3, the battalion killed three partisans and wounded two more. On September 5, *SS-Grenadier* Haberland was killed in action, but the battalion claimed thirty-five to forty partisans killed and ten to fifteen wounded. Finally on September 7, the *Sonderkommando* reported seizing 213 work-fit persons for shipment back to the Reich.

On September 3, *SS-Gruppenführer* Glücks sent a communiqué to all military districts requesting that they once again look through their

The Cruel Hunters

district for poachers who had the potential to be sent to *Sonderkommando* Dirlewanger.[58]

On September 11, 1943 Dirlewanger reported the following strength of the *Sonderkommando*: eight officers, forty-three non-commissioned officers and three hundred sixty men for a total of four hundred eleven.

In response to a request by Himmler to provide accurate personnel figures, the Higher SS and Police Leader for Central Russia and White Russia submitted a detailed status report. In it Police Regiment 31 reported 1,868 men, SS-Police Regiment 2 showed 2,310 men, SS-Police Regiment 26 listed 1,799 men and Dirlewanger reported 550 men.[59]

On September 13 the main office of the Waffen-SS sent a message to Dirlewanger stating that new field post office numbers would be instituted. The regimental staff would retain 00512, the 1st Battalion (consisting of 1st through 4th Companies) would use 03824, the 2nd Battalion (with the 5th through 8th Companies) would get 01499, and the 3rd Battalion (with the 9th through 12th Companies) would receive 02678.[60]

On September 14 the *Sonderkommando* received a message from the SS Court that *SS-Untersturmführer* August Zeller, from the reconnaissance battalion, 4th SS *"Polizei"* Division had been convicted in a court martial and sentenced to five months imprisonment. However, the *SS-Reichsführer* had changed the sentence to four weeks confinement to quarters and an additional four months to be served in the *Sonderkommando*.[61] *SS-Untersturmführer* August Zeller was born August 31, 1914. He would killed in action with the *Sonderkommando* November 13, 1943.[62]

On September 20 *SS-Obergruppenführer* Jeckeln awarded the Iron Cross 1st Class to *SS-Unterscharführer* Franz Eder.

Wilhelm Kube, who had complained earlier about Dirlewanger, was assassinated in Minsk on September 22, 1943 when a servant placed a bomb under his bed. With his death, the Higher SS and Police Leader for Central and White Russia ordered that any organization using Russians as domestic workers must have those workers screened by the SD.[63]

Kube was an unusual Nazi administrator. He spent a short time in 1936 in a concentration camp – as a prisoner, for insinuating that the wife of Walter Buch, the President of the Nazi Party Tribunal, was partly Jewish. Rosenberg and Göring did not want Kube placed in command of

White Russia, but Hinrich Lohse, the Reichs Commissioner for *Ostland* convinced Hitler to approve the appointment. Kube had a reputation for promiscuity and loose morals during his stay in Minsk; on the other hand, he wanted to cultivate a reputation for humanity in his dealings with the Russians. After Kube's death, Himmler stated that had it not been for the assassination, he would have had to put Kube in a concentration camp again.[64]

In a response to a request for information, the 1st Company reported that two soldiers had five or more children; Gerhard Henze with eight and Eugen Hanser with five.

On September 29, 1943 five *SS-Grenadier* from 2nd Company ran over a mine in their truck and had to be taken to the SS hospital at Minsk. Wounded were Walter Augustin, Walter Richter, Arthur Heimsch, Willi Rossa and Werner Leuendorf.

SS-Untersturmführer Dr. Heinrich Wehninck was assigned to the *Sonderkommando* as a physician, due to a history of trouble. Previously convicted of theft, he was sentenced by an SS court in September to fourteen days arrest for having sex with a captured female Polish prisoner. Wehninck, who joined the Nazi Party May 1, 1937 (party number 4,837,758) and the SS in 1940, was also diagnosed as being severely psychotic. Prior to service in the *Sonderkommando*, he was assigned to the SS *"Totenkopf"* Division.[65]

On October 23, 1943 the battalion was ordered by the SS Economic Office, Section D – Concentration Camps, to send four Russian volunteers as prisoners to the Mauthausen concentration camp. There were no charges or allegations listed in the report.[66]

The same day the *Sonderkommando* submitted a request for dogs to help in combating the elusive partisans. They asked for twenty tracking dogs and forty-two guard dogs.[67]

By the beginning of November, Soviet regular army forces threatened a breakthrough on the northern flank of Army Group Center. Police Battle Group von Gottberg was dispatched to the fluid sector northwest of Vitebsk and ordered to hold on November 5. The next day Soviet forces broke through at Dretun. On November 7, heavy fighting occurred around the town. On November 8, 1943 *SS-Grenadier* Theodor Kalbe, Fritz Krüger, Wilhelm Brencher, Georg Gröbner, Erich Bax, Karl Schmidt,

Heinrich Möhle, Herbert Zahn, Ludwig Beniger, Walter Wegner and Otto Grabs were killed in action. On November 11, *SS-Grenadier* Karl Flesch was killed in action. The same day, perhaps reflecting the ferocity of the fighting, *SS-Gruppenführer* von Gottberg, commander of Battle Group von Gottberg, gave out allocations for awards to units in his command. To the *Sonderkommando* he stated he would approve ten Iron Cross 2nd Class and two Bars to the Iron Cross 2nd Class.[68]

On November 13, *SS-Untersturmführer* August Zeller and *SS-Grenadier* Alfred Ciesewski, Rudolf Faust, Fritz Reel and Walter Lange were killed in action and *SS-Grenadier* Friedrich Kaelber was wounded. This assault at Kosari was later designated as an assault day for the purposes of the Infantry Assault Badge. The same day *SS-Standartenführer* Heinz Lammerding took command of Battle Group von Gottberg.[69] On November 14 the *Sonderkommando*, with two attached companies of army Security Regiment 797, attacked elements of the Red Army near Kosari. *SS-Hauptsturmführer* Rudolf Stöweno, *SS-Rottenführer* Hans Miketta and *SS-Grenadier* Alois Smoliner, Hans Baur, Viktor Lempa, Erhard Jokiel, Willi Schütze and Georg Binzer were killed in action north of the village of Kalinki. *SS-Oberscharführer* Erich Hähnle was awarded the Iron Cross 2nd Class on this day.

SS-Hauptsturmführer Rudolf Stöweno was an early Nazi. Born April 11, 1901, he entered the Nazi party with a party number of 181,489 and an SS number 16,489. He was promoted to *SS-Untersturmführer* on June 12, 1933 to *SS-Obersturmführer* on May 9, 1934 and to *SS-Hauptsturmführer* on June 1, 1935.

The losses continued. On November 15, *SS-Oberscharführer* Erich Selzer, *SS-Unterscharführer* Willi Rett and *SS-Grenadier* Fritz Brehm, Siegfried Reinhard and Fritz Raml were killed in action. The next day *SS-Unterscharführer* Hans Pfab and *SS-Grenadier* Ewald Bujara fell. The *Sonderkommando* launched another attack on November 17 along with SS-Police Regiment 24. *SS-Funker* (radioman) Jürgen Sten and *SS-Grenadier* Siegfried Krause, Eugen Ulmer, Erich Lebin and Karl Weber were killed in the attack. On November 20 *SS-Grenadier* Heinrich Kuhlmann was killed. On November 24 *SS-Grenadier* Franz Planitzer was killed in action.

The Anti-Partisan Years - 1943

The *Sonderkommando* reported the following overall losses for October and November 1943: two officers, four NCOs, thirty-five men killed and one officer, seventeen NCOs, 125 men wounded. A further eight men were reported sick. Replacements to the unit totaled just five for the same period.[70]

Apparently the combat with the Red Army unnerved more than a few *Sonderkommando* troops and some ran in the face of the enemy. In an attempt to alleviate this, the battalion put out an order on December 1 that anyone showing cowardice in the face of the enemy would receive a sentence of death.[71]

On December 2, 1943 the *Sonderkommando* and enemy forces attacked and counterattacked over defensive positions. Nine troops were wounded – foxhole strength was reported to be down to two hundred sixty-four. Many men had dysentery as well. Later that morning the enemy attacked again in battalion strength and took several positions losing some seventy to eighty killed but inflicted nineteen more casualties on the Germans.[72] On December 6, 1943 Colonel of Police Stahn assumed command of Battle Group von Gottberg. On December 7, 1943 *SS-Hauptsturmführer* Walser, on behalf of the officers and men of the battalion, sent a telegram congratulating Dirlewanger for being awarded the German Cross in Gold. Dirlewanger was recuperating at the time at his home at Esslingen.[73] With the appearance of regular Soviet Army troops it became imperative that the men of the *Sonderkommando* learn how to kill tanks. On December 7, the battalion sent a request through SS-Police Regiment 24 for *SS-Unterscharführer* Axman, Daub and Plattner, and *SS-Sturmmann* Bochum, Heck, Katz, Jokiel, Lehrmann, Stein, and Jung to attend the tank destruction course. On December 8, 1943 *SS-Obersturmführer* Othmar Walchensteiner died of his wounds at the aid station in Polota. December 20, 1943 was declared an assault and close combat day for the purpose of the Infantry Assault Badge and the Close Combat Clasp, for *Sonderkommando* troops fighting south of Stradansee.[74]

By December 1943, the battalion had a thirty-two man supply section under *SS-Obersturmführer* Otto Gast, assisted by *SS-Oberscharführer* Rudolf Liers and Ludwig Schopf, *SS-Sturmmann* Bertsch and *SS-Grenadier* Asum and Mehr. *SS-Oberscharführer* Alfred Mammitsch was the weapon's officer. He, in turn, was assisted by *SS-Grenadier* Hartl, Klunker and Herkt. In command of all motorized vehicles was *SS-Oberscharführer* Günther Credner. *SS-Unterscharführer* Gerhard Kellkamp was in charge of the mess. On December 23, 1943, a reinforced reconnaissance troop under *SS-Sturmbannführer* Weisse conducted an operation against enemy positions south of Malt-Puschtscha/Dretun. Weisse pushed through the enemy positions and caused considerable damages to the enemy in hand-to-hand fighting. On December 24, the SS-Latvian Company reported a strength of one officer, seven NCOs and 160 troops. The next day the battalion submitted a status report for the period October 21 to November 20. It read:

Personnel:

| 5 officers German | 24 NCOs | 172 men |
| 0 officers Foreign | 0 NCOs | 166 men |

Weapons:

146 rifles	40 pistols	9 MP
8 light MGs		
4 heavy MGs	3 light mortars	5 heavy mortars

Vehicles:

| 1 command car | 8 motorcycles | 8 medium trucks |
| 1 radio van | | |

Animal Transport:
82 horses

Heavy Weapons:
5 howitzer (76.2mm) 3 anti-tank guns (45mm)

On December 29 the battalion dug in, completing four hundred sixty meters of trenchline, all behind wire entanglements. The Germans also built fifty living and ammunition bunkers, fifteen light machine-gun firing positions, four heavy machine-gun firing positions, and several positions for the anti-tank guns and mortars. The *Sonderkommando* laid ninety meters of anti-tank mines and two hundred forty meters of anti-personnel mines – all in all a formidable defensive position.[75]

Nineteen forty-three had seen the maturing of the *Sonderkommando* into one of Germany's most formidable anti-partisan units in central Russia. Operating in numerous counter-guerilla operations, Dirlewanger's forces had killed thousands of partisan combatants and murdered thousands of civilians. But the handwriting for Germany was on the wall. The end of 1943 saw the *Sonderkommando* once again in a precarious situation. The following year would lead the unit west to Warsaw at the frontiers of the Reich itself. Perhaps with a sense of foreboding, on December 31, 1943 the Higher SS and Police Leader for Central and White Russia, *SS-Gruppenführer* Curt von Gottberg extended his best wishes to all units in his command:

DAILY ORDER

> At the change of year I communicate my best wishes to all leaders, non-commissioned officers and men. I hereby extend my thanks to each of you for your actions this past year. In the fanatical belief in Final Victory we call in the new year.
>
> Hail to the Führer
>
> von Gottberg
> *SS-Gruppenführer*

ENDNOTES

[1] judenrein/Jew-free
[2] Büchler. "Kommandostab Reichsführer-SS.", p.20.
[3] Kampfgruppe Kutschera, Ia, Einsatzbefehl, 4.1.43, Washington, D.C: National Archives Microfilm Publication T354, Roll 650.
[4] SS-Sonderbataillon Dirlewanger, Befehl, 5.1.43, Washington, D.C: National Archives Microfilm Publication T354, Roll 650.
[5] SS-Sonderbataillon Dirlewanger, Befehl, 10.1.43 & 14.1.43, Washington, D.C: National Archives Microfilm Publication T354, Roll 650. Once again, the ratio of captured weapons to enemy dead suggest that many of the fallen Russians were unarmed.
[6] Personalakt Egyd Ingruber, Washington, D.C: National Archives Microfilm Publication A3343, Records of SS Officers from the Berlin Document Center, Roll SSO-126A.
[7] Einsatzgruppe Griep, Einsatzbefehl, 15.1.43, Washington, D.C: National Archives Microfilm Publication T354, Roll 650.
[8] SS-Sonderbataillon Dirlewanger, Abschlussbericht, 25 Januar 1943, Washington, D.C: National Archives Microfilm Publication T354, Roll 650.
[9] SS-Sonderbataillon Dirlewanger, Abschlussbericht, 28 Januar 1943, Washington, D.C: National Archives Microfilm Publication T354, Roll 650.
[10] Reitlinger. *The House Built on Sand.* p.239. The exagerated ratio of Russian killed in action to prisoners of war suggest that the Germans clearly were not inclined to keep captured partisans alive.
[11] Ziemke, Earl F. *Stalingrad to Berlin: The German Defeat in the East.* (Washington, D.C: Center of Military History, United States Army, 1968), p.113.
[12] Brief "Kragenspiegel für Sonderkommando Dirlewanger", 26.1.43, Washington, D.C: National Archives Microfilm Publication T175, Roll 18.
[13] SS-Sonderbataillon Dirlewanger, Message to Kampfgruppe Binz 7.2.43, Washington, D.C: National Archives Microfilm Publication T354, Roll 650.
[14] SS-Sonderbataillon Dirlewanger, Befehl, 7.2.43, Washington, D.C: National Archives Microfilm Publication T354, Roll 650.
[15] SS-Sonderbataillon Dirlewanger, Befehl, 7.2.43, Washington, D.C: National Archives Microfilm Publication T354, Roll 650.
[16] SS-Sonderbataillon Dirlewanger, Befehl, 15.2.43, Washington, D.C: National Archives Microfilm Publication T354, Roll 650.
[17] Die Höhere SS und Polizeiführer Russland Mitte, Ia, Befehl, 12.2.43, Washington, D.C: National Archives Microfilm Publication T354, Roll 650.
[18] Personalakt Curt von Gottberg, Washington, D.C: National Archives Microfilm Publication A3343, Records of SS Officers from the Berlin Document Center, Roll SSO-024A.
[19] Hilberg. *The Destruction of the European Jews (Revised and definitive edition).,* p.383.
[20] SS-Sonderbataillon an den Reichsführer-SS (SS-Hauptamt-Ergänzungsamt der Waffen-SS), 17.3.43, Washington, D.C: National Archives Microfilm Publication T354, Roll 650.
[21] SS-Sonderbataillon Dirlewanger, Befehl, 13.3.43, Washington, D.C: National Archives Microfilm Publication T354, Roll 650.
[22] SS-Sonderbataillon Dirlewanger, Befehl, 22.3.43, Washington, D.C: National Archives Microfilm Publication T354, Roll 650.
[23] Einsatzstab Schimana, Einsatzbefehl, 30.3.43, Washington, D.C: National Archives Microfilm Publication T354, Roll 649.
[24] Die Kommandeur Sicherheitspolizei und des SD Weisruthenien, Feindlage, 29 März 1943, Washington, D.C: National Archives Microfilm Publication T354, Roll 650.
[25] Einsatzstab Schimana, Einsatzbefehl, 3.4.43 & 7.4.43, Washington, D.C: National Archives Microfilm Publication T354, Roll 649.
[26] Sonderbataillon Dirlewanger, Einsatzbefehl, 7.4.43, Washington, D.C: National Archives Microfilm Publication T354, Roll 649.
[27] Personalakt Oskar Dirlewanger.
[28] SS-Sonderbataillon Dirlewanger, Letter, 11.4.43, Washington, D.C: National Archives Microfilm Publication T354, Roll 649.

The Anti-Partisan Years - 1943

[29] Der Führer des Unternehmens "Zauberflöte", Einsatzbefehl, 15. April 1943, Washington, D.C: National Archives Microfilm Publication T354, Roll 649.

[30] Ibid.

[31] Ibid.

[32] Personalakt Karl Praefcke, Washington, D.C: National Archives Microfilm Publication A3343, Records of SS Officers from the Berlin Document Center, Roll SSO-391A.

[33] Der HSSPF Russland Mitte und Weissruthenien Nachrichtenführer, Decknamenliste 1, 29.4.43, Washington, D.C: National Archives Microfilm Publication T354, Roll 650.

[34] Ibid.

[35] SS-Sonderbataillon Dirlewanger, Einsatzbefehl, 10.5.43, Washington, D.C: National Archives Microfilm Publication T354, Roll 649.

[36] SS-Sonderbataillon Dirlewanger, Gefechtsbericht, 10.5.43, Washington, D.C: National Archives Microfilm Publication T354, Roll 649.

[37] Personalakt Erwin Walser, Washington, D.C: National Archives Microfilm Publication A3343, Records of SS Officers from the Berlin Document Center, Roll SSO-219B.

[38] Personalakt Wilhelm Reiner, Washington, D.C: National Archives Microfilm Publication A3343, Records of SS Officers from the Berlin Document Center, Roll SSO-020B.

[39] Weingartner. "Law and Justice in the Nazi SS.", p. 287.

[40] Berger was promoted to SS-Obergruppenführer on June 21, 1943.

[41] SS-Sonderbataillon Dirlewanger, Brief, 8.6.43, Washington, D.C: National Archives Microfilm Publication T354, Roll 650.

[42] Personalakt Richard Glücks, Washington, D.C: National Archives Microfilm Publication A3343, Records of SS Officers from the Berlin Document Center, Roll SSO-17A.

[43] Der Reichsführer-SS, Chef des SS-Hauptamtes, Amt AI3, Brief, 17. Juni 1943, Washington, D.C: National Archives Microfilm Publication T354, Roll 650.

[44] Der Reichsführer-SS, Chef des SS-Hauptamtes, Amt AI, Brief, 24. Juni 1943, Washington, D.C: National Archives Microfilm Publication T354, Roll 650.

[45] Kampfgruppe Korsemann, Ia, Einsatzbefehl, 28.6.43 & 6.7.43, Washington, D.C: National Archives Microfilm Publication T354, Roll 649.

[46] SS-Sonderbataillon Dirlewanger, Gefechtsbericht, 9.7.43, Washington, D.C: National Archives Microfilm Publication T354, Roll 649.

[47] SS-Sonderbataillon Dirlewanger, Bataillonsbefehle, 10.7.43, Washington, D.C: National Archives Microfilm Publication T354, Roll 650.

[48] Ibid.

[49] Personalakt Kurt Weisse, Washington, D.C: National Archives Microfilm Publication A3343, Records of SS Officers from the Berlin Document Center, Roll SSO-232B.

[50] Kampfgruppe von Gottberg, Ia, Einsatzbefehl, 7.7.43, Washington, D.C: National Archives Microfilm Publication T354, Roll 649.

[51] Der HSSPF Russland Mitte und Weissruthenien, Ic, Brief, 11.8.43, Washington, D.C: National Archives Microfilm Publication T354, Roll 650.

[52] *Trials of War Criminals before the International Military Tribunal, Volume XIII, The Ministries Case, Case No. 11.*, pp. 314-315.

[53] Klausch, Hans-Peter. *Antifaschisten in SS-Uniform.* (Bremen, Germany: Edition Temmen, 1993), pp. 62, 64.

[54] Personalakt Oskar Dirlewanger.

[55] Reitlinger. *The SS: Alibi of a Nation.*, pp. 173-174.

[56] SS-Sonderbataillon Dirlewanger, Bataillonsbefehl - Nr. 15, 16.8.43, Washington, D.C: National Archives Microfilm Publication T354, Roll 650.

[57] SS-Sonderbataillon Dirlewanger, Bataillonsbefehl 12, 13.8.43, Washington, D.C: National Archives Microfilm Publication T354, Roll 650.

[58] SS Hauptamt Amt BI, Wilddiebereiverdächtige Brief, 3 Sep. 1943, Washington, D.C: National Archives Microfilm Publication T354, Roll 650.

[59] Der HSSPF Russland Mitte und Weissruthenien, Ia, Kraftübersicht, 31.8.43, Washington, D.C: National Archives Microfilm Publication T354, Roll 650.

[60] SS-Fuhrungshauptamt, Kommandoamt der Waffen-SS, Ic, Brief, 13. Sep. 43, Washington, D.C: National Archives Microfilm Publication T354, Roll 650.

[61] Der Reichsführer-SS, Hauptamt, SS-Gericht, Brief, 14 Sep. 1943, Washington, D.C: National Archives Microfilm Publication T354, Roll 650.

[62] Personalakt August Zeller, Washington, D.C: National Archives Microfilm Publication A3343, Records of SS Officers from the Berlin Document Center, Roll SSO-019C.
[63] Der HSSPF Russland Mitte und Weissruthenien, Brief, 22.9.43, Washington, D.C: National Archives Microfilm Publication T354, Roll 650.
[64] Reitlinger. *The House Built on Sand.*, pp. 156-157.
[65] Personalakt Heinrich Wehninck, Washington, D.C: National Archives Microfilm Publication A3343, Records of SS Officers from the Berlin Document Center, Roll SSO-225.
[66] SS Wirtshafts-Verwaltungshauptamt, Amtsgruppe D, Brief, 23.10.43, Washington, D.C: National Archives Microfilm Publication T354, Roll 650.
[67] SS-Sonderbataillon Dirlewanger, Fernschrift, 23.10.43, Washington, D.C: National Archives Microfilm Publication T354, Roll 650.
[68] Kampfgruppe von Gottberg, Tagesbefehl 2, 11.11.43, Washington, D.C: National Archives Microfilm Publication T354, Roll 648.
[69] Later commanded the 2nd SS Division "Das Reich"; implicated in the 1944 Oradour-sur-Glane massacre in France.
[70] SS-Sonderbataillon Dirlewanger, Zustandsbericht, 25.12.43, Washington, D.C: National Archives Microfilm Publication T354, Roll 650.
[71] SS-Sonderbataillon Dirlewanger, Befehl, 1.12.43, Washington, D.C: National Archives Microfilm Publication T354, Roll 650.
[72] SS-Sonderbataillon Dirlewanger, Morgenmeldung, 2.12.43, Washington, D.C: National Archives Microfilm Publication T354, Roll 650.
[73] It is not known when Dirlewanger left Russia in this instance.
[74] Numerous soldiers in the Sonderkommando received the Close Combat Bar in Bronze for fifteen days designated as close combat with the enemy. Several received the Close Combat Bar in Silver for thirty designated days of close-in fighting. None were awarded the Close Combat Bar in Gold for fifty days of close combat with the enemy, which was awarded to only five hundred thirty-eight soldiers in the entire Wehrmacht — of whom ninety-seven were in the Waffen-SS. Source: Dörr, Manfred und Franz Thomas. *Die Träger der Nahkampfspange in Gold.* (Osnabrück, FRG: Biblio Verlag, 1986.)
[75] Einheit FPN 00512, Stellungsbau in der HKL, 29.12.43, Washington, D.C: National Archives Microfilm Publication T354, Roll 650.

4

FAREWELL TO RUSSIA
1944

The tactics, to put terror against terror, succeeded marvelously.
- SS-Brigadeführer Walter Stahlecker[1]

January 3, 1944 was a quiet day. The battalion continued to improve its positions and was not shelled by the enemy. One man was wounded, two were sick. The battalion strength was five officers and 221 men. On January 4 both the Germans and Russians continued to improve their positions. The enemy fired some sixty tank rounds, seventy mortar rounds and two hundred small arms rounds at the German positions, which killed one man and wounded another. The *Sonderkommando* strength dropped to five officers and 238 men. On January 5 quiet returned to the front and the arrival of some replacements raised the strength of the *Sonderkommando* to five officers and 279 men. There were no casualties for the day. On January 6, the battalion had one man wounded and three sick. The Germans expended forty mortar rounds but ran out of ammunition for the anti-tank guns. Fortunately for the *Sonderkommando* there was no Soviet tank attack that day. The SS-Latvian Company reported no special occurrences and a strength of one officer, nine NCOs and 144 men.

The defensive stalemate continued at Lake Beresno on January 7. The Russians fired about eighty mortar rounds which wounded one German soldier. Three soldiers were sick but the overall strength of the battalion increased to five officers and 286 men. The situation remained unchanged the following day. The Russians fired about eighty more mortar rounds wounding two. Once again the personnel strength increased – to five officers and 299 men. On January 9, the battalion continued to work on its positions. Strength increased to five officers and 304 men. No men were wounded but two soldiers reported sick. On January 10 the battalion had one man killed and one wounded as once again the Soviets bombarded the *Sonderkommando* with approximately sixty mortar rounds during the day.

On January 13 the Soviets increased their mortar fire against the battalion to approximately one hundred forty rounds, which wounded two men. The battalion's artillery battery reported a strength of two officers and fifty-five men. The battery additionally had four howitzers with caissons, eight horse-drawn wagons, a horse-drawn kitchen and sixty-five horses. The Germans were bombarded again on January 15 with approximately forty mortar rounds. One soldier was wounded. The following day the *Sonderkommando* reported receiving 122mm howitzer fire from positions about one kilometer distant. Two casualties were incurred, but overall strength increased to four officers and 307 men.

On January 17 losses rose somewhat to one killed, three wounded and two sick. The battalion used its anti-tank guns, which now had am-

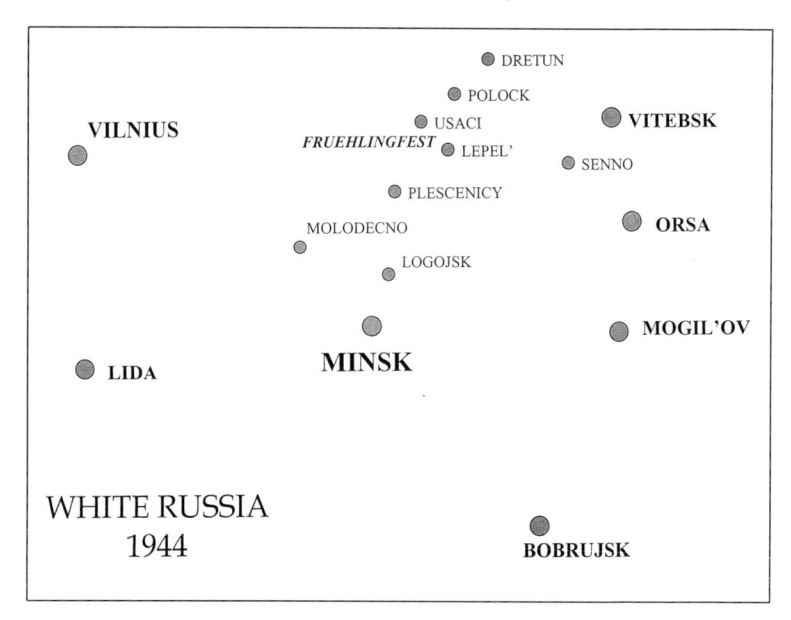

```
                              ● DRETUN
                           ● POLOCK
                        ● USACI         ● VITEBSK
     VILNIUS      FRUEHLINGFEST ● LEPEL'
        ●                          ● SENNO
                        ● PLESCENICY
              MOLODECNO                  ● ORSA
                   ●
                      ● LOGOJSK

                         ●              ● MOGIL'OV
     ● LIDA           MINSK


  WHITE RUSSIA
      1944                        ●
                              BOBRUJSK
```

152

Farewell to Russia - 1944

munition, to fire at the Russian positions. *SS-Unterscharführer* Schmitt was in charge of receiving reports at the battalion headquarters, while *SS-Unterscharführer* Sievers conducted a reconnaissance for a supply point further to the rear – an indication of imminent movement. The following day the *Sonderkommando* began to deploy troops to this new area as strength in sector decreased to four officers and 244 men. Two men were wounded and two reported sick.

On January 21 the battalion provided a detailed report of its strength. The German battle group had four officers, two hundred twenty men, thirty-one horses, three field kitchens, nine motorcycles with sidecars, one command car, eight trucks, three anti-tank guns, forty-seven winter sleighs and thirty-two *panje* wagons (Russian horse-drawn carts). The Russian Company, meanwhile had one officer, 160 men, eighteen horses, ten winter sleighs, seven *panje* wagons and one field kitchen. The attached 1st Battery *Schuma* Artillery Battalion 56 had two officers, fifty-five men, sixty-five horses, four howitzers with caissons, one field kitchen and eight horse-drawn wagons. The battalion reported that a further thirty-seven horses were sick and were located at the horse hospital at Polock. This was not a blitzkrieg-equipped force. Like its combat ethos, it was almost a throwback to the Middle Ages in equipment.[2]

On February 8, 1944 the battalion reported a strength of six officers, forty-four non-commissioned officers and 209 soldiers. Additionally, the unit had 201 foreign troops assigned.[3]

On February 18 the *Sonderkommando* sent the personnel files of twelve troops who had been killed in the last several weeks to the Waffen-SS information office for war casualties at Bamberg. The dead included Johannes Klekamp, Johann Gamsjaeger, Kurt Haberland, Herbert Kalix, Georg Cichon, Karl Winkler, Erwin Gorn, Karl Busse, Gerhard Keusch, Alfred Schlicht, Ferdinand Dorfer and Friedrich Bunn.[4]

As the war progressed, the German High Command recognized both the importance and difficulty of combating partisans. The mission was originally handled by the Army but in October 1942 it transferred to the SS and *SS-Obergruppenführer* von dem Bach-Zelewski was subsequently named chief of anti-partisan warfare. On January 30, 1944 Himmler instituted a special war badge for all soldiers – not just SS, engaged in this type of warfare. Named the Anti-Partisan War Badge, it was awarded in bronze for twenty days of anti-partisan duty, in silver for fifty days and in gold for one hundred fifty days.[5] It was Himmler's desire to present the version in gold personally – the first award of this highest grade occurred in February 1945.[6]

In late February Dirlewanger requested two hundred award documents for the badge in bronze, thirty for it in silver and twenty for the badge in gold.

On February 20, 1944 Himmler sent an order to the Chief of the SS Leadership Main Office, the Chief of the SS Main Office, the Chief of the SS Court Main Office and the Chief of the Reich Security Main Office. In it, he delineated the authority of Dirlewanger within his unit:[7]

> The *Einsatz-Bataillon* Dirlewanger consists of German men who have been previously convicted of poaching. The nucleus is considered to be good and even very good: concentration camp inmates who are suitable for the assignment; former members of the SS, who, after having served their time, are assigned for rehabilitation purposes to front service. In combat the commander has jurisdiction over life and death of all members of these battalions, which consist of these different components. The rehabilitation of the former poachers will be undertaken, without participation of the SS Court Main Office, through *SS-Obergruppenführer* Berger and *SS-Gruppenführer* Nebe in the Reich Security Main Office through the Reich Ministry of Justice. The accomplished rehabilitation will be reported by *SS-Obergruppenführer* Berger to the SS Court Main Office. The commander of the battalion, *SS-Obersturmbannführer* Dirlewanger, will have jurisdiction over life and death of the concentration camp inmates in rest area and field garrison. The poachers will be under SS jurisdiction after their rehabilitation. As long as they have not been rehabilitated, the commander has also the power over life and death in rest area and field garrison. Former SS men, assigned for rehabilita-

tion, are under SS jurisdiction in rest area and field garrison.

Dirlewanger and the *Sonderkommando* were merely at the tail end of the SS judicial system. On October 17, 1939 the Ministerial Council for the Defense of the Reich set up a special judicial system for cases involving members of the SS. The special SS courts were empowered to handle all military and non-military crimes committed by members of the SS or police. Infractions committed before enlistment could also be looked into. SS and police courts were located at the headquarters of each HSSPF. There was an additional SS and police court attached to the SS Legal Department to deal with offenses of special importance where investigations were particularly difficult. Different officials could convene a court depending on the circumstances of a case. Hitler was the convening authority in the case of death sentences on death sentences of all commanders and officers or in the case of certain serious offenses by senior officials. Himmler was the convening authority on any case he reserved for himself which included cases against SS members with an SS number below 15,000. As befitting a special court, the Chief of the SS Legal Department served as the convening authority for all cases specially delegated to him by Himmler. Finally, the chief of a *Hauptamt* and commanders of HSSPF within their area of responsibility were also convening authorities when the above circumstances did not apply.[8]

On February 23, 1944 *SS-Obersturmbannführer* Dirlewanger reported that on the previous day *SS-Unterscharführer* Riegler had died a hero's death. *SS-Oberscharführer* Hans Lühr was killed the same day.[9]

On March 11, 1944 Dirlewanger radioed a message to a wounded *Sonderkommando* soldier, *SS-Oberscharführer* Schmidt at the reserve hospital in Dresden extending his congratulations on Schmidt for winning the Infantry Assault Badge in Silver. Schmidt had been an early SS man with an SS number of only 9,157.

The same day Dirlewanger sent a message back to through *SS-Hauptsturmführer* Blessau, the adjutant for the Chief of the *SS-Hauptamt*, to *SS-Obergruppenführer* Berger. In the message Dirlewanger stated that the wolf hunting area was prepared for Berger to fly out the following week for a hunting trip. Berger could catch a courier flight from Berlin to

Minsk and from there take a Fieseler Stork light aircraft to bring him to the *Sonderkommando*. In the second part of the message, Dirlewanger stated that the Russian girls that *SS-Obersturmbannführer* Otto wanted had been captured and would be sent back to Germany with the next group of men going on leave. The price for each girl would be two bottles of schnapps.

Dirlewanger continued to amuse himself with Russian girls near Minsk as well. Two members of the *Sonderkommando* corroborated the following description of events:[10]

> One evening when I was on guard duty at the Castle of Lahoisk, which housed the officers, I was told by an orderly that the officers who were completely drunk were whipping and mistreating eight naked women in the hall....I have seen these naked women myself, through the open door. The next morning three or four women who had been shot and most miserably molested were lying in front of the castle. These women were then buried by us. Such murderous excesses did not stop Dirlewanger who always was carrying a dog whip to confront his "poachers."

SS-Hauptsturmführer Werner Blessau, the adjutant for the Chief of the *SS-Hauptamt*, had previously been assigned to the *Sonderkommando* as a company commander and adjutant. Born May 18, 1918 in Besskow, he possessed Nazi Party number 3,807,016 and SS number 290,636. Blessau served in Poland with the *Leibstandarte Adolf Hitler* being wounded in the foot on September 12, 1939. He spent 1940 and 1941 recuperating from this wound. Assigned next to the *SS-Hauptamt* until 1943, his personnel file shows he was charged with stealing a diamond ring while stationed in Berlin. He was transferred to Dirlewanger in June of 1943 and apparently did well with the unit. He won the Eastern People's Medal 2nd Class for Bravery on June 26, 1943 and the Iron Cross 1st Class on August 8. Blessau was severely wounded on August 7, 1943 and was transferred back to Berlin. He continued to do well in the SS, returning to the *SS-Hauptamt* and receiving the War Service Cross 1st and 2nd

Classes, the Eastern People's Medal for Bravery 1st Class with Swords, the Wound Badge in Silver and the Anti-Partisan Badge. These last three awards were for his service in the *Sonderkommando*. The following is an efficiency report covering the period Blessau was in the *Sonderkommando*:[11]

> During the time of June 12, 1943 to August 7, 1943, *SS-Obersturmführer der Reserve* Werner Blessau was ordered from the Chief of the *SS-Hauptamt* to this unit. Tasked with the leadership of a company, he has participated in all engagements of the unit, among them two large endeavors against Bolshevik bandits and has proven to be a circumspect, daring and brave soldier. Despite the injuries sustained during the Poland Campaign which still caused him problems in walking, he marched and stormed at the front of his company against the enemy, always a good example for his men. His military know-how and his youthful dare-devil behavior often led to great successes. To his leaders in rank below him and to his men he was always an example of courage and bravery. Because of his correct, military and open comradely behavior, within a very short time he gained the confidence of his superiors and the entire leadership group. In addition, he was always appreciated and respected by the leaders below him and the men. For extraordinary bravery against the enemy, *SS-Obersturmführer* Blessau was awarded the Eastern People's Bravery Medal in Silver on June 26, 1943, and on August 8, 1943 he was awarded the Iron Cross 1st Class. For a successful assault attack, he was awarded the Infantry Assault Badge in Silver on August 14, 1943. As far as his character is concerned, Blessau exemplifies fully the requisites of an SS leader. His premature transfer back to the SS-Main office on August 7, 1943 was due to injuries he had sustained.

Many of the officers serving in the *Sonderkommando* received the Eastern People's Bravery Medal. This award was established on July 14, 1942 to recognize heroic actions in the field and services rendered by the more than one million volunteers from the various Soviet republics, Lithuania, Latvia and Estonia who helped German forces. The award came in two classes first and second. It was further subdivided by color, bronze, silver and gold for successive contributions; and was further subdivided with swords for heroism and without swords for service. After October 29, 1942 German troops serving with Eastern People's combat units were eligible for the award providing they already held the Iron Cross 1st or 2nd Class.[12]

On March 17, 1944 *SS-Sturmbannführer* Ernst-Günther Heidelberg was assigned to the *Sonderkommando*. Heidelberg was born May 1, 1908 in Beuthen, Upper Silesia. He was an accredited architect; he joined the Nazi Party April 1, 1933 with a party number of 1,684,992. He subsequently joined the SS and received SS number 209,649. Heidelberg was married with two children. He started his SS career as a department head for construction in the *Wirtschafts und Verwaltungshauptamt*, the Economics and Administration Head Office of the SS, charged with the administration of the concentration camps.

In 1941 Heidelberg was assigned to the *SS-FHA* before going east in 1942 to assume duties as the supply chief for the SS and Police Leader for South Russia. Later assignments included commander of the SS training area at Böhmen and later as a supervisor for construction of defensive positions with the Vth SS Corps.[13] He had one black mark in his career. In 1942 he was charged in an incident at the Debica training area.

Dirlewanger received a reply from *SS-Hauptsturmführer* Blessau on March 19. It began "Dear Oskar" and stated that unfortunately *SS-Obergruppenführer* Berger would not be able to go wolf hunting. It went on to state that concerning Dirlewanger's price of two bottles of schnapps, the *SS-Obergruppenführer* had a hearty laugh that Dirlewanger was so clever a merchant.

On March 18, 1944 Dirlewanger forwarded correspondence to the SS Main Office requesting that 337 his troops be declared rehabilitated.[14] One of those men Dirlewanger considered rehabilitated was *SS-Oberscharführer* Alfred Mammitsch. Mammitsch had an outstanding record winning the Iron Cross 2nd Class on May 20, 1942, the Infantry Assault Badge on June 21, 1943 and the Eastern Front Medal. He had been promoted July 1, 1941 to *SS-Sturmmann*, April 20, 1942 to *SS-Rottenführer*, August 11, 1942 to *SS-Unterscharführer* and June 21, 1943 to *SS-Oberscharführer*.[15]

On March 19 *SS-Obersturmbannführer* Dirlewanger was promoted to *SS-Standartenführer*. Despite his new rank, Dirlewanger was still desperately short of troops. In his ongoing attempt to procure reinforcements for the *Sonderkommando*, Gottlob Berger again went to Himmler. On March 22, 1944 Berger submitted the following draft order to the *SS-Reichsführer* for his approval:[16]

> In view of the difficult reinforcement situation, it is my desire that *SS-Obersturmbannführer* Dirlewanger [*SS-Standartenführer* by this date] or a special representative nominated by him in agreement with *SS-Obergruppenführer* Berger and experienced in anti-guerrilla warfare, should select from the inmates of the SS and Police punishment camps and other prisons those Waffen-SS men suited by their character and the nature of their offense for employment in the Dirlewanger unit. In view of the urgency and importance of anti-guerrilla warfare, regulations should be interpreted liberally. By showing courage, the men selected have the opportunity to rehabilitate themselves. This instruction will take precedence over all general and special instructions regarding the serving of sentences. In pending or future cases of investigation against Waffen-SS men, investigating officers will check whether their character and the nature of their offense is such that they could be made available to *SS-Obersturmbannführer* Dirlewanger and, if the answer is in the affirmative, they will be made so available. Summaries of evidence will be held by *SS-Obersturmbannführer* Dirlewanger until the conclusion of the probationary period.

Himmler refused to sign the order fearing that its result would mean the end of the SS legal system of justice – under Berger's proposal, any Waffen-SS soldier accused of a crime could be sent to the *Sonderkommando*!

On April 1, 1944 the *Sonderkommando* reported the following strength: [17]

Personnel:
German	9 officers	321 NCOs and men
Foreign	0 officers	246 men

Weapons:
529 rifles 28 light machine-guns 8 heavy machine-guns
6 light mortars 12 medium mortars

Vehicles:
2 command cars 14 motorcycles 7 medium trucks
1 radio van

Animal Transport:
102 horses 82 *panje* wagons

Heavy Weapons:
2 anti-tank guns (45mm)

On April 11, 1944 the *Sonderkommando* received orders to participate with Battle Group von Gottberg in *Operation Frühlingsfest* (Operation Spring Festival), an anti-partisan operation in the Lepel'-Usaci area. The operation was to run from April 11 to May 10. Other German units included SS-Police Regiment 2, SS-Police Regiment 24, SS-Police Regiment 26, two *Schuma* battalions, SD Battalion 23, 3rd Battalion Police Regiment 31, 2nd Battalion Police Regiment 36 and Group Kaminski. The army took part in the operation as well. The 3rd Panzer Army contributed Security Regiment 64, Engineer Battalion 743, 3rd Company Anti-Tank Battalion 256 and three armored trains.[18]

The Germans estimated the strength of the partisans in the area to be

Oskar Dirlewanger. (BAK, 573495)

Dirlewanger's armored train. (Edition Temmen)

Roll Call, Sachsenhausen concentration camp. (USHMM)

Odilo Globocnik. (USHMM)

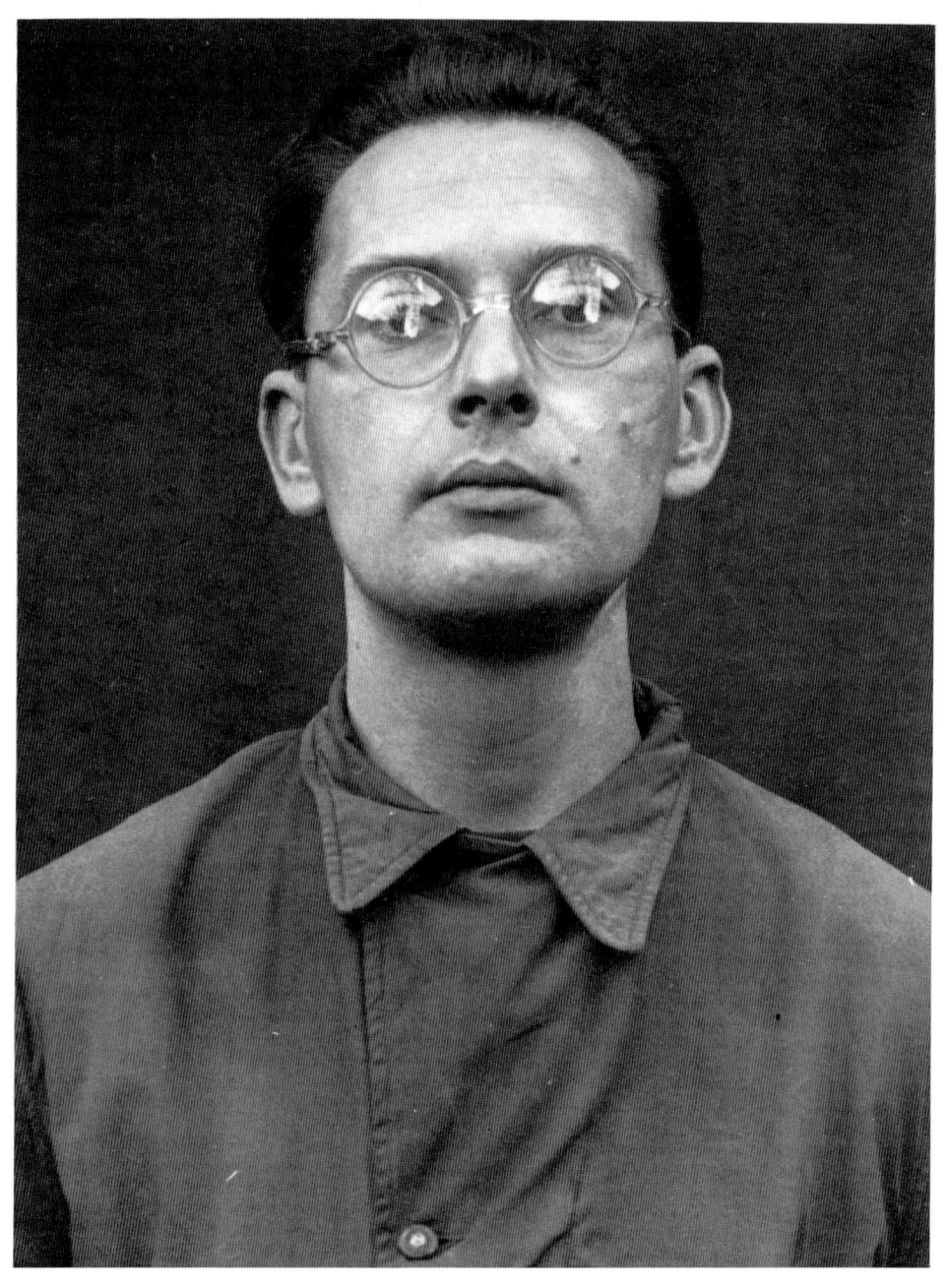

Rudolf Brandt, Himmler's personal secretary, shown here at Nürnberg War Crimes Trial. (USHMM)

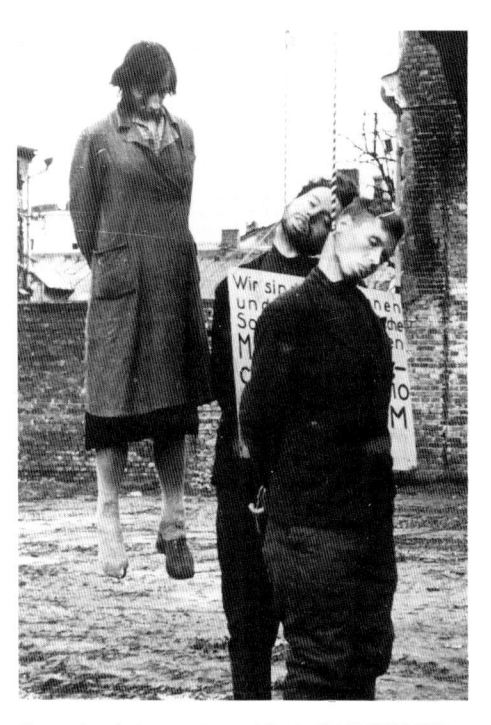

Hanged and shot partisans, Minsk. (BAK, 70/43/50)  "Attention, Danger from partisans from 3pm to 6am. No traffic in individual vehicles." *(BAK, 31/2427/19a)*

Dead partisan as warning to German troops, 1942 Minsk. (BAK, 76/127/23a)

Execution of Jews by members of an Einsatzkommando. (USHMM)

Mass execution of Russians. (USHMM)

Dirlewanger troops – probably recon platoon. (Edition Temmen)

Dirlewanger troops. (Edition Temmen)

Erich Naumann. (USHMM)  *Pre-war photo of Bach-Zelewski. (BAK, 88/24/2a)*

Von dem Bach (left) with Kurt Daleuge (center) Chief of German Police. (BAK, 96/57/15a)

Naumman's handiwork – execution in progress. (USHMM)

Dirlewanger and Staff. (Edition Temmen)

Dirlewanger collar insignia.

Burning partisan dwellings. (BAK, 88/3721/11a)

SD troops questioning suspected partisan. (BAK, 74/132/4a)

Friedrich Jeckeln, Higher SS and Police Leader. (USHMM)

Operation Frühlingsfest. (BAK, 90/86/2)

Wehrmacht rocket launcher advance on Warsaw. (BAK, 696/435/11a)

Dirlewanger troops move in on Warsaw. (BAK, 695/425/31)

German troops prepare rockets for launching in Warsaw. (BAK, 696/426/10)

Rockets Away – launch of rockets against Uprising. (BAK, 696/426/15)

More rockets – Note empty launch frames indicating massive volleys. (BAK, 696/426/19)

Still more – these rockets were not precision weapons and were designed to suppress large areas, hence non-combatants were often the casualties. (BAK, 696/426/20)

Rocket launcher advances down a Warsaw street. (BAK, 96/57/12a)

German quad-20mm anti-aircraft gun in Warsaw square shown here in ground-attack mode. (BAK, 73/113/20)

German troops advance through rubble in Warsaw. (BAK, 73/113/21)

German infantry and assault guns attack a large concentration of Poles. (BAK, 73/113/22)

SS flamethrower team advances cautiously in the city. (BAK, 77/143/21)

"Each nest of partisans must be burned and smoked out." (BAK, 96/57/10a)

Many blocks were left with no one alive. (BAK, 96/57/11a)

Germans advance past burning Warsaw houses in Wola. (BAK, 695/408/8a)

Barricades stop German assault guns from advancing. (BAK, 96/57/14a)

German troops prepare to rush a building. (BAK, 96/57/19a)

SS troops consult a map before proceeding. (BAK, 695/412/17)

Inner city carnage. (BAK, 96/57/13a)

SS troops take a rest during the fighting. (BAK, 696/426/21)

Aserbajani troops prepare for fighting. (BAK, 695/425/20)

Aserbajani soldier – note scimitar insignia on cap. (BAK, 696/426/2)

Karl in firing position. (BAK, 695/424/23a)

Shell being hoisted prior to loading. (BAK, 695/424/10)

Lifting the massive shell from ammunition carrier. (BAK, 695/424/8a)

Loading the shell; the breech-block is slid to the right to permit loading. (BAK, 695/424/18a)

Karl firing. (BAK, 695/424/26a)

German engineers prepare Goliath for operation. (BAK, 695/412/19)

German troops appear interested in their new "toy." (BAK, 695/411/6)

Goliath operator – control box has toggles and buttons for operation; signals sent to Goliath are via a thin metal wire. (BAK, II 438)

Polish sisters comfort people of Warsaw. (BAK, 96/57/8a)

Slovak partisan reconnaissance unit of "Jan Zizka" Brigade. (BAK, NO 708/328)

Slovak partisans. (BAK, CO 902/53/12)

Slovak partisans attack near Banska Bystrica. (BAK, H 1119/203/15)

Slovak partisans attack near Kosuty. (BAK, 19000/3818)

Slovak aircraft camouflaged against German air attacks. (BAK, 96/57/7a)

Paul Hausser (right) with Heinz Lammerding. (BAK, 73/96/2)

(L-R) Otto Ohlendorf, Heinz Jost, Erich Naumann and Erwin Schultz, former Einsatzkommando leaders, receive indictments at Nürnberg. (USHMM)

Einsatzkommando leader Ernst Biberstein pleads "not guilty." (USHMM)

Former grave of Oskar Dirlewanger. (Rudolf Multer)

The "Hopfendarre" – hop drying house at Altshausen where Oskar Dirlewanger met his fate on June 6-7, 1945. (Rudolf Multer)

Grave of Karl Wolf. (Author photo)

Grave of von dem Bach-Zelewski. (Author photo)

Anti-partisan badge. (Author photo)

Farewell to Russia - 1944

at least 14,000. There were numerous partisan brigades which were named after their commanders and included: the 2,500 man "Melnikov" Brigade, the 1,000 man "Tjabuth" Brigade, the "Bareyka" Brigade, the 1,000 man "Lenin" Brigade, the "Kosmin" Brigade, the 1,500 man "Romanov" Brigade, the 1,500 man "Utkin" Brigade, the 2,000 man "Lobanek" Brigade, the 3,000 man "Alexejew" Brigade, the 1,000 man "Smolensker" Brigade (commanded by Ssadtschikov), the 1,000 man "Raizev" Brigade, the 600 man "Korotkin" Brigade, the 400 man "Medwedjew" Brigade and the 500 man "Rodianov" Brigade.[19]

The overall object of the operation was to surround and destroy the partisan groups. The concept of the operation was to have elements of the 3rd Panzer Army attack west on April 11 to secure a line on the west bank of Lake Gomel, Lake Janovo, Lake Tettscha, Lake Werkudskoje, Lake Otelove and Lake Beloje. The panzer army's operation was codenamed *Operation Regenschauer* (Operation Rain Shower). Battle Group von Gottberg meanwhile, would attack from the southwest and south in four groups: Krehan, Kaminski, Anhalt and Rehdans. These four units would advance toward the 3rd Panzer Army, effectively overrunning the partisans. Battle Group von Gottberg's operation was codenamed *Operation Frühlingsfest*. The Dirlewanger *Sonderkommando* was part of Group Anhalt as were SS-Police Regiment 2, SS-Police Regiment 24 and *Schuma* Battalion 62.[20]

On April 15 the battalion reported a strength of eight officers, thirty-eight non-commissioned officers and 388 men. Three days later, the battalion was located on the northwest bank of Lake Medsosol with its headquarters at Czernizka. There were no signs of partisans as the battalion seized three men, three women, fourteen head of cattle and two horses for shipment back to the Reich. The 4th Company was detached from the battalion and was temporarily assigned to SS-Police Regiment 24 from April 20 to 24. The company was involved in heavy fighting along a wooden corduroy road northeast of Hornowo-Sswatki. On April 21, during the occupation of the village of Hornowo II, the company fought against "massive enemy resistance." The following day the company seized Hornung-Asory III, again reporting "intense resistance." On April 23, during movement through thickly wooded terrain west of Chernizka, the company once again was engaged in intense combat.[21]

Meanwhile, on April 22, the enemy attacked the left flank of the battalion at 5:00 AM, killing one soldier and wounding another. Sometime earlier, four men had apparently been injured by a mine – and three had already died. Replacements were on the way, however. On April 25 the battalion was notified by the SS Main Office that on April 17 twenty-seven prisoners from the Sachsenhausen concentration camp began transportation to the *Sonderkommando*.[22]

SS-Sturmbannführer Andreas Mayer-Mader, who had previously served in the 13th SS Division "*Handschar*", reportedly was serving with the *Sonderkommando* at this time. His SS personnel file lists him as being killed in action at Hornowo-Wiercinski on May 2, 1944 – but the circumstances surrounding his death remain unclear. During the night of May 3, the enemy tried to break through the battalion defenses at Krownica and Hornowo-Wiercinski. One German was killed. On May 8, the enemy again put pressure on the *Sonderkommando*, probing both flanks.

Dirlewanger provided a summary of the operation on May 17. Nineteen *Sonderkommando* soldiers had been killed and forty-three wounded. Dirlewanger reported killing sixty-five partisans and capturing two deserters. Additionally, the Germans destroyed two partisan camps and captured a good amount of munitions and foodstuffs.

Sometime during the spring, Dirlewanger was involved in another circumstance. At Minsk, he was involved in a whipping incident. We do not know who the victim was or if Dirlewanger himself beat the individual or ordered a subordinate to do so. In any case Reichs Leader Rosenberg sent a letter of complaint to Himmler, who forwarded it in turn to *SS-Obergruppenführer* Berger. Berger drafted a reply for Himmler which read:[23]

> Dear Party Member Rosenberg:
> On principle I share your view, and I am not at all pleased when an incident such as the one in Minsk occurs. However, I am convinced that you can fully understand if I cannot at present involve *SS-Standartenführer* Dr. Dirlewanger in an investigation, as I need him most badly for the safeguarding of that area.

Heil Hitler
Yours,
Berger

Enlisted personnel received awards as well as officers. On May 3, *SS-Grenadier* Adam Pres was awarded the Iron Cross 2nd Class and the Eastern People's Bravery Medal 2nd Class in Silver. The next day *SS-Oberscharführer* Jakob Dett was awarded the Iron Cross 1st Class.

Sonderkommando troops came from unusual sources. On April 14 the battalion prepared a list of all personnel. On the list were six SS volunteers (*SS-Freiwilliger*) from Spain: Valenzia-Haras, Praga-Rodrigues, Castellanos, Ovadio-Inglesios, Lopez and Rodriguez-Garcia. The Spaniards quite likely transferred from remnants of the Spanish Blue Division who remained in Germany after the unit redeployed to Spain. This unit had originally been provided by *Generalissimo* Franco to Hitler for the fight in Russia as a partial pay-back for German help during the Spanish Civil War.[24]

Many of the Russian soldiers in the *Sonderkommando* were former members of the Red Army who had been captured by the Germans. They included ranks of private through lieutenant and included personnel from not only the army but also the air force. Former Russian officers who were members of the unit included Ivan Melnitschenko, Leonid Sakhno, Ivan Holtwjanik, Nikolai Roschko, Ivan Teretschenko, Pawel Romanenko, Ivan Susuija, Wasil Jalinskij, Alexander Radkowski, Piotr Teretschuk, Stepan Slobodjanik, Nestor Cjhonkow and Ivan Goldwianik.

The *Sonderkommando* continued to have army troops assigned as well. A 1944 personnel report showed that Corporal Egeon Thieme, Private First Class Heinz Krause and Private Richard Tölkner were assigned to Dirlewanger. The same report showed a four man SD commando assigned as well – led by *SS-Untersturmführer* Heinrich Amann.

On May 8, the *Sonderkommando* received a warning order that Fritz Sauckel had decided that 2,000-3,000 Eastern Muslims (*Ostmusselin*) and possibly 1,000 soldiers from North Caucasian areas might be assigned to the battalion in about six weeks.[25] Fritz Sauckel served as the Plenipotentiary for Labor and Manpower. Born October 27, 1894, he was an early member of the Nazi Party holding party number 1,395. In the 1930s he was the *Gauleiter* of Thuringia. He was convicted at Nürnberg and hanged.[26]

SS-Untersturmführer Hans Schäftlmeier reported for duty in the unit on May 15, 1944. Born June 18, 1910 in Stuttgart, he had a Nazi Party number of 5,459,706 and an SS number of 244,253. Schäftlmeier previously served at SS training centers at Heidelager and Münsingen. While with Dirlewanger he received the Eastern Front Medal, the Iron Cross 2nd Class, the Eastern People's Bravery Medal in Silver and the war Service Cross 2nd Class with Swords. Married with three children, he had a clean record.[27]

In reviewing Schäftlmeier's record, along with other personnel in the unit, it is apparent that a relatively large number of personnel came from the Stuttgart, Heilbronn and Esslingen areas – Dirlewanger's home grounds. From the record, Dirlewanger took numerous leaves and trips to the area during the war. It is quite possible that he undertook recruiting campaigns while in the area and convinced these men to join him.

In response to an inquiry from the *SS-Hauptamt*, the *Sonderkommando* reported on May 23 that the following men who had served in the *Reichspost* (Reich Postal Service) were now assigned as radio operators: Martin Fuchs, Gerhard Labette, Heinrich Spern, Heinrich Gerards, Kurt Thiel, Heinrich Flohr, Heinrich Kehl, Walter Ledermann, Erich Koch, Engelbert Geschler and Josef Scheber. Two other former postal service members had been in the unit but were no longer: Leopold Heuschneider had been released from service and had returned to Vienna, and Paul Kunze who had been killed in action February 22, 1944.

The same day 287 men were reported ready at the concentration camp at Sachsenhausen for transportation to Dirlewanger. On May 27, the *Sonderkommando* received a telegram stating that 182 men were ready to be transported from the Auschwitz concentration camp to the unit.

On the 29th Dirlewanger sent a message to Berger stating that *SS-Untersturmführer* Feiertag had radioed to the *Sonderkommando* that one thousand Eastern Muslims were currently in Oslo, Norway awaiting transport to the unit.

The *Sonderkommando* would need these additional troops. As of June 1944, according to Soviet sources, there were 150,000 partisans – grouped into some one hundred fifty brigades and forty-nine detachments in White

Russia. Many of these brigades were grouped into what was termed a partisan complex. There were more than a dozen partisan complexes in White Russia. The largest included one of 15,000 men in Rossono Rayon north of Polock, one of 18,000 between Borisov and Lepel', one of 8,000 near Minsk, another of 9,000 in the vicinity of Senno and one of 14,000 men near Vitebsk.[28]

On June 1, the battalion reported a strength of eight officers, fifty non-commissioned officers, four hundred eight German troops and two hundred forty-one foreign troops. That day they received former Captain of Police Franz Ambros for assignment. Additionally, Dirlewanger received a message that the *Sonderkommando* would receive Lieutenant of Police Rack, who was being relieved of his duties in Croatia. Part of the instructions to Dirlewanger included that Rack would serve in an officer position when he arrived. Dirlewanger fired back a message to the Chief of the SS Main Office asking why, if Rack was deemed unsuitable to serve as a lieutenant in Croatia, should he continue to serve as a lieutenant and not a private?[29]

Dirlewanger did not seem to mind when former officers came to the units as privates – having been reduced in court martial proceedings. A case in point concerned Georg-Wilhelm Eggers. A former *SS-Hauptsturmführer*, Eggers was born March 8, 1904 in Hildesheim. He entered the Nazi Party March 1, 1931 and received party number 468,113. He joined the SS shortly thereafter with a membership number of 8,736. Eggers had a good record in the SS, serving in several SD positions. However, in Göttingen in the early morning hours of February 22, 1944, Eggers pulled out his service pistol and fired several shots during a night of carousing. The fact that he was intoxicated was not a mitigating circumstance, and Eggers was reduced to a private and sentenced to three months in prison. In lieu of prison, his sentence was changed to service in the *Sonderkommando*, where he reported on August 2, 1944.[30]

On June 2 Dirlewanger sent a message to *SS-Obergruppenführer* Berger thanking him for giving the *Sonderkommando* an 88mm flak battery. Dirlewanger also asked if it might be possible to obtain a 20mm flak battery as well, as this weapon would be excellent in anti-partisan operations.[31]

Dirlewanger may have celebrated the arrival of the 88s by falling to one of his old vices – drunkenness, as he became involved in another incident that night. Late in the evening Dirlewanger began to berate several junior officers present, which led one of them to write a letter to Berger seeking redress. The letter, from one *SS-Hauptsturmführer* Walter Brandenburg, written on June 9, 1944 follows, and reveals the bullying nature Dirlewanger frequently displayed toward subordinates:[32]

> During an official trip to the occupied East Area during the time of May 31 to June 8, 1944, I [*SS-Hauptsturmführer* Brandenburg] was invited for an evening gathering at the house *dacha* of *SS-Gruppenführer* von Gottberg. Among others who attended this gathering were the supply chief of Army Group Center *Oberst* von Unhold, the SS leader of the Hitler Youth for the area *Hauptbannführer* [equivalent to major] Nickel, and a number of leading personalities of the General Commissariat Administration and *SS-Standartenführer* Dr. Dirlewanger. Completely unprovoked, my honor as *SS-Führer* was damaged to the utmost by *SS-Standartenführer* Dirlewanger at around 1:30 at night. Shortly before this, *SS-Standartenführer* Dirlewanger had brought up the subject of war service evasion. Out of the blue, *SS-Standartenführer* Dirlewanger attacked me with the following verbal insult: "That Brandenburg, he is also a shady bird, who during the five years of war has done nothing except hang around in Berlin being in charge of the East Ministry with his big mouth." This remark was that much more insulting because, prior to it, the subject of war evasion had been discussed extensively. After this remark I waited another moment in hopes that the most senior of the attending SS leaders and the host, *SS-Gruppenführer* von Gottberg would step in to defend my honor. Since no reaction came from them, I got up, announced my exit to *SS-Gruppenführer* von Gottberg

by referring to the insult which was made and left. As was reported to me [later] by others in attendance, *SS-Standartenführer* Dirlewanger continued to rub-in my supposed evasion of war duty. During those remarks he declared that all men who were capable to serve in the war but who had not been at the front during these five years were to be considered "scoundrels", and since this was true in my case, I was a "scoundrel" also. The attending Luftwaffe officers and also other members of the civilian administration, many of whom did not yet possess war awards were insulted by him when he opined that no decent soldier would wear the War Service Cross. When from among the people present, including the Assistant General Commissar, *SS-Standartenführer* Freitag, the assistant commander of the Security Police and of the SD, *SS-Sturmbannführer* Gornig, *Hauptbannführer* Nickel and *Oberbannführer* Schulz energetically protested what *SS-Standartenführer* Dirlewanger had said about me, *SS-Standartenführer* Dirlewanger declared that he could prove it in writing that I was a "scoundrel" since he had in his hands a letter from *SS-Obergruppenführer* Berger in which was written that I had avoided service at the front by doing "SD-Tours" and that, therefore, it was high time for me to now become a soldier. During the course of his additional remarks, *SS-Standartenführer* Dirlewanger referred to me as a "scoundrel" at different occasions. As it was reported to me afterwards, *SS-Gruppenführer* von Gottberg was requested to intercede and to defend me. Nothing happened in this connection from him. When several of the persons who attended – among them Luftwaffe officers – requested permission to leave the house in protest of the behavior of *SS-Standartenführer* Dirlewanger against me, they were ordered to remain by *SS-Gruppenführer* von Gottberg. Only *SS-Sturmbannführer*

The Cruel Hunters

Sepp of the commander of the Security Police and the SD was allowed to depart.

Personally it is completely unclear to me what motivated *Standartenführer* Dirlewanger to make these insults and deprive me of my honor. I have known *SS-Standartenführer* Dirlewanger only very slightly during occasional contact in Berlin; the evening as a whole went in complete harmony. In the usual custom, about two hours before this incidence *SS-Standartenführer* Dirlewanger toasted me and there was no general indication during the evening for such insults. In addition, I have referred this matter to the commander of the Security Police and the SD in this connection.

The same day, by order of the *SS-Reichsführer*, *SS-Hauptsturmführer* Grohmann was relieved of his duties and reduced to *SS-Schutze*. The following day *SS-Standartenführer* Dirlewanger radioed the SS and police punishment camp at Danzig-Matzkau that *SS-Hauptsturmführer* Plaul should bring Grohmann back to the unit as a private.[33]

SS-Hauptsturmführer Josef Grohmann was born in Weidenau in the Sudetenland on November 1, 1908. He was convicted in Czechoslovakia of spying for Germany and sentenced to three years imprisonment. He later joined the SS and received SS number 207,848. He was promoted to *SS-Untersturmführer* on January 30, 1938. One year later he made *SS-Obersturmführer* and was promoted again on January 30, 1940 to *SS-Hauptsturmführer*. His early service was with an SD detachment in Gleiwitz and later an SD detachment at Kattowitz. In 1943 he was sentenced to seven months confinement for a weapons violation, being drunk on duty and for making false official statements. He was then sent to the *Sonderkommando*, where he served as the commander of 4th Company. There is no record of what his latest disciplinary problem was.[34]

His escort, *SS-Hauptsturmführer* Wolfgang Plaul, also had a history of problems. Born April 13, 1900 at Grimma, Saxony he was an early member of the Nazi Party with party number 18,213. He had served in the very last months of World War I with the 22nd Engineer Battalion and in 1919 had served with *Freikorps* Menke. In 1934 he joined the police at

Farewell to Russia - 1944

Dresden and later served in Hamburg. With an SS number of 59,933 and a date of rank to *SS-Hauptsturmführer* of November 9, 1937, he served in Serbia from October 1941 to November 1943. He was then court-martialed for misappropriation of government property and sentenced to eleven months confinement. He was subsequently transferred to the *Sonderkommando* on April 17, 1944 and won the War Service Cross in his first month with the unit.[35]

On June 4 Dirlewanger sent a telegram to *SS-Obersturmführer* Ingruber, now with the Main SS Economic Office, congratulating him on being awarded the Iron Cross 1st Class and the Anti-Partisan Badge. Dirlewanger also sent another message to *SS-Gruppenführer* Jurs, in the SS Main Office informing him that *SS-Untersturmführer* Feiertag, who was assigned to the SS Main office – but had previously been assigned to the *Sonderkommando* as an *SS-Oberscharführer*, was hereby awarded the Anti-Partisan Badge in Silver. Dirlewanger understood that it was always good to have friends in high places and took every opportunity to maintain contact with them.

Heinz Feiertag had been elevated to officer rank after departing the *Sonderkommando*. He was promoted to *SS-Untersturmführer* January 30, 1944 and would be promoted to *SS-Obersturmführer* on June 21, 1944. Born December 20, 1914 at Herne, he entered the SS in 1932 shortly after turning eighteen. He served with the *Leibstandarte Adolf Hitler* in Poland and the *Totenkopf* in France in 1940. He received the Iron Cross 2nd and 1st Class, the War Service Cross 2nd Class with Swords, the Infantry Assault Badge, the Anti-Partisan Badge in Silver and the Wound Badge in Silver among his many decorations.[36]

On June 5 the *Sonderkommando* received a telegram instructing Dirlewanger to inform every member of his command that they could volunteer to participate in an operation as a member of *SS-Sturmbannführer* Otto Skorceny's [sic Skorzeny] SS-Jäger Battalion 502 (a special commando unit). The message stated that the *SS-Reichsführer* wanted to ensure that every soldier was aware of the opportunity. It is not known if any soldiers from the *Sonderkommando* volunteered or were accepted into the program. Dirlewanger also received a telegram informing him that *SS-Obersturmführer* Gast was enroute to the *Sonderkommando* with two hundred ninety-three men from the concentration camp at Oranienburg.

SS-Obersturmführer Otto Gast served in the *Sonderkommando* as the administrative officer. Born July 6, 1908 he joined the SS in May 1940 with an SS number of 177,886 and was promoted to *SS-Untersturmführer* on November 9, 1940. He had previously served two months in the German army with the 12th Infantry Regiment. In 1941 he served at the Oranienburg concentration camp and the *WVHA – Wirtschafts und Verwaltungshauptamt*, the Economics and Administration Head Office of the SS charged with the administration of the concentration camps. He served in the SS *"Totenkopf"* Division in 1942 and transferred to the *Sonderkommando* in 1944. He was a recipient of the War Service Cross 2nd Class, the Infantry Assault Badge, the Iron Cross 2nd Class and the Eastern People's Bravery Medal. He subsequently left the unit on August 28, and returned to the *WVHA*, and still later in the war went to the 18th Waffen-SS Infantry Training Battalion.[37]

On June 8 the 2nd Battalion of the *Sonderkommando* conducted an action against the Sowch Kommune Ssejatel. They captured seventeen men, twenty-four women and twenty-eight children for slave labor and took two horses and six cows as well.[38]

On June 18, the regimental staff company reported that the following men who had served in the *Sonderkommando* since its inception were now declared to be fully rehabilitated: *SS-Hauptscharführer* Strumpf, *SS-Oberscharführer* Mammitsch and Heinrich Kraus, *SS-Unterscharführer* Walther, Rau, Maas, Georg Kraus and Hellcamp, and *SS-Rottenführer* Drabeck, Graminski and Simoner.

On June 21, Dirlewanger sent a radio message to *SS-Gruppenführer* von Gottberg congratulating him on receiving the Infantry Assault Badge.

On June 22, 1944, Josef Stalin launched *Operation Bagration* – the Soviet attack to destroy Army Group Center. The *1st Baltic, 3rd Belorussian, 2nd Belorussian* and *1st Belorussian Fronts*, with some 2,500,000 Russian troops, backed by a revitalized air force, smashed into Field Marshal Busch's 400,000 overextended German troops. The ground force ratios, exasperated by Soviet control of the air, combined with the element of surprise almost guaranteed that Red Army gains would be swift and massive.

It is at this point that the continuous *Sonderkommando* battle reports, as found in the National Archives microfilm rolls, stop. On June 30, the

Farewell to Russia - 1944

strength of the *Sonderkommando* was reported to be nine hundred seventy-one.[39] It is likely that Dirlewanger and his men found themselves a part of Battle Group von Gottberg during the German attempted defense of White Russia, although no available sources specifically confirm this. Von Gottberg had at his disposal parts of SS-Police Regiments 2, 4, 17, 22, 26, 34 and 36. He additionally had under his command Heavy Artillery Detachment 861 and Police Panzer Companies 12 and 20.[40]

On July 2, 1944 Battle Group von Gottberg was assigned directly to the German 4th Army. Von Gottberg had forces near Smilovici, Smolevici and Logojsk. His mission was to delay the Soviet advance on Minsk and the capture of the city; to maintain communications with pockets of surrounded German troops and to cover the withdrawal of various combat service support units which had remained forward.[41]

By 9:00 AM on July 3, von Gottberg reported that the defense of Minsk had collapsed. His forces would attempt to withdraw to Ivenec, but many of the roads were blocked by destroyed vehicles and fleeing units. German aerial reconnaissance showed that Minsk had been abandoned.[42]

On July 4, as ordered by 4th Army, von Gottberg reported to the tactical command post of the German VIth Corps west of Volozin. How-

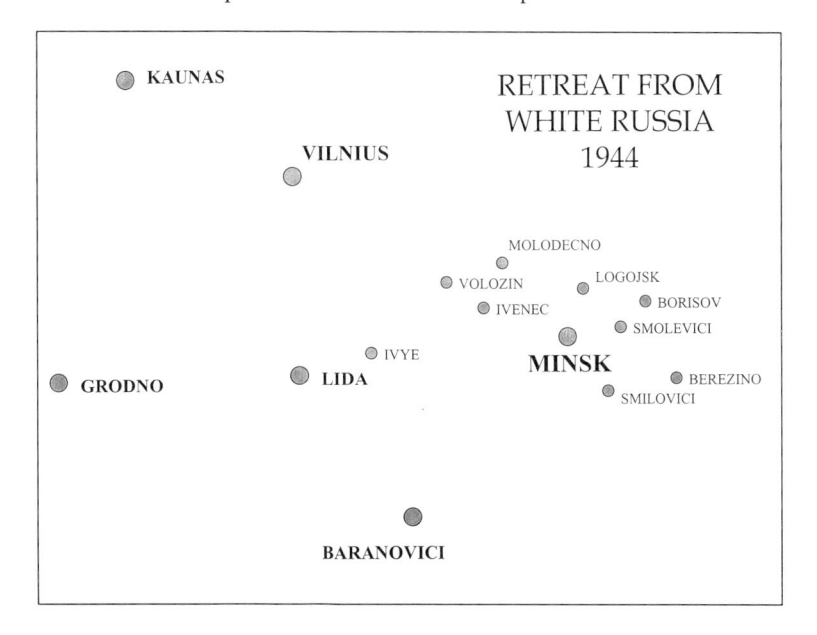

RETREAT FROM WHITE RUSSIA 1944

ever, he declined to be subordinated to the VIth Corps as he had been ordered by 4th Army, stating that his formations had been seriously mauled. Instead, he ordered his SS and Police units to continue to withdraw west and reform at Lida. On July 5, elements of Battle Group von Gottberg assumed defensive positions east of Lida, to the south of the Molodecno-Lida railroad. These positions consisted of old World War I strong points which provided some degree of protection but were seriously overgrown.[43]

Some replacements still trickled in during this time, despite the gravity of the German retreat. *SS-Untersturmführer* Helmut Lewandowski reported for duty on July 5. Lewandowski, born April 1, 1906 in Liegnitz, previously served in the *SS-Hauptamt* in Berlin. In 1943 he was convicted in an SS court of an unspecified crime.[44]

By July 6, von Gottberg established a screen of police troops along the railroad and had concentrated his defense east of Ivye. This was the only German force in position between units from the 4th and 9th Armies. They remained in this position through July 7.[45] On July 7 the *Sonderkommando* was reported to have been in position southeast of Lida. During the day Soviet forces attacked; the *Sonderkommando* matched this with a counterattack into the flank of the enemy. Both *SS-Sturmbannführer* Weisse and Dirlewanger were singled out as performing well in this engagement – although the *Sonderkommando* was forced to withdraw under heavy infantry pressure and artillery bombardments.[46]

By the evening of July 8 Soviet troops captured Lida. On July 9 Hitler met with Field Marshall Model and Colonel General Friessner and ordered that *SS-Obergruppenführer* von Gottberg would reform his units at Grodno. Von Gottberg did, but the Red Army captured Grodno on July 16.[47]

Sometime in July the Eastern Muslim SS-Regiment was attached to the *Sonderkommando*. It was commanded from July 29 to August 30 by *SS-Sturmbannführer* Franz Liebermann. The regiment had a reported strength of four thousand men.[48]

The *Sonderkommando* was pulled out of the debacle in time to save it from the Soviet maw, and was reportedly reassembled at Neuhammer, Silesia. From there the unit traveled to Lyck, East Prussia, from where it would soon deploy into infamy.[49]

Farewell to Russia - 1944

ENDNOTES

[1] International Military Tribunal Nürnberg. *Trials of War Criminals before the International Military Tribunal, Volume IV, United States of America vs. Otto Ohlendorf, et al., Case No. 9.*, p.168.

[2] SS-Sonderregiment Dirlewanger, Funkspruch, 21.1.44, Washington, D.C: National Archives Microfilm Publication T354, Roll 648.

[3] SS-Sonderregiment Dirlewanger, Funkspruch, 8.2.44, Washington, D.C: National Archives Microfilm Publication T354, Roll 648.

[4] SS-Sonderregiment Dirlewanger, IIB, Personalbogen Gefallener, 18.2.44, Washington, D.C: National Archives Microfilm Publication T354, Roll 650.

[5] See rear dust jacket for illustration.

[6] Littlejohn, David and Dodkins, COL C..M. *Orders, Decorations, Medals and Badges of the Third Reich.* (Mountain View, CA: R. James Bender, 1968), p.156.

[7] *Trials of War Criminals before the International Military Tribunal, Volume XIII, The Ministries Case, Case No. 11.*, pp. 531-532.

[8] Krausnick, Helmut & Hans Buchheim, Martin Broszat and Hans-Adolf Jacobsen. *Anatomy of the SS State.* New York: Walker and Company, 1968. pp. 250-253.

[9] SS-Sonderbataillon Dirlewanger, Brief an SS-Hauptamt - Chefadjutantur, 23.2.44, Washington, D.C: National Archives Microfilm Publication T354, Roll 650.

[10] Klausch. *Antifaschisten in SS-Uniform.*, pp. 86 - 87.

[11] Personalakt Werner Blessau, Washington, D.C: National Archives Microfilm Publication A3343, Records of SS Officers from the Berlin Document Center, Roll SSO-076.

[12] Angolia. *For Führer and Fatherland.*, pp. 410-411.

[13] The Germans used Arabic numerals (1,2,3, etc.) for divisions and roman numerals (I,II,III, etc.) for corps.

[14] SS-Sonderbataillon Dirlewanger, Rehabilitierungsanträge, 18.3.44, Washington, D.C: National Archives Microfilm Publication T354, Roll 650.

[15] SS-Sonderbataillon Dirlewanger, Rehabilitierungsantrag, 6.3.44, Washington, D.C: National Archives Microfilm Publication T354, Roll 650.

[16] Krausnick, Helmut & Hans Buchheim, Martin Broszat and Hans-Adolf Jacobsen. *Anatomy of the SS State.*, p. 383.

[17] SS-Sonderbataillon Dirlewanger, Funkspruch an HSSPF, Abt Ia, 1.4.44, Washington, D.C: National Archives Microfilm Publication T354, Roll 650.

[18] Kampfgruppe von Gottberg, Einsatzbefehl, 11.4.44, Washington, D.C: National Archives Microfilm Publication T354, Roll 650.

[19] Der HSSPF Russland-Mitte und Weissruthenien, Ic, Feindlage, 11 April 1944, Washington, D.C: National Archives Microfilm Publication T354, Roll 650.

[20] Kampfgruppe von Gottberg, Einsatzbefehl, 11.4.44, Washington, D.C: National Archives Microfilm Publication T354, Roll 650.

[21] SS-Bataillon Dirlewanger, Sturm-und Bandenkampftage Brief, 5.5.44, Washington, D.C: National Archives Microfilm Publication T354, Roll 650.

[22] Der Reichsführer-SS, SS-Hauptamt, BI4, Brief, 25.4.44, Washington, D.C: National Archives Microfilm Publication T354, Roll 650.

[23] *Trials of War Criminals before the International Military Tribunal, Volume XIII, The Ministries Case, Case No. 11.*, pp. 533-534.

[24] 00512, Namentliche Liste aller am Einsatz Beteiligten Batl.-Angehörigen, 14.4.44, Washington, D.C: National Archives Microfilm Publication T354, Roll 650.

[25] HSSPF Russland-Mitte und Weissruthenien, Ia, Abschrift, 8.5.44, Washington, D.C: National Archives Microfilm Publication T354, Roll 650.

[26] Krausnick, Helmut & Hans Buchheim, Martin Broszat and Hans-Adolf Jacobsen. *Anatomy of the SS State.*, p.592.

[27] Personalakt Hans Schäftlmeier, Washington, D.C: National Archives Microfilm Publication A3343, Records of SS Officers from the Berlin Document Center, Roll SSO-068B.

[28] Ziemke. *Stalingrad to Berlin.*, p.304.

[29] SS-Sonderregiment Dirlewanger, Funkspruch an den Chef SS-Hauptamt, 1.6.44, Washington, D.C: National Archives Microfilm Publication T354, Roll 650.

[30] Personalakt Georg-Wilhelm Eggers, Washington, D.C: National Archives Microfilm Publication A3343, Records of SS Officers from the Berlin Document Center, Roll SSO-174.

[31] SS-Sonderbataillon Dirlewanger, Fernschreiben, 2 Juni 1944, Washington, D.C: National Archives Microfilm Publication T354, Roll 650.

[32] Personalakt Oskar Dirlewanger.

[33] SS-Sonderregiment Dirlewanger, Funkspruch an den Strafvollzugslager der SS und Polizei, 3.6.44, Washington, D.C: National Archives Microfilm Publication T354, Roll 650.

[34] Personalakt Josef Grohmann, Washington, D.C: National Archives Microfilm Publication A3343, Records of SS Officers from the Berlin Document Center, Roll SSO-033A.

[35] Personalakt Wolfgang Plaul, Washington, D.C: National Archives Microfilm Publication A3343, Records of SS Officers from the Berlin Document Center, Roll SSO-302A.

[36] Personalakt Heinz Feiertag, Washington, D.C: National Archives Microfilm Publication A3343, Records of SS Officers from the Berlin Document Center, Roll SSO-199.

[37] Personalakt Otto Gast, Washington, D.C: National Archives Microfilm Publication A3343, Records of SS Officers from the Berlin Document Center, Roll SSO-004A.

[38] II./SS-Sonderregiment Dirlewanger, Brief an SS-Sonder Regt. Dirlewanger, 8.6.44, Washington, D.C: National Archives Microfilm Publication T354, Roll 650.

[39] Munoz, Antonio J. *Forgotten Legions: Obscure Combat Formations of the Waffen-SS*, (Boulder, CO: Paladin Press, 1991), p.366.

[40] Hinze, Rolf. *Das Ostfront-Drama 1944: Rückzugskämpfe Heeresgruppe Mitte.* (Stuttgart, FRG: Motorbuch Verlag, 1988), p.439.

[41] Niepold, Gerd. *Battle for White Russia: The Destruction of Army Group Center June 1944.* (London: Brassey's Defense Publishers, 1987), p. 187.

[42] Ibid., p. 195.

[43] Ibid., pp. 208, 218.

[44] Personalakt Helmut Lewandowski, Washington, D.C: National Archives Microfilm Publication A3343, Records of SS Officers from the Berlin Document Center, Roll SSO-259A.

[45] Ibid., pp. 226, 236.

[46] Personalakt Oskar Dirlewanger and Personalakt Kurt Weisse, Washington.

[47] Niepold. *Battle for White Russia.*, pp. 256-257.

[48] Munoz. *Forgotten Legions.*, pp. 166, 167, 176.

[49] Reitlinger. *The House Built on Sand.*, p.371. It is more likely that the Sonderkommando went straight west to Lyck, which was only fifty miles from Dirlewanger's last position, as part of Battle Group von Gottberg. Silesia is hundreds of miles to the southwest of Grodno and Lida; if the Sonderkommando did in fact deploy there, then it had to turn right around and head back in the direction from which it came. Given the stretched state of the German rail system, backtracking does not make sense.

5

WARSAW

Mein Führer, das sind wirkliche Strolche.
(My Führer, they are real low-lifes)
- SS-General Hermann Fegelein speaking to Hitler about the
Dirlewanger Regiment in the Warsaw Uprising, 1944.[1]

On August 1, 1944 the Red Army reached the Vistula River on a broad front and even had reconnaissance detachments on the west bank in the Warsaw suburb of Praga. Receiving reports that Soviet tanks were visible on the horizon east of Praga and believing that liberation was imminent, Polish insurgent leader General Bór-Komorowski called his 35,000 man Home Army to fight the Germans in the Polish capital.[2]

General Tadeusz "Bór" (his pseudonym) Komorowski had served as Commander-in-Chief of the *Armia Krajowa* (Home Army) since 1943 when his predecessor, General Grot-Rowecki had been arrested by the Germans. He was assisted by the commander of Home Army troops in the Warsaw district Colonel Antoni "Monter" Chrusciel. They had a substantial force – by the summer of 1944 the strength of the Home Army in total stood at 350,000 with 34,000 of them in Warsaw. The figures were misleading, however. At the end of July 1944 there were only small arms to equip some 6,000 men. Crew served weapons were in equally short supply: at the start of the Uprising, the Home Army in Warsaw probably had only sixteen mortars, thirty-nine heavy machine-guns, 130 light machine guns and thirty-six anti-tank rifles. With these meager stocks, the basic tactical unit in the Home Army was the platoon, with thirty to fifty men in each. There were six hundred platoons located throughout War-

The Cruel Hunters

saw on August 1. With this size of a formation it was possible to defend individual buildings and perhaps conduct a simple defense of an area, but attempts to conduct coordinated counter-attacks would prove difficult.[3]

Warsaw was composed of eight districts on the west bank of the Vistula: Old Town, Wola, Ochota, Zoliborz, Mokotów, Czerniaków, Okecie, and the Inner City. On the east bank was the district of Praga. The insurgents had units in all; the most important districts were considered to be Old Town and the Inner City as these two contained the five major bridges over the river. In the Old Town and Inner City areas there were two highway and two railroad bridges. These bridges could be used by advancing Soviet forces to enter the capital.[4]

The morning of the 1st, some twenty-five men of the Home Army secretly made their way to their designated posts. A further four thousand were sent just outside of Warsaw to block key avenues through which the Germans would be expected to reinforce the city. The Poles expected a short battle with the Germans and then the arrival of units of the Red Army. General Bór-Komorowski had requested aid from the western allies as well but learned that although some supply air drops would be made, there would be no large-scale support.[5]

The Uprising commenced at 5:00 PM on August 1: a late hour in the day, but a time which was designed to catch the Germans by surprise. By the end of the day the insurgents held the bulk of the Old Town and had defeated initial local German counterattacks. Within three hours the Polish flag was proudly flying from the highest building in the city.[6]

The Polish Uprising, as it came to be called, threatened to cut the lines of supply and communication to the German 9th Army fighting further to the east. Colonel General Heinz Guderian, the German Army Chief of Staff, requested to Hitler that the Army be allowed to put down the revolt and that the city correspondingly be declared part of the army operations zone. Hitler refused Guderian's request and gave the mission to *SS-Reichsführer* Heinrich Himmler as Commander in Chief of the Replacement Army. Himmler, in turn, placed a senior SS general in charge.[7]

Himmler later explained the situation and his decision to a group of army district commanders:[8]

> When I heard the news of the rising in Warsaw I went immediately to the Führer. I should like to tell you this is an example of how one should take news of this kind quite calmly. I said, '*Mein Führer*, the time is disagreeable. Seen historically [however] it is a blessing that the Poles are doing it. After five or six weeks we shall leave. But by then Warsaw, the capital, the head, the intelligence of this former 16-17 million Polish people will be extinguished, this *Volk* [people] that has blocked us in the east for 700 years and has stood in our way ever since the first battle of Tannenberg. Then the Polish problem will no longer be a large problem historically for our children who come after us, nor indeed for us.'

This philosophy was expressly manifested in the conduct of the *Sonderkommando*. During the defeat of the Uprising, the Dirlewanger Brigade burned prisoners alive with gasoline, impaled babies on bayonets and stuck them out of windows and hung women upside down from balconies – all according to Himmler to create sheer violence and terror which would extinguish the revolt in just a few days.[9]

SS-Obergruppenführer von dem Bach-Zelewski was selected to crush the uprising, in part, because of his special expertise in anti-partisan operations. Additionally, by making the suppression of the revolt an SS affair, it was intended to leave the army free to face the Russians. Finally, the SS also wanted a free hand to crush the Poles without interference by "squeamish" elements.[10]

Von dem Bach was initially located near Lötzen. On August 2 he reported to Zoppot to receive his orders to crush the rebellion. Later that day he flew back to Lötzen. On August 3 he flew to Breslau and on August 4, drove to Cracow. Von dem Bach stated after the war that he received the following guidelines from Hitler and Himmler:[11]

> 1. Captured insurgents ought to be killed regardless of whether they are fighting in accordance with the Hague Convention or not.

2. The part of the population not fighting, women and children, should likewise be killed.

3. The whole town must be leveled to the ground, i.e. houses, streets, offices – everything that is in the town.

Von dem Bach modified these orders and attempted to stop the mass murder of civilians – as he felt the harshness of Hitler's orders would only add to the resolve of the defenders. It appears, however, that these executions continued to occur until August 12.

The massacres were not confined to the German side. On August 1, a group of Azerbaijanis soldiers fighting for the Germans were surrounded at their barracks on Koszykowo Street. After several hours of fighting the German allied unit was offered its freedom if they laid down their arms. The Azerbaijanis agreed and surrendered – they promptly had their throats slit by the Polish insurgents.[12] An Azerbaijani unit was later placed under Dirlewanger's command.

On August 2, the German commander for Warsaw, Luftwaffe Brigadier General Rainer Stahel, broadcast the following order over loudspeakers:[13]

I order that as of this moment Warsaw is in a state of siege. Civilians who go out into the streets will be shot. Buildings and establishments from which Germans are shot at will be leveled to the ground.

The fighting immediately was fierce. By the end of the first full day of fighting, over two thousand Poles were killed. Stahel had some 13,000 troops in Warsaw proper including police troops, an army infantry regiment, some rear area SS forces, and some Luftwaffe troops at the two airports. On August 3, General Bór sent a message to London describing the scope of the Uprising and its progress:[14]

The people of the capital join the Army in the fight and even the unarmed youth, carried away with enthusiasm, build anti-tank barricades. Women vie with the

Warsaw

men to serve and fight, all of them in great obedience and with the spirit of sacrifice. Ammunition stocks diminish hourly and this accompanied by the shortage of arms is an increasing concern. As a result, volunteers reporting *en masse* cannot be sent into action.

The regiment was stationed at Lyck, East Prussia (50km southeast of Rastenburg) prior to the Uprising. The advance guard of the *Sonderkommando*, one battalion with three hundred sixty-five men arrived in Warsaw on August 4. Two more battalions, a submachine-gun company, a mortar company and an anti-tank company arrived shortly thereafter. In all, the regiment had sixteen officers and 865 men, plus the attached Azerbaijani troops. During the Uprising the *Sonderkommando* received two thousand five hundred replacements, of which about one thousand nine hundred came from the SS punishment camp at Matzkau near Danzig. By the end of the revolt, the strength of the regiment stood at only six hundred forty-eight men.[15] Dirlewanger was in Berlin on August 4 and apparently did not share his superiors sense of urgency. Ordered to Warsaw, he caused the airplane waiting to fly him to the battle zone to sit idly at the airfield. Himmler was incensed and sent the following letter:[16]

> *SS-Standartenführer* Dirlewanger
> via
> Chief, SS-Main Office, *SS-Obergruppenführer* Berger
> B e r l i n
>
> As much as I am satisfied with your endeavors, as I recently told you personally, I must express my displeasure about the fact that, despite having been warned to immediately proceed [directly]to your regiment on the airplane which was reserved for you, you spent several more hours in Berlin.
>
> I am used to prompt and immediate obedience.
> H. H i m m l e r

By August 4, although much of the city was in insurgent hands, none of the original objectives of the Uprising had been achieved by the Poles: the Germans still controlled the bridges over the Vistula and still retained the main arteries of communication, the airport and the railway stations.[17] The Home Army also failed to capture the Gestapo headquarters. Unit "Jalen" was completely destroyed in attacks on this position. Unit "Wysocki" was also hit badly as it did battle with Luftwaffe flak and mechanized units near the airport.[18]

Already though, the Germans began fierce reprisals. That day, a Catholic priest, lying in a hospital in the Wolski area witnessed this scene:[19]

> The Germans took the house opposite and executed all the inhabitants on the pavement in front of it, I suppose about sixty to a hundred people. I also saw how the Germans grabbed hold of one woman with a small child who in fear was visibly running away from the burning house, and throw them both back through the window into the flames.

But the Germans needed more troops and began reinforcing the area. By August 5, von dem Bach had the following units in Warsaw to combat the Poles:

Police Group Posen	45 officers	2695 men
SS-Sturm Brigade RONA		1700 men
SS-Sonderkommando Dirlewanger	16 officers	865 men
Army Security Regiment 608	20 officers	598 men
Aserbajani Detachment	5 officers	677 men

Arrived later during the Uprising:

One armored train	1 officer	48 men
Assault gun training detachment	3 officers	157 men
Panzer Detachment 302		
Assault Panzer Company 218	1 officer	77 men

Warsaw

Heavy Artillery Battery 638	3 officers	110 men
Heavy Rocket Launcher Battery 201	2 officers	62 men
Assault Mortar Company 1000	2 officers	54 men
Assault Engineer Battalion 500	1 officer	52 men
Flame-thrower Battalion Krone	10 officers	292 men

The German plan was to recapture the city district by district, killing or at the least driving out all Poles from every block and every house. In this manner, the insurgents would be compressed into an ever constricting perimeter, with mounting logistical concerns as non-combatant civilians fleeing the Germans, would migrate into these areas. Additionally under this plan, there would be no insurgents to the German rear once the Nazis took a district.

The *Sonderkommando* swung into full action on August 5, as Battle Group Reinefarth moved to clear the district of Wola in western Warsaw. The battle plan was to first have the Luftwaffe conduct a massive attack on the area using incendiary bombs. Then, Reinefarth would have Dirlewanger advance west to east through Wola south of the Ulica Wolska Street, the main road running through this district. Police Group Posen, meanwhile, would advance in the same direction north of Ulica Wolska

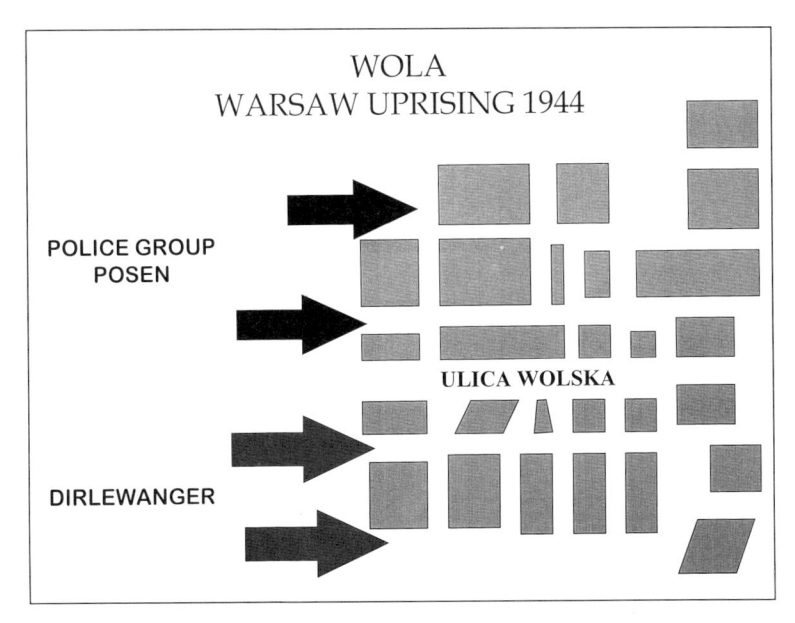

WOLA
WARSAW UPRISING 1944

POLICE GROUP POSEN

ULICA WOLSKA

DIRLEWANGER

Street. The fighting was especially gruesome. On that day German soldiers shot two thousand civilians near Wilski Hospital and burned the hospital down, killing patients inside who had been unable to flee. The Nazis also burned St. Lazarus Hospital and killed three hundred patients. By the end of August 5, Dirlewanger had gained almost one half mile and had reached the intersection of Ulica Wolska and Korotkowa streets, in an attempt to move east toward the Vistula. On August 6 they destroyed the Charles and Mary Hospital. One hospital was saved, the St. Stanislaw Hospital – which Dirlewanger commandeered as a headquarters.[20]

Wola was defended by an elite Home Army unit, the "Kedyw" battalion. This formation was some 1,650 men strong.[21]

On August 6 the *Sonderkommando* had advanced through Chlodna and Elektoralna streets and had broken through to Brigadier General Stahel and his beleaguered forces at the Brühl Palace.[22] Fighting in the area was fierce. Dirlewanger's men spread out along the square and with armor support, rooted out several insurgent positions. Then the *Sonderkommando* attempted to advance further using a shield of Polish women and children in front of them – but the Poles fired anyway and drove the Germans back.[23]

Dirlewanger's men quickly saw that fighting in a large city was quite different then the combat they had been used to in the swamps and forests of Russia. On August 6 the *Sonderkommando*, therefore, sent one officer and twenty-four soldiers to a training session with the 9th Army engineers on the operation and tactical use of flame-throwers. An SS soldier remembered the fighting:[24]

> At pivotal points and everywhere where it was extremely critical or threatened to be critical, sooner or later the unit "Dirlewanger" surfaced. Dirlewanger was a fellow with a pronounced, remarkable look of a hanging bird. During normal times, any loyal citizen, whether a private person or in the police, would have taken this monster into custody away from the street and would have brought him behind locks, with the accusation following! This crowd [the *Sonderkommando*] fought with incredible harshness and granted no pardon.

Across from our former recuperation squadron there was a sizable multi-storied building and in it there were rebels. They dominated the surroundings near and far. Among them were excellent sharp-shooters. It was not advisable to raise one's nose within three blocks of houses from there. One day we attacked and had to withdraw after having suffered a loss of 50% of our people. We employed the little explosive tank "Goliath" but had no success with it. Not more than the spacious entrance was scratched. It was a fight for a house in the big city of Warsaw... So we continued and it was easy to see even without the use of a calculator when the last of the man would be delivered to the mass grave on the athletic field behind the staff building at the Siegesallee [Victory Boulevard]. That's when the Dirlewanger crowd was thought of. "The crowd" arrived, took a look and stormed in. About 50 men rushed across the street. Approximately 30 men remained lying there and did not move anymore. The remainder vanished into the house and during the next ten minutes, both corpses and living people flew out of the windows of the fourth and fifth floor. The Dirlewanger people did not stop by giving long speeches. This is how the houses of Warsaw were cleaned up.

By August 7 Dirlewanger had occupied the Saxon Gardens and had linked up with German troops at the Kierbedzia Bridge.[25]

Several enlisted soldiers in the *Sonderkommando* displayed great bravery during the fighting. Dirlewanger requested and received permission to promote *SS-Hauptscharführer* Max Schreiner, Paul Zimmermann and Karl Staib to *SS-Untersturmführer*.

Max Schreiner was born June 21, 1899 in Esslingen. He arrived at the *Sonderkommando* on June 9, 1943 and served with the unit until his death on September 9, 1944. Schreiner was highly decorated and won the War Service Cross, the Infantry Assault Badge, the Bar to the Iron Cross 2nd Class, the Iron Cross 1st Class, the Eastern People's Bravery Medal

2nd Class in Silver with Swords, the Wound Badge in Silver and the Anti-Partisan Badge in Bronze. Dirlewanger submitted Schreiner for the German Cross in Gold. *SS-Obergruppenführer* von dem Bach warmly endorsed the recommendation which read:[26]

JUSTIFICATION

SS-Untersturmführer Schreiner has been a member of the *SS-Sonderregiment* Dirlewanger since June 9, 1943.

Schreiner has participated in all missions of the unit and, due to his military know-how, has always substantially contributed to the full success of the undertakings.

In missions against bandits in mid-Russia and "Weissruthenien", as well as in engagements at the front southwest of Newel, he has been an example of readiness to his because of his exemplary courage and enormous decisiveness. Always at the front line, he led his men to great success due to his circumspection and decisive force. Especially noteworthy are the following:

When crossing the Drissa on November 7, 1943, the bridge was under heavy anti-tank fire, which caused considerable losses to our own troops.

Making a quick decision, *SS-Untersturmführer* Schreiner went with a group of volunteers in a float across the Drissa, flanked the anti-tank position and destroyed the occupants in close combat. Two guns and one MG were captured.

On November 13, 1943, during the storm attack on Conibor southwest of Newel, the attack by strong enemy grenade fire was just about brought to a halt. Here it was again Schreiner, who worked himself and a group of courageous men towards the enemy positions by taking advantage of natural cover and were able to put the grenade throwing positions out of commission by throwing hand grenades towards it. Because of this courageous decision, the attack could continue and was a complete success with heavy losses too the enemy.

On November 14, 1943, he was again one of the first at the enemy when it meant that the positions of the enemy near Allessy were to be taken by storm. During this fight, *SS-Untersturmführer* Schreiner was wounded in the calf of his leg, but he remained at the main field hospital and was able to return to the troop as early as November 22, 1943. Immediately thereafter he took part in the fighting.

On February 22, 1944, he again showed great courage and was a dare-devil in the attack on strong groups of bandits which had attacked one of our motor convoys between Minsk and Usda. Despite heavy machine-gun and automatic weapons fire, he encouraged his men; he also led the attack so cleverly that the bandits were beaten into retreat and left 31 counted dead of theirs in the process.

During the general retreat movements at the front in mid-Russia, on July 3, 1944 on the route Rakow-Lida the motor convoy of the unit was again attacked by heavy bandit forces. Without hesitation and disregarding the heavy fire from the enemy, he had two machine-guns brought into position and responded to the fire. It was due to his decisiveness that the attack could be put down immediately before greater friendly losses would have resulted.

During the heavy street fighting in Warsaw during August of 1944, Schreiner proved himself as fighting group commander.

On August 8, 1944, he led a group on the right side along the market hall which made it possible to cut of the path of retreat for the enemy which resulted in their complete annihilation. This also caused the enemy to retreat because of the surprise advance at the Adolf Hitler Square which made the immediate occupancy off the Palais Brühl possible.

On August 12, 1944, *SS-Untersturmführer* Schreiner was at the front of his men when they stormed a building in the Dlugastrasse which was heavily occupied by bandits and heavily barricaded. Despite severe counter attack, in which Schreiner was shot in the chin, he succeeded in having the house set on fire and the bandits in it, who were defending themselves desperately, were completely annihilated. Despite being wounded, Schreiner stayed with his troops. Due to his courageous behavior our attack in the Dlugastrasse continued and, despite considerable losses, led to the planned destination.

Dirlewanger
SS-Oberführer

During the storming of a heavily occupied house block at the banks of the Weichsel, *SS-Untersturmführer* Schreiner, while storming at the head of his men, died the death of a hero on September 6, 1944.

Kampfgruppe Reinefarth   September 29, 1944

The candidate has proven extra-ordinary courage on many occasions. Therefore, I endorse the recommendation.

Reinefarth
SS-Gruppenführer

—

However, Himmler disapproved the award in November 1944.

Paul Zimmermann was one of the oldest soldiers in Dirlewanger's command. Born in Landsberg on August 22, 1888, he fought in World War I and won the Iron Cross 2nd Class in that conflict. In World War II he received the Bar to the Iron Cross 2nd Class, the Infantry Assault Badge, the Eastern People's Bravery Medal 2nd Class in Silver, the Close Combat Bar in Bronze and the Anti-Partisan Badge in Silver. Zimmermann was married with three children. There is no record of any disciplinary proceedings in his personnel file.[27]

Karl Staib came from Auerstein, where he was born on January 12, 1901. During the war his family lived in Heilbronn. Staib won the Iron Cross 2nd Class and the Eastern People's Bravery Medal 2nd Class in Silver with Swords during his service with the *Sonderkommando*. Like Zimmermann, he appears to have had no previous discipline problems.[28]

On August 8 the *Sonderkommando* commenced an attack on a Polish cemetery and continued to advance through the 10th. On August 11 the cemetery fell.[29] During the first week of the Uprising between 40,000 and 50,000 people were killed, most in the Ochota and Wola districts of the city where the *Sonderkommando* operated.[30]

Corpses often remained unburied for weeks and made parts of the city look like a morgue. The Germans pressed Polish prisoners into service to remove the bodies. These work details often used long poles with hooks for the job – frequently causing the carcasses to fall apart and frightening the swarms of rats who had been feeding on the decaying flesh.[31]

Dirlewanger believed he was responsible only to Himmler and therefore disliked many of his immediate superiors. He told von dem Bach that he would kill *SS-Standartenführer* Golz, Bach's chief of staff. At one point in the battle, part of the *Sonderkommando* threatened von dem Bach's headquarters with machine-guns.[32]

Another SS unit at Warsaw gained a notorious reputation and must be mentioned here as well. The Kaminsky Brigade, also known as *SS-Sturm Brigade RONA,* consisted of Ukrainian renegades who had also fought in numerous anti-partisan operations prior to coming to Warsaw. Led by Bratislav Kaminsky, they advanced south of Dirlewanger and also killed thousands of civilians. The unit was withdrawn from the fight after they became a drunken mob which could not be controlled; Kaminsky was secretly murdered by the SS outside of Warsaw – probably to pre-

The Cruel Hunters

vent him from coming back to haunt von dem Bach, should the German effort at Warsaw taken a turn for the worse.[33]

During this period Dirlewanger operated under the immediate command of *SS-Gruppenführer* Heinz Reinefarth. Dirlewanger hated Reinefarth intensely and challenged him to a duel. Both appeared to have gone out of their way to avoid meeting each other.[34]

In addition to the horrible civilian casualties, the Germans completely looted Warsaw as well. During the first ten days of the Uprising, German forces loaded seven thousand rail cars with booty and shipped them to the Wartheland area of the Reich.[35] In the middle of the fighting German troops used crowds of women and children as human shields while advancing on rebel strong points. Additionally, sick and wounded Polish citizens were taken out of hospitals and shot *en mass*. "Rape and the cutting of throats were commonplace."[36]

The Germans also used more sophisticated weapons and tactics in the fight for the city. On August 14 the Germans introduced thirty-five "Goliaths" in Panzer Detachment 302 and a 38cm storm mortar in Assault Mortar Company 1000. On August 18 they brought in the 60cm mortar "Karl" in Heavy Artillery Battery 638.[37]

The 60 cm mortar "Karl" was the biggest German artillery piece to ever be mounted on a self-propelled carriage. Capable of firing a huge explosive projectile with a high trajectory to penetrate underground fortifications, it was initially designed for use against the French Maginot Line. Six weapons were built and used at Brest-Litovsk and Sevastopol earlier in the war. They were initially constructed with 60 cm barrels but several were refitted with 54 cm pieces to increase the weapon's range. The weapon at 132 tons was actually too heavy to travel far on its self-propelled carriage and would be transported by train, suspended between two special railway cars on a special steel truss. The "Karl" was then detrained at set up in a local firing position. An accompanying special ammunition loader, based on a Mark IV tank chassis and equipped with a 2.5 ton crane, would load the ammunition into the "Karl's" huge loading tray prior to firing.[38]

The "Karl" piece at Warsaw, nicknamed the "Ziu", at a range of 6.8 kilometers (about 4 miles) and could fire between six and twelve rounds per hour. The huge projectiles could penetrate 2.5 meters of concrete before exploding. In a city fight like Warsaw, this meant the round would travel completely through the roof and all floors of a building and lodge deeply in the foundation before exploding. The subsequent detonation would destroy not only that structure but also many surrounding buildings.[39]

The second technological marvel was the radio-controlled demolition vehicle "Goliath." This small tracked robot, which weighed about eight hundred pounds, carried an explosive charge of between one hundred sixty and two hundred twenty pounds. The theory behind the weapon was that it would be guided by a remote human operator to an obstacle or structure that needed to be destroyed – but that was too heavily defended for an open assault by troops. Some models were controlled by signals sent through a wire connected to the vehicle, while others were radio controlled. Once in position, the operator detonated the explosive charge which destroyed the "Goliath" and the target as well.[40] There were two ways to attempt to attack a "Goliath." First, the defenders could attack the small vehicle with machine-guns or *molotov* cocktails, hoping to explode the demolition charge on the robot. This was difficult to do as the "Goliath" was a fairly small target. Second, the defenders could attempt to locate the remote human operator and kill him. The operator was forced to be in a position where he could see both the moving vehicle and the intended target. Sometimes it was possible for the Poles to predict this location and dispatch the German controller.

About this time the Germans turned their attention to the Old Town. For this district the Germans attacked from four sides. Dirlewanger would attack from the east and south, Battle Group Schmidt from the north and Battle Group Reck from the west.

The Germans began the attack on August 12. On the 13th, they booby trapped a tank and left it where the Poles would gather to look at the equipment. It exploded and killed over four hundred people. The Allies tried to airdrop supplies into the city, but most did not fall into insurgent hands. The cellars and basements were soon overcrowded as civilians feared that they would suffer the same fate as the thousands who had been killed in Wola in the mass executions.

The Luftwaffe played a role as well, with attacks by Stukas bombing and strafing. By August 31, the insurgents prepared to evacuate this dis-

The Cruel Hunters

trict of the city as the Germans continued to close in. Dirlewanger's troops continued to loot and plunder in the district as well as advance toward the Old Town Market. Dirlewanger suffered the highest losses of the three groups but also made the most progress. The Germans sent roughly 50,000 Poles, who had crossed the lines from Old Town, to a transit labor camp. Sadly enough, probably 40,000 Poles – including many women and children – were killed in this district alone.[41]

The attack into Old Town featured not only an extensive aerial bombardment, but also an overwhelming artillery barrage. One source has estimated that during the two-week fight for this part of the city, some 3,500 to 4,000 tons of shells fell on an area only three quarters of a square mile.[42]

As resistance in Old Town collapsed, the insurgents prepared to escape. Colonel Chrusciel sent them the following order:[43]

> Armed units will retreat via the sewers to the Midtown sector. I am concerned that as many people as possible cross with arms and ammunition. They will be needed for further fighting.

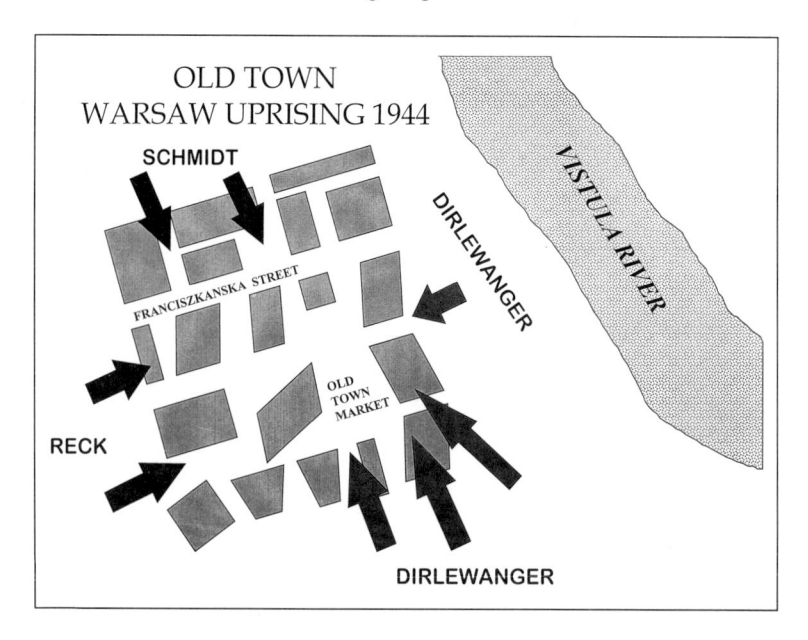

OLD TOWN WARSAW UPRISING 1944

Warsaw

The rebels complied and tried to use the extensive sewer system to escape. Often the Germans detected these movements and then poured gasoline into the sewers and ignited it with hand grenades. Another technique for the Germans was to increase the water flow through the sewers and drown those seeking to flee.[44]

A more sophisticated method for clearing sewers was the use of the *Taifun* (Typhoon) system. In this method, specialized German engineers would blow an explosive gas into a segment of the sewer thought to contain insurgents. Shortly thereafter the gas was ignited which produced a chain reaction explosion similar to that in coal mining disasters. The overpressure of the explosion caused rats, cats and humans to be plastered to the walls of the sewer shafts.[45]

On September 3 the Soviet 47th Army attacked German forces in Praga in an attempt to gain at least the east bank of the Vistula. The German 73rd Infantry Division was forced to retreat, and German army units then destroyed the bridges over the Vistula. But the insurgents remained in the western districts of the city, and posed a threat of creating a bridgehead should Soviet units cross the river.[46]

Dirlewanger then turned south to clear the remaining west bank of the Vistula of insurgent forces concentrated at the Warsaw district of the Inner City. The German attacks began in this area on September 11, but five days later two Polish regiments with the Soviet Army on the east bank of the Vistula attempted to cross the river, link up with the insurgents and gain bridgeheads in the area. Dirlewanger was forced to fight in two directions and inflicted some 2,000 casualties on the Poles, forcing the survivors back by September 23.[47]

For his part in quelling the uprising, Dirlewanger was promoted to *SS-Oberführer* on August 12 and was recommended for the Knight's Cross of the Iron Cross. The following is the award recommendation:[48]

> On April 25, 1944, heavy bandit forces crowded together between the Berezina and the Tschernitza and dug themselves in. Enormous enemy fire from heavy and infantry weapons did not allow our advancing. *SS-Oberführer* Dirlewanger made the decision to attack the enemy in the flank and from behind by taking ad-

vantage of nature cover. Fighting himself in the front line, he succeeded to surprise the enemy due to his decisiveness and personal involvement, to cut off their retreat and to cause heavy losses for them.

During the general retreat at the front in mid-Russia, on July 7, 1944, acting on his own decision, *SS-Oberführer* Dirlewanger with parts of his regiment occupied a bolt position southeast of Lida. This resulted in the fact that the enemy who was in hot pursuit was held up for some time and that his own supplies as well as the supplies of other units could be channeled through the highway Lida-Grodno without extensive losses. Fighting at the front line, he was an example of dedication and decisiveness and motivated his men to defend themselves in a tough and unrelenting way against an enemy with far superior numbers. However, in order to avoid heavier own losses, strong enemy pressure and heavy artillery shooting forced a retreat. The mission to retrieve parts of the regiment who had been left be-

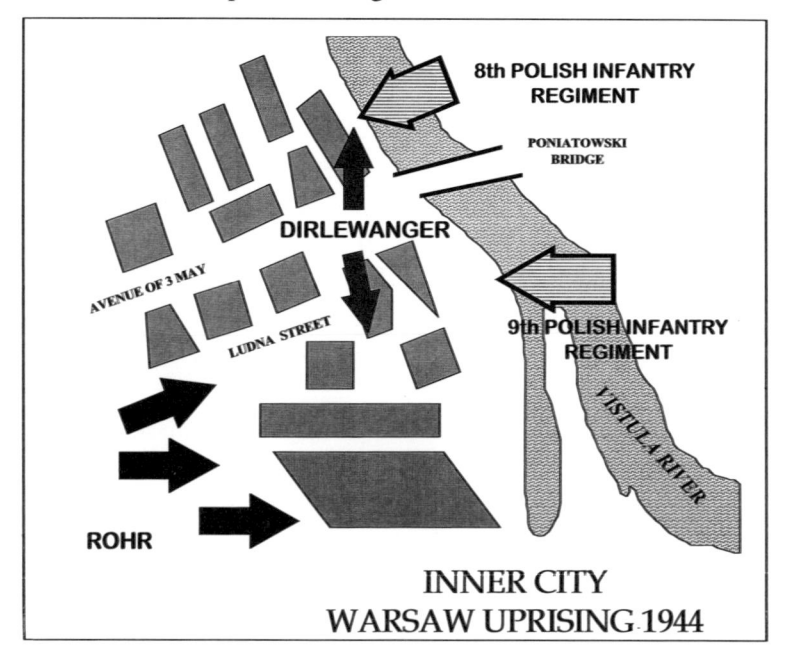

INNER CITY WARSAW UPRISING 1944

hind was accomplished through his heroic action, because otherwise they would not have escaped the surrounding enemy and certain capture.

In order to thwart the rebellion of Polish and Bolshevik bandits in Warsaw, the *SS-Sonderregiment* Dirlewanger was put into action on August 5, 1944 at the western border of the city. Shortly after leaving their post, heavy street fighting developed. Well camouflaged and heavily barricaded bandit posts had to be fought down. It was only through the tactical capabilities, the bravery and dare-devil spirit of *SS-Oberführer* Dirlewanger that the attack went smoothly and that the order of the day was executed. Also here, *SS-Oberführer* Dirlewanger demonstrated decisiveness of the highest order and he fought in front of his men with a weapon in his hand so that the nests of the enemy were destroyed. Also in this case, he was an example of courage, bravery and duty for his men. At first, barricades and mine fields at Litzmannstadtstrasse [Ulica Wolska Street] did not allow further advancing. After Stukas, tanks and other heavy weapons were put into play, *SS-Oberführer* Dirlewanger started the attack. He caused heavy losses for the enemy with hand grenades and forced them to give up their positions. During further heavy street fighting, the attack was conducted purposefully due to the bravery of *SS-Oberführer* Dirlewanger and as soon as August 8, 1944, the Adolf Hitler Platz could be taken and the unhindered connection to the front over the Vistula was restored. During the defeat of enemy forces in the basin at the Old Town Market on September 2, 1944, *SS-Oberführer* Dirlewanger demonstrated great military know-how, bravery and a dare-devil attitude. Again and again, he was fighting at the front line with his men, destroyed enemy nests and sharp shooters. The complete cleansing of this area was already accomplished around noon of September 3,

1944. On September 4, 1944, the advance at the eastern rim of the south basin and the cleansing of the Vistula banks was started. Heavy enemy fire did not hold *SS-Oberführer* Dirlewanger back. Again fighting at the front line, inspiring his men through dare-devil acts and bravery towards a fast advance, even though there were some losses among themselves, the banks of the Vistula was completely clean.

SS-Oberführer Dr. Dirlewanger who was already 50% disabled in the World War demonstrated through repeated acts that he belongs to the bravest of the brave. I recommend that he be awarded the Knight's Cross of the Iron Cross.

—

Headquarters, October 10, 1944

I warmly endorse the recommendation.

The successes achieved are primarily the personal reward of *SS-Oberführer* Dirlewanger who has always been a shining example for his men due to his personal courage and dare-devil attitude. *SS-Oberführer* Dirlewanger was wounded a total of 11 times so far.

von dem Bach
SS-Obergruppenführer
und General der Polizei

SS-Obersturmführer Adelbert Trattenschegg was severely wounded during the fighting and taken to an aid station where he died on September 21, 1944. He had been convicted in April of misappropriating company monies, stealing foodstuffs, plundering, misusing official paperwork and having sex with a fifteen year old girl. For this he received one year in prison which was changed to service in the *Sonderkommando*.

Trattenschegg was from Bruko, a Croatian of German descent, born May 29, 1905 with three children. He had served in the Yugoslavian Army prior to German occupation, and received the Croatian Bravery Medal. In the *Sonderkommando* he served as a supply officer. In 1945 he received an official posthumous pardon.[49]

On September 15, 1944 *SS-Hauptsturmführer* Ewald Ehlers took command of one of the regiments in the *Sonderkommando*. Ehlers was born in the town of Lelm near Helmstedt on January 3, 1910. From 1928 to 1934 he served in the army and subsequently served four more years in the Luftwaffe. He entered the SS on October 1, 1938 with SS number 309,725. His first assignment as an *SS-Untersturmführer* was with the Death's Head unit *"Thüringen"* and then transferred in 1939 to Oranienburg. It is possible that he met Dirlewanger there in 1940. On September 1, 1941 Ehlers was promoted to *SS-Hauptsturmführer*. Later assignments took Ehlers to SS Infantry Regiment 9, SS Police Panzer Grenadier Regiment 1, SS Division *"Totenkopf"* and SS Division *"Polizei."* During his service in Russia, he won the War Service Cross 2nd Class with Swords, the Infantry Assault Badge in Bronze and the Eastern Front Medal. In 1942 he was charged with "cowardice in the face of the enemy" but was not convicted of this accusation. While serving in the *Sonderkommando* he was promoted to *SS-Sturmbannführer*. The following report on Ehlers provides a look into his character:[50]

> *SS-Hauptsturmführer* Ehlers is a short, strapping appearance with an open character. He values a civilized look. Ehlers has good theoretical knowledge which he understands to put into practice. In the training of recruits under his command he achieved good results and he has taken care of his men with diligence and circumspection. Simulations and teaching fall on fertile ground in his case. His is temperamental and driven in the good sense, and due to his fresh unencumbered willingness to get involved, he is well liked by the men below him and the troops. Ehlers fulfills his task well.

SS-Hauptsturmführer Hans Bünger reported to the *Sonderkommando* on September 25. Born in Haan on July 28, 1908, he entered the Nazi Party on March 1, 1933 and received a party number of 1,550,461. He entered the SS the same year and received SS number 144,264. Bünger served in the Economics and Administration Head Office of the SS before transferring to Dachau for a short time and then moving to the *Sonderkommando*. Bünger listed his religion as Catholic, was married with two children and had a spotless record.[51]

By September 26 it was obvious to all that the Uprising had failed. On that day General Bór Komorowski sent representatives to the Germans to negotiate a truce. On October 2 the Polish representatives signed the capitulation.[52] It is hard to assess overall casualties for the Uprising. Probably 9,700 men of the Polish Home Army were killed in action with a further 6,000 missing and presumed dead. Over 150,000 civilians were killed as well. German losses too were high. Von dem Bach estimated that 10,000 German troops were killed and 7,000 missing – the missing, in all likelihood, killed as the Poles took understandable vengeance against prisoners especially those in SS uniforms. The *Sonderkommando* was hard hit losing some 2,700 men.[53]

Like the Mongols, who invaded Poland centuries before, the *Sonderkommando* inspired fear and terror in the Polish population in Warsaw. And again, as during the Mongol onslaught, Catholic Poland prayed for deliverance – the following is one of their prayers authored during the Uprising:[54]

> *From bombers and fighter planes – save us, O Lord,*
> *From tanks and 'Goliaths' – save us, O Lord,*
> *From bullets and grenades – save us, O Lord,*
> *From minethrowers – save us, O Lord,*
> *From fires and being burnt alive – save us, O Lord,*
> *From being shot – save us, O Lord,*
> *From being buried alive – save us, O Lord.*

For upwards of a quarter million people, the prayer was not answered.

ENDNOTES

[1] Seaton, Albert. *The Russo-German War 1941-45*. (Novato, CA: Presidio Press, 1990), p.456.

[2] Höhne. *The Order of the Death's Head,*, p.544.

[3] Prados, John. "Warsaw Rising: Revolt of the Polish Underground, 1944." *Strategy & Tactics*. (Lake Geneva, WI: Dragon Publishing), Number 107, May-June 1986, pp. 19-20.

[4] Krannhals, Hanns von. *Der Warschauer Aufstand 1944*. (Frankfurt am Main: Bernhard & Grafe Verlag, 1964), p.107.

[5] Prados. "Warsaw Rising.", pp. 20-21.

[6] Hanson, Joanna K. M. *The Civilian Population and the Warsaw Uprising of 1944*. (Cambridge, England: Cambridge University Press, 1982), pp. 74-75.

[7] Höhne. *The Order of the Death's Head,*, p.544.

[8] Padfield, Peter. *Himmler: Reichsführer-SS*. (New York: Henry Holt and Company, 1990), p.524.

[9] Clark, Alan. *Barbarossa: The Russian-German Conflict, 1941-45*. (New York: William Morrow and Company, 1965), p.391.

[10] Ibid., p.391.

[11] Hanson. *The Civilian Population and the Warsaw Uprising of 1944.*, pp. 85-86.

[12] Ready, J. Lee. *The Forgotten Axis: Germany's Partners and Foreign Volunteers in World War II*. (Jefferson, North Carolina, 1987), p.350.

[13] Hanson. *The Civilian Population and the Warsaw Uprising of 1944.*, p.84.

[14] Ibid., pp. 76-78.

[15] Krannhals. *Der Warschauer Aufstand 1944.*, p.126.

[16] Personalakt Oskar Dirlewanger.

[17] Hanson. *The Civilian Population and the Warsaw Uprising of 1944.*, p.79.

[18] Prados. "Warsaw Rising.", pp. 21-22.

[19] Hanson. *The Civilian Population and the Warsaw Uprising of 1944.*, p.87.

[20] Ibid., p. 88.

[21] Lukas. *The Forgotten Holocaust.*, p.196.

[22] Ibid., p.197.

[23] Ready. *The Forgotten Axis.*, p.353.

[24] Michaelis. *Die Grenadier Divisionen der Waffen SS*, pp.172-173.

[25] Orpen, Neil. *Airlift to Warsaw: The Rising of 1944*. (Norman, OK: University of Oklahoma Press, 1984), p.64.

[26] Personalakt Max Schreiner, Washington, D.C: National Archives Microfilm Publication A3343, Records of SS Officers from the Berlin Document Center, Roll SSO-101B.

[27] Personalakt Paul Zimmermann, Washington, D.C: National Archives Microfilm Publication A3343, Records of SS Officers from the Berlin Document Center, Roll SSO-023C.

[28] Personalakt Karl Staib, Washington, D.C: National Archives Microfilm Publication A3343, Records of SS Officers from the Berlin Document Center, Roll SSO-149B.

[29] Ready. *The Forgotten Axis.*, p.354.

[30] Hanson. *The Civilian Population and the Warsaw Uprising of 1944.*, p.85.

[31] Lukas. *The Forgotten Holocaust.*, p.209.

[32] Zawodny, J.K. *Nothing But Honor: The Story of the Warsaw Uprising, 1944*. (Stanford, CA: Hoover Institution Press, 1978), p.56.

[33] Windrow, Martin. *The Waffen-SS*, Osprey Men at Arms Series 34, (London: Osprey Publishing Ltd, 1982), p.24.

[34] Krannhals. *Der Warschauer Aufstand 1944.*, p.250.

[35] Lukas. *The Forgotten Holocaust.*, p.204.

[36] Seaton. *The Russo-German War 1941-45.*, p.456.

[37] Krannhals. *Der Warschauer Aufstand 1944.*, p.141.

[38] Crow, Duncan. *Armored Fighting Vehicles of Germany*. (New York: Arco Publishing Company, 1973), p.231.

[39] Engelmann, Joachim und Horst Scheibert. *Deutsche Artillerie 1934-1945: Eine Dokumentation in Text, Skizzen und Bildern*. (Limburg/Lahn, FRG: C.A. Starke Verlag, 1974), p.142.

[40] Spielberger, Walter J. and Uwe Feist. *Sonderpanzer: German Special Purpose Vehicles, Armor Series Volume 9.* (Fallbrook, CA: Aero Publishers, 1968).
[41] Hanson. *The Civilian Population and the Warsaw Uprising of 1944.*, pp. 107-117, and von Krannhals. *Der Warschauer Aufstand 1944.*, pp. 145-150.
[42] Lukas. *The Forgotten Holocaust.*, p.210.
[43] Bielecki, Tadeusz and Szymanski, Leszek. *Warsaw Aflame: The 1939-1945 Years.* (Los Angeles, CA: Polamerica Press, 1973), p.149.
[44] Ibid.
[45] Deschner, Gunther. *Warsaw Rising. Ballantine's Illustrated History of the Violent Century — Politics in Action Number 5.* (New York: Ballantine Books, 1972), p.117.
[46] Ziemke. *Stalingrad to Berlin.*, p.344.
[47] Krannhals. *Der Warschauer Aufstand 1944.*, pp. 151-157.
[48] Personalakt Oskar Dirlewanger.
[49] Personalakt Adalbert Trattenschegg, Washington, D.C: National Archives Microfilm Publication A3343, Records of SS Officers from the Berlin Document Center, Roll SSO-019C.
[50] Personalakt Ewald Ehlers, Washington, D.C: National Archives Microfilm Publication A3343, Records of SS Officers from the Berlin Document Center, Roll SSO-175.
[51] Personalakt Hans Bünger, Washington, D.C: National Archives Microfilm Publication A3343, Records of SS Officers from the Berlin Document Center, Roll SSO-118.
[52] Ziemke. *Stalingrad to Berlin.*, p.345.
[53] Krannhals. *Der Warschauer Aufstand 1944.*, pp. 214-215.
[54] Hanson. *The Civilian Population and the Warsaw Uprising of 1944.*, p.250.

6

THE MONSTER DIES

Our SS formations have put up a wretched show.
- Josef Goebbels, March 1945[1]

Shortly after the start of the Warsaw Uprising, Slovak politicians and several units of the Slovak Army revolted against the Germans as well, and threatened to block German units withdrawing from Galicia. The revolt apparently started on August 27, when insurgents stopped a train at St. Martin and killed twenty-two Germans returning from the Wehrmacht military mission to Romania. President Josef Tiso requested help from his capital at Bratislava.[2]

On September 1, Gottlob Berger, the Head of the *SS-Hauptamt* was named Wehrmacht commander in chief for Slovakia.[3] Berger deployed several army and Waffen-SS units to halt the revolt. On the northwest perimeter of rebel held territory was the army's Panzer Division "*Tatra*." This division consisted of about 6,000 troops and was reinforced by the 178th Infantry Division. Due north of the rebellion was SS Battle Group "Schaefer." It was made up of 1,200 troops of the 18th SS Division "*Horst Wessel*", and a further 1,200 soldiers from the 86th Infantry Division. To the southwest was SS Regiment "Schill" composed mostly of troops from the SS Training School Bohemia/Moravia. Due south was SS Battle Group "Wildner." This unit was a hodgepodge of SS units and totaled about 1,500 men.[4]

The Germans slowly started to constrict the perimeter but their offensive stalled by September 7. Berger was subsequently replaced by *SS-*

Obergruppenführer Hermann Hoefle, who then became the HSSPF for Slovakia. The Germans continued making limited advances and used the first weeks of October to reinforce the area. On October 15, the 14th SS Division *"Galizien"* arrived and was sent to relieve the Panzer Division *"Tatra"* northwest of the rebels. *SS-Sturmbrigade* Dirlewanger arrived the following day and was reported to have approximately 4,000 men organized into two regiments and some artillery. The arrival was not without misfortunes. On October 16, three La-5FN Soviet-made fighter aircraft, belonging to the Slovak Air Force, strafed and bombed elements of the *SS-Sturmbrigade* at the railroad station at Diviaky.[5] Dirlewanger relieved SS Battle Group "Schaefer." Additionally, the 271st *Volksgrenadier* Division and the 708th *Volksgrenadier* Division deployed to the area. Both divisions were understrength at 7,200 and 6,000 men respectively. From the south, the rest of the 18th SS Division *"Horst Wessel"*, approximately 8,000 men, was deployed from Hungary.[6] On October 18 the Germans again mounted a major offensive. *SS-Sturmbrigade* Dirlewanger attempted to take Ostro Mountain, a well-entrenched position along the northwest sector of the rebellion. After hard fighting, Dirlewanger was thrown back. Two days later Dirlewanger attacked again but could make no progress. Finally, on October 25 the brigade seized the towns of Necpaly and Biely Potok – between Trencín and Zvolen, after fierce fighting and

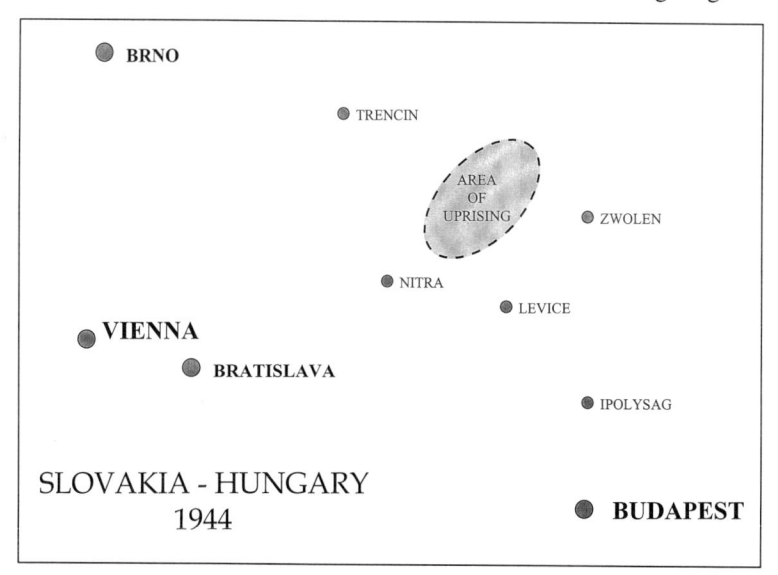

SLOVAKIA - HUNGARY 1944

The Monster Dies

advanced some six kilometers. Between October 27 and 30 Dirlewanger eliminated small pockets of rebels as the insurgent defense became disorganized. During the insurrection Dirlewanger was subordinated for a time to the 14th SS Division "*Galizien*", but did not conduct any actions with this unit – as always, Dirlewanger remained fiercely independent.[7]

By now Dirlewanger was more well-known throughout Germany, stemming from his award of the Knight's Cross. The former convict was even congratulated by the Lord Mayor of Würzburg, Dirlewanger's hometown:[8]

> The Lord Mayor of the City of Würzburg October 17, 1944
>
> I request that the enclosed letter addressed to *SS-Oberführer* Dr. Oskar Dirlewanger, Commander of a Brigade of the Waffen-SS, to send him congratulations from his home town of Würzburg on the occasion of his being awarded the Knight's Cross, be forwarded to him since I do not have his address.

Dirlewanger also was given an audience with Hans Frank, the Governor General of occupied Poland on October 16, 1944. Frank must have forgotten that he had approved kicking Dirlewanger out of Poland in early 1942 as evidenced by Frank's diary entry describing the visit:[9]

> The Governor General received *SS-Oberführer* Dirlewanger and *SS-Untersturmführer* Amann in the presence of *SS-Sturmbannführer* Pfaffenroth. *SS-Oberführer* Dirlewanger reports to the Governor General on the employment of his combat group in Warsaw. The Governor General thanks *SS-Oberführer* Dirlewanger and expresses to him his appreciation for the excellent employment of his combat group in the fighting in Warsaw.... Lunch on the occasion of the presence of *SS-Oberführer* Dirlewanger.

Congratulations though, did not alone bring new recruits to the *Sonderkommando* which was still seriously understrength from the fighting in Warsaw. On October 7, 1944 Dirlewanger sent the following letter to Himmler:[10]

> *Reichsführer!*
>
> During my presence at musterings in concentration camps I was advised both by *SS-Gruppenführer* Glücks as well as *SS-Standartenführer* Pister [a concentration camp commander] to make an experiment to form a unit consisting of former enemies of the National Socialist movement.
>
> There are men in the camps who in February 1933 and perhaps even after March 5, 1933 did not camouflage themselves externally as National Socialists. For the time being they remained loyal to their point of view, thereby demonstrating their character, in contrast with many hundreds of thousands who swung to the stronger, and in spite of their opposition raised their right hand to our greeting immediately after March 5, 1933.
>
> I approve the proposition of *SS-Sturmbannführer* Zill [another concentration camp commander] and obediently request that you order the following:
>
> 1. The commanders of the concentration camps personally select per camp up to 250 former political opponents to the movement who have, according to the personal firm conviction of the camp commander, changed their point of view and desire to prove that fact by participation in the struggle for the German Reich. Their age can be up to 45, in exceptional cases up to 50.
>
> 2. 3. 4. 5. 6. [paragraphs concerning administrative details]
>
> Dirlewanger
> *SS-Oberführer*

The Monster Dies

• • •

In Dirlewanger's twisted logic, he wanted political prisoners who had remained faithful for many years, not to Germany, but to their own beliefs such as communism! Himmler approved the concept on October 15. On November 3, 1944 the *WVHA*, Section D IV gave all concentration camps a quota for suitable prisoners to send to the regiment. The quotas, which totaled 1,910 men, were as follows:[11]

Auschwitz	400 men
Buchenwald	150 men
Dachau	300 men
Flossenbürg	45 men
Gross-Rosen	30 men
Mauthausen	10 men
Neuengamme	130 men
Ravensbrück	80 men
Sachsenhausen	750 men
Stutthof	15 men

Since the end of 1943, Neuengamme concentration camp, near Hamburg, had been sending criminal inmates to the *Sonderkommando*. In early November, in response to this new quota, camp officials assembled seventy-three political prisoners for transport to Dirlewanger. First, however, the inmates were "treated" to a demonstration. On November 5 at roll call all foreign inmates were released to return to their barracks. All German prisoners, including the seventy-three, remained in formation. SS guards then led Franz Hobelsberger, a former inmate from Sachsenhausen who had been in the *Sonderkommando* until he deserted, from his cell to a gallows in the center of the roll call square. There, as a warning to those prisoners about to depart for service with Dirlewanger, the camp commandant Max Pauly, publicly hanged Hobelsberger.[12]

The strict discipline did not always deter new arrivals from violating Dirlewanger's strict regimen. A survivor reported on justice in the *Sonderkommando* about this time:[13]

From former members of the above-named battalion [II/SS-Rgt 2] we found out that on a Sunday evening, somewhere during the time between October and early December 1944, approximately twenty members of that unit were executed by legal order of the brigade commander Dirlewanger because they left the unit without permission. Among the men who were shot were Ukranians and foreign German nationals (most probably former members of the Ukranian 14th Waffen-Grenadier-Division of the SS), and also political persecutees from German concentration camps, who were transferred to the Brigade Dirlewanger. For the execution, the whole battalion had to stand there forming an open square, the approximately twenty men were kneeling in the middle, stripped down to a shirt, and who were then shot in the neck by the chauffeur of the battalion commander. Light was provided by the headlights of cars.

Some officers arrived as well. *SS-Hauptsturmführer* Johannes Karnop, *SS-Untersturmführer* Georg Wild and *SS-Obersturmbannführer* Erich Brandt reported for duty in November. Karnop was a former police officer. Born in Altendorf on October 1, 1897, he had a Nazi Party number of 5,211,483 and an SS number of 314,222. He had a terrible record of infractions; four times sentenced (twice because of women trouble, of which once due to suspicion of abetting an abortion, once because of heavy drinking) with one child born in 1941 out of wedlock. In 1943 an SS court convicted Karnop of having an affair with the wife of an SS man who was away at the front in Riga, and sentenced him to six months imprisonment. The following is a summary of the proceedings:[14]

Legal Proceedings Against Johannes Karnop
March 27, 1944

1. Karnop is being sentenced by the court to six months of imprisonment because of insubordination.

The Monster Dies

2. For this punishment, Karnop has to spent four weeks in strict house arrest. The remainder of the sentence is waived to afford Karnop the opportunity to prove himself as a company leader in the Sonderkommando Dirlewanger.

Important factors for this sentencing by the SS-Reichsführer:

1. the serious breach of confidence of Karnop towards a subordinate, when his wife came to him for advice and assistance.

2. prior disciplinary sentencing of Karnop.

Appropriate action is to be taken.

Dr. Wehser
SS-Sturmbannführer

SS-Obersturmführer Erich Brandt came from Grevesmühlen, where he was born on November 14, 1912. With a Nazi Party number of 5,179,553 and an SS number of 168,720, he entered the SS in 1935 and spent the early war years in various headquarters units in Germany. Brandt had no record of disciplinary proceedings against him.[15]

SS-Untersturmführer Georg Wild served in several regular Waffen-SS units during the war including the divisions "*Das Reich*", "*Polizei*" and "*Hitlerjugend.*" Born in Baden by Vienna April 7, 1915, he entered the SS in 1941 and held an SS number of 423,850. Wild was demoted to the rank of *SS-Mann* shortly after arriving at the *Sonderkommando*. He was shot and killed on December 17, 1944 near Polost, Hungary as he attempted to desert to the Red Army.[16]

On November 23, *SS-Sturmbrigade* Dirlewanger moved to the southwest of Trencín to combat other Slovakian partisan groups. On December 3, the *SS-Sturmbrigade* Dirlewanger, along with elements of the 167th and 182nd Divisions from the army, killed one hundred thirty-six Slovakian partisans near Trencín.[17]

Despite successes in the fight with the partisans, the *Sonderkommando* experienced problems with the local civilians. The following is part of an SD report on the unit's conduct during the Uprising:[18]

The Cruel Hunters

> That bad behavior of the Dirlewanger members as for instance in Jastrabie has led to numerous complaints. Many SS-members were supposed to have behaved "worse than partisans," were said to have entered stores by force, served themselves without paying for the goods, were said to have demanded food and drink from the population, while abducting the men and intending to sleep with their wives, and they were said to have taken the shoes off an innocent farmer robbing him of everything he had with him.. This troop which proved itself most capable and necessary at the front must be withdrawn as soon as possible if the last connecting thread with the local population is not to be torn apart.

On December 1, 1944 *SS-Obersturmbannführer* Erich Buchmann took command of one of the regiments in the brigade. Buchmann was born in Berlin-Charlottenburg May 23, 1896. He joined the Nazi Party October 1, 1930 with party number 334,035 and joined the SS fifteen days later with SS number 5,118. He had a distinguished military record in World War I winning the Iron Cross 2nd Class in 1916 and the 1st Class in 1917. He also received the Golden Military Service Cross in 1918 for service in the 20th Infantry Regiment. The justification for this award follows:[19]

> Sergeant Buchmann who belonged to the regiment since the beginning of the war has participated in all large battles and in November of 1917 he was already awarded the Iron Cross 1st Class. He especially excelled again in the great battle in France when near Golancourt he personally took over the servicing of a heavy machine-gun with his company already severely damaged and in this way he beat back three enemy counterattacks and a cavalry attack while causing heavy damages to the enemy. After that he gathered together the infantry men around him whose leader was killed in action, went in front of them and lead them to attack

The Monster Dies

the village of Collezy which he conquered. Also during the most recent battles Buchmann often went into battle independently and decided them in our favor; especially in the attack on the village of Muscourt and the Beauregard-Ferme. Under cover of a light machine-gun, Buchmann advanced in this battle and attacked the stubbornly defending enemy from the back with such enormous firing that they left their position and a large portion of them threw away their weapons and let themselves be captured. It is Sergeant Buchmann's merit that this important elevation was captured whereby through his circumspect action he spared the battalion from heavy losses.

After the war Buchmann, like Dirlewanger and many other officers of the unit, served in the *Freikorps* and then returned to his trade as a baker in northern Berlin. During the 1930s he rose steadily in the SS to *SS-Standartenführer* in 1937. He then got into disciplinary problems including misuse of official vehicles and was reduced to *SS-Sturmbannführer* and posted to several backwater SS positions in the early days of the war. In 1943 he received the War Service Cross 1st Class with Swords and was transferred to the staff of the HSSPF *Alpenvorland*. He apparently had heart problems but received good ratings from both *SS-Gruppenführer* Jürs and *SS-Obergruppenführer* Berger. Berger's report is shown below:[20]

> For some time Buchmann has been engaged as leader of an auxiliary position and has always garnered great successes in the auxiliary field through his diligence and experience. Physically severely handicapped by a heart defect, Buchmann volunteered for duty at the front and is taking over a regiment of the *SS-Sturmbrigade* Dirlewanger.

Buchmann continued to serve with the unit until the last days of the war. He would survive the *Sonderkommando* and World War II.

Other soldiers came to the unit during this time due to disciplinary problems. A former officer describes his fall from rank:[21]

> In June of 1942 I was transferred to the administration of Concentration Camp Majdanek. In May of 1943 I got to a *Junkerschule* [Officer Training School] in Germany. After returning to Majdanek in January of 1944, I was occupied again in the administration of the camp until February of 1944. On expressed desire, I was transferred to the Buchenwald Concentration Camp as company leader; because as a soldier and officer I did not want to become a murderer of innocent women and children. In Weimar, I gave among other things cigarettes to prisoners who were working there, and this was reported to the commander. After a heated discussion, I got drunk and did not report to duty the next day. I was taken into custody after that and a trial against me was initiated. I was sentenced to two years imprisonment, was demoted to *SS-Grenadier* and was transferred to Dirlewanger on November 7, 1944. The company to which I belonged was completely wiped out. After I was quickly put into a fighting group with other comrades, I was taken prisoner near Ecseg in the area of Ladzani at the border between Hungary and Slovakia....

Another new addition was *SS-Hauptsturmführer* Dr. Bruno Wille, who arrived at the unit to serve as the SS judge of the formation. He also survived the war. In 1946 he commented on his assignment with Dirlewanger.[22]

> I was the deputy judge at the field courts of the 16th SS-Panzergrenadier-Division, when I received transfer instructions to the *Sturmbrigade* "Dirlewanger" in November of 1944 from my superior office, the main office SS-Court. Prior to that, the unit was only known

to me by hearsay as a battalion for the rehabilitation of poachers. I was told by *SS-Standartenführer* Burmeister, the commander of the rehabilitation department, that this *Sturmbrigade* also in part consisted of sentenced SS-soldiers for rehabilitation by expressed command of Himmler, and that I was being sent there to straighten out the rehabilitation cases for these soldiers, since no cooperation between the main office of the SS court and Dirlewanger could be arrived at. I learned from the chief of the main office, *SS-Obergruppenführer* Breithaupt that no SS-court to which I could be sent as SS-judge existed at the *Sturmbrigade*, but that for newly punishable SS-members and former SS-members the nearest SS- and police court would be applicable, while for all other members of the Brigade the commander, *SS-Oberführer* Dirlewanger, had unlimited control over life and death, which he had obtained by reason of a command by the *Reichsführer-SS*, which was granted as a "Secret Commando-Case."...I arrived at the brigade in Slovakia early December 1944. The situation which I found was such that I did not believe I could justify proceeding slowly and cautiously, in the interest of humanity and justice... The unit was neither by their composition nor by their leadership a SS-unit, besides the pure appearance when only a few wore SS-uniform. From several remarks by Dirlewanger and observations during the short time of my presence, I believe I can say that the central command of the total Waffen-SS, the SS-command main office, had no power or commanding force over the *Sturmbrigade*, but that Dirlewanger took care of all questions concerning him directly with Himmler with whom he enjoyed an especially preferred position, with *SS-Obergruppenführer* Nebe of the *Reichskriminalpolizeiamt* [Government Criminal Police Office] or with his intimate friend *SS-Obergruppenführer* Berger who did everything possible for him. Inquiries and complaints from other offices, among them the main offices, landed in the waste paper basket when they were inconvenient, whereby Dirlewanger always quoted his position with Himmler. Legal justice within the Brigade was shocking. Factual reports were not handed over to a SS or police court, but Dirlewanger took care of everything himself, greatly misusing his authority over life and death, no matter if it concerned somebody who had a prior record or not, whether it concerned a member of the concentration camp, army or former SS. Punishment consisted only of thrashing or death, while the leadership of the whole unit was based only on corporal punishment...Already on the third day of my presence after I had some insight did I point out to Dirlewanger the unpardonable circumstances and made recommendations to him for change....When I persisted further and told him that all that was happening in the Brigade is plain murder and when I, by pointing out my oath as a judge, refused the slightest activity under these circumstances, it came to a breaking up so that I had no influence whatsoever from then on. Since I could not dare to speak up in front of the brigade, I used the first possible occasion, namely an official trip to the SS- and Police court in Pressburg to give a truthful report about the bad situation within the Brigade....Partly due to the expected hostility of Dirlewanger towards me because of my behavior, and because a cooperation in the sense of justice was not to be accomplished, partly because of reasons for my personal safety, I was transferred to another unit.....

On December 5, 1944 Soviet Marshal Malinovsky's *2nd Ukrainian Front* with the 6th Guards Tank Army and the 7th Guards Army attacked from Hatvan, a city located northeast of Budapest, west along the boundary between the German 6th and 8th Armies. Within eight days the Red

Army had gained some sixty miles and had outflanked Budapest to the north. Meanwhile, on December 10, the *Sonderkommando* took up positions between Nitra and Levice, along the Slovakian-Hungarian border. On December 12, the *Sonderkommando* was at Ipolysag with a strength of four battalions. By December 14 the Soviets had taken the town of Ipolysag. The next day troops from the *Sonderkommando* blew up part of the town. On December 21, the *Sonderkommando* moved toward Polost. On the 22nd, Dirlewanger attacked enemy forces near Polost and pushed them back, gaining important high ground. Dirlewanger continued the attack on December 23 seizing more high ground southwest of Polost. On December 26 enemy forces struck the right flank of the brigade. Dirlewanger ended the month in the area of Masovce, Priewitz. The brigade had five battalions, one heavy rocket launcher battery, one artillery battalion with two batteries, and numerous support troops.[23]

On December 19, the *Sonderkommando* was listed in the Wehrmacht organizational files as *SS-Sturmbrigade* Dirlewanger. It was listed as being comprised of two regiments, each of three battalions which each had four companies. Additionally, the *SS-Sturmbrigade* was reported to have a mixed reconnaissance company and two batteries of artillery. It was subordinated to the IVth Panzer Corps of the 8th Army.[24]

Sometime during December, Colonel General Johannes Friessner, the commander of Army Group South, visited the Dirlewanger Brigade which had given ground during the onslaught. Friessner found Dirlewanger sitting at a desk with a monkey on his shoulder. Neither Dirlewanger nor his staff knew what was going on at the front, but the SS commander proposed to withdraw. Friessner countermanded him and ordered the brigade to stay in place. Later that evening Friessner, who thought the SS troops were an undisciplined and unruly mob, returned to Dirlewanger's headquarters to ensure his orders were being carried out – but found that Dirlewanger had left.[25]

Dirlewanger, perhaps realizing that he still had powerful enemies within the SS, used his reception of the Knight's Cross to further cement ties with powerful SS leaders. After the award, several SS dignitaries wrote to Dirlewanger expressing their congratulations. *SS-Obergruppenführer* Maximillian von Herff was one who sent congratulations; he served as the chief of the SS-Personnel Main Office from August 1942 to the end of the war. This office managed personnel files, promotions and officer replacements. It was a subordinate element of the *SS-Führungshauptamt*, the SS Leadership Main Office.[26] The following is Dirlewanger's response from December 30, 1944 to von Herff:[27]

> To the Chief of the SS-Personnel Main Office
> *SS-Obergruppenführer* von Herff
> Berlin-Charlottenburg
>
> Very esteemed *SS-Obergruppenführer*,
>
> I am sending you my most humble thanks for your congratulations and the praising words on the occasion of my being awarded the Knight's Cross. Once again we have difficult weeks behind us, and my brigade has suffered heavy and bloody losses.
>
> May I wish you all the best for 1945.
>
> *Heil dem Führer,*
> Your very devoted
> O. Dirlewanger

On January 2, 1945 the *SS-Sturmbrigade* was located near Zvolen, Slovakia. On February 2, 1945 the *SS-Sturmbrigade* was located northeast of Bratislava.

The SS Legal Office finally replied to Himmler's personal staff on the conduct of the investigation against Dirlewanger which was last addressed in April 1943, on January 25, 1945. An *SS-Sturmbannführer* stated in a message to the *SS-Reichsführer* staff stamped "SECRET":[28]

> After its presentation, the *SS-Reichsführer* ordered the discontinuation of the proceedings against *SS-Oberführer* Dr. Dirlewanger.

The Monster Dies

How had Himmler decided in the case against Dirlewanger without his personal staff knowing the outcome? Had Berger or Breithaupt engaged in a personal request with the *SS-Reichsführer*, or had the case run its course with Konrad Morgen failing to amass required documentation to bring Dirlewanger to trial? It appeared that after being in and out of legal proceedings since 1934, Dirlewanger was now free from the shadow of the court.

• • •

At the beginning of the new year, a junior non-commissioned officer in the unit wrote an unusual letter to Heinrich Himmler. It read:[29]

My dear Reichsführer!

This year I am too late to send you the usual wishes for happiness, health and a long life at the New Year. But please accept these wishes even now. May destiny keep you alive for a long time. With fervent toughness and a fanatical belief in our victory we will stand by our beloved Führer, as we have always done during our time in battle. You, my Reichsführer, must therefore live as our true leader and must strengthen the spirit of the SS with us old fighters and to help lead us. May the year 1945 turn out better for our struggle than the old one. This, my dear Reichsführer, is my sincerest desire which I, as a simple SS-Unterscharführer, pose to you – but it comes from a pure, devoted heart.

According to your command, I am with the Dirlewanger Brigade and have reported for service at the front. Thus, the first hard lot reached me in Warsaw when I was taken prisoner by the bandits, but I was able to escape after eleven hours. Now I am in Ipolinik fighting against the Russians, where unfortunately our leader, SS-Untersturmführer Pollack, was lost. The soldiers and lower echelons of command were daring and courageous to the last man. Unfortunately, a lot of blood was shed – but Ivan will remember the Dirlewanger Brigade.

Now, Reichsführer, I have one request – in Warsaw I was recommended for an award by SS-Stabscharführer Schmitt, who lost both legs; here in the battle I was again recommended for an award, but to date I received neither the first nor the second.

I now have one wish – to be transferred out of the unit Dirlewanger to another one, because what have I really done so wrong that I must serve under such people who are looting and getting drunk – and if one doesn't participate in it, they shun you. I don't have any enemies in the unit, no, but please do not misunderstand me, dear Reichsführer: ten years have passed since I made a mistake and in the ensuing ten years, in private life as well as the military, I have demonstrated that I have faithfully done my duty according to my oath, and I will continue to do so. I have risked my life when I rescued the medical supplies for the IIIrd Battalion, so that when I arrived here, the commander had the highest praise for me. However, it is a strange feeling when you have to be around comrades from the concentration camps who have spent six to eight years or more behind prison walls. Dear Reichsführer, I truly believe that I have suffered enough because of a mistake which unfortunately was made.

May the year 1945 also for me bring the hour, after a long battle, when I, as in the past, can continue to live as a fanatical, faithful fighter with unbreakable allegiance to our Reichsführer, and move around without restraint.

Once again, all the best possible to you, dear Reichsführer, especially a long life and may you, together with our Führer, experience victory and full health.

My Honor is Loyalty!
Heil Hitler
Andreas Schillinger

We do not know if Himmler took any actions – positive or negative – against Schillinger or his chain of command for this letter.

The division then entrained and moved from Slovakia to Dresden. On February 15 the *SS-Sturmbrigade* was reported at having seized the villages of Sommerfeld, Christianstadt and Naumburg. The following day the Germans captured another two villages in the area. On February 17 the *SS-Sturmbrigade* counterattacked a strong Soviet attack near Sommerfeld and destroyed one tank. The next day the *Sonderkommando* continued the attack.[30]

Dirlewanger continued his harsh treatment of the men during this time. A political prisoner from a concentration camp, who had been assigned to the *Sonderkommando*, revealed a personal run-in with the commander:[31]

> I made the personal acquaintance of Dirlewanger in February of 1945. He had watched me through the field-glass as I was hurrying with a horse-drawn am-

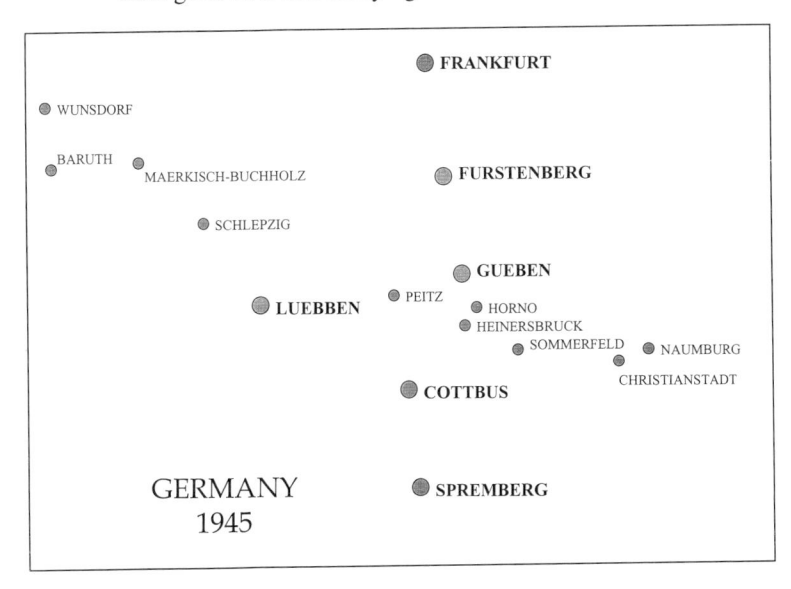

GERMANY 1945

- FRANKFURT
- WUNSDORF
- BARUTH
- MAERKISCH-BUCHHOLZ
- FURSTENBERG
- SCHLEPZIG
- GUEBEN
- LUEBBEN
- PEITZ
- HORNO
- HEINERSBRUCK
- SOMMERFELD
- NAUMBURG
- CHRISTIANSTADT
- COTTBUS
- SPREMBERG

munition car through a barrage. He stopped me and accused me of being a coward because I did not shoot back. When I replied that nothing prompted me to do so, he beat me so that I fell to the ground, covered in blood. Three days later I suffered an additional thirty lashings – 'due to cowardice in front of the enemy' – by order of Dirlewanger.

SS-Obersturmführer Theodor Krätzer arrived in February to lend his expertise with concentration camp inmates to Dirlewanger. Krätzer was born November 30, 1914 in Nürnberg, and held SS number 276,344 and Nazi Party number 4690977. He served at Buchenwald concentration camp from 1939 to 1941 and at Auschwitz from 1941 until early 1945.[32]

SS-Oberführer Dirlewanger was probably wounded on February 15, 1945 leading his unit in a counterattack and was replaced by *SS-Brigadeführer* Fritz Schmedes.[33] In addition, Dirlewanger's old chest wound began bothering him again, and he was placed on a sick-leave.[34]

Fritz Schmedes was born October 7, 1894 in Schwarme near Verden, the son of a minister. On February 20, 1913 he entered military service as an officer candidate in the Ostfriesiche Field Artillery Regiment 62 and was promoted to lieutenant June 23, 1914. During World War I he served on the Western Front, ending the conflict with the 84th Strassburg Field Artillery Regiment. He later entered the *Freikorps*, first as the commander of "Volunteer Battery Schmedes" in *Freikorps* Hasse in Berlin and Silesia, and later his old 62nd, fighting communists in the Ruhr. Schmedes later served in the police as a staff officer in Erfurt, rising to police lieutenant colonel and commander of the *Schutzpolizei* in Erfurt in 1939. From March 1939 to June 1941 he served with the inspectorate of the Order Police in Kassel. At the start of *Operation Barbarossa*, Schmedes was assigned to the artillery regiment of the SS *"Polizei"* Division and soon rose to be the regimental commander. He received the active rank of *SS-Obersturmbannführer* on April 1, 1942, *SS-Standartenführer* on April 20, 1942, *SS-Oberführer* on June 10, 1943, and *SS-Brigadeführer* on November 9, 1943. Schmedes was named commander of the 4th SS Division *"Polizei"* on June 10, 1943 and received the German Cross in Gold the same day. He commanded this unit during 1943 and 1944.[35]

Schmedes was well thought of. The following is an efficiency report for his earlier service:[36]

> Since December 1, 1941, *SS-Standartenführer* Schmedes has been in charge of the artillery regiment in my Division. A quiet balanced personality. Schmedes led his regiment very successfully in all attacks and defensive battles. Clever, a personality on the highest level as far as artillery is concerned. The successes of the infantry were mainly the merit of the energetic leadership, skillfully adapting to each situation. He shows courage and bravery so that Schmedes has been recommended for the German Cross in Gold. During the critical days of February 10th to the 13th, he lead the Division with great success while I was absent and he mastered the difficult situation of the Division during that time. Because of his great merit in leading the troops, I recommend that Schmedes be promoted to *SS-Oberführer*.
>
> Wunnenberg
> *SS-Gruppenführer*

• • •

Schmedes had been submitted for a Knight's Cross in 1944 but the award was turned down. The following is the justification for the decoration:[37]

> From September 1943 as commander of the 4th SS Grenadier Division *Polizei*, *SS-Brigadeführer* Schmedes has proven himself extraordinarily in all missions to date. With the newly established division, he was especially effective in the bandit fights in the Serbian and Greek areas. Engaged in the Rumanian-Hungarian area after the treacherous fall of Rumania,

SS-Brigadeführer Schmedes <u>was successful</u> with his division during the time of 25th to 27th of September 1944 <u>through personal decisiveness and exemplary personal bravery</u>, which had the <u>ultimate importance</u> for the continuation of battle in the Hungarian area.

The fast advance of Russian and Rumanian forces on a broad front made it necessary that already from September 15th on the division had to use all weak infantry troops that had arrived in the new war theater for action in the area of Temeschburg. Up to September 25th, the division which had by then arrived in full numbers succeeded in brave attacks and hardest defensive battles, while depending only on themselves, without any support to the right or left, to bring the Russian attack peak to a standstill and to form a defensive front in the line west of Temeschburg and Pesak (40 km southwest of Arad).

While at this front numerous attacks from highly superior forces were averted, the enemy pushed new troops on both sides of the Maros along the left wing of the division towards Szeged. At the same time, an advance by the Soviets towards Gross-Betschkerek threatened an interruption of our own supply lines. In addition, due to the great distance from the corps, relaying of commands to the division could only be done by radio which suffered atmospheric disturbance many times, so that *SS-Brigadeführer* Schmedes was faced again and again during these battles to make his own decisions. He has proven himself in the best possible way!

Disregarding the threatening outflanking, *SS-Brigadeführer* Schmedes decided, while knowing that he was weakening his defensive front, to lead a strike to the north into the flank of the enemy to reach the Maros and by that to cut off and destroy the enemy forces located at the south of the Maros. Against a far superior enemy as to material and number of troops, Periam was taken on September 27th and with that the sealing off of the enemy forces accomplished. By providing new infantry, artillery and tanks, the enemy tried to break through the front which was now about 50 km wide, however, all attacks of the enemy which concentrated on Pesak – Periam to replace the locked in forces were broken off under high bloody losses for the enemy.

With the last battalion of the division which had arrived in the meantime, *SS-Brigadeführer* Schmedes made the personal decision – despite advances by the enemy from the south to the back of our own forces – to continue the attack to the west against the encircled enemy forces in the area of Sannicolau Mare – Cenadul Mara. In long, most severe street fights the villages were taken and the enemy suffered heavy losses of men and material. The brave decision paid off!

For the division to have accomplished these decisive successes, the <u>power of decision</u>, the unshakable calm and the <u>exemplary bravery</u> of *SS-Brigadeführer* Schmedes were the factor. The commander stood always in the middle of the battle and succeeded in complete accomplishment of the tasks initially planned through his personal example, circumspect actions and direct involvement in the leadership of the battle groups. During the battles of the division in those days, the following were the losses to the enemy:

Personnel:	1,013 counted dead
	2,700 estimated dead
	288 prisoners
Weapons:	1 Panzer KV 1
	3 Panzer T 34
	1 Flak 8.8 cm

28 Pak 7.62 cm
4 Pak 3.7 cm
10 medium mortars
64 anti-tank weapons
42 heavy machine-guns / 99 light machine-guns
900 rifles
97 machine-pistols

Equipment:
24 trucks
2 cars
22 field telephones
3 radios
160 baggage wagons
200 horses

Due to the high merit of *SS-Brigadeführer* Schmedes, he deserves the award of the Knight's Cross of the Iron Cross.

The Commanding General
Kirschner
Lieutenant General

Schmedes would survive the war.

On February 20, the SS-*Sturmbrigade* Dirlewanger was reorganized for the final time as the 36th *Waffen-Grenadier Division der SS*. It had the following composition:

36th Waffen-SS Grenadier Division
    72nd Waffen-SS Grenadier Regiment
    73rd Waffen-SS Grenadier Regiment
    SS Artillery Detachment 36
    SS Füsilier Company 36
    SS Signal Company 36
    Army Panzer Detachment Stahnsdorf 1

The Monster Dies

Army Panzer Jäger Detachment 681
Army Engineer Brigade 687
Army Grenadier Regiment 1244

Both SS grenadier regiments owned ten fighting companies, organized in two battalions. SS Artillery Detachment 36 was a weak formation with only two batteries of guns; with three maneuver elements this meant that one would always be out of artillery support. The *füsilier* company was in effect a reconnaissance company, while the signal company provided communications support for the division

The 1244th Grenadier Regiment brought a confusing mix of soldiers to the division. Fifty percent of the personnel had previously served as students in the non-commissioned officer schools at Treptow, Prenzlau, Freiberg, Mengerskirchen, Eutin and Deggendorf. A further twenty-five percent of the regiment were *Volkssturm* recruits – old men and young boys pressed into service. The regiment fielded ten company-size units, organized in two battalions. Panzer Detachment Stahnsdorf 1, another army formation, joined the division with three companies – a company of mixed types of tanks and two companies fielding fourteen *sturmgeschütz* assault guns each. Panzer Jäger Detachment 681 came from Spremberg and featured 88mm heavy anti-tank guns organized in two companies. It had recently fought as part of the 1st Army on the western front in the Saarpfalz region. The 687th Engineer Brigade, with two battalions, joined the division from Rathenow.

On March 1, 1945 the 36th SS Division was located near Güben as part of the XXXXth Panzer Corps. On March 20, 1945 the 36th SS Division was located just east of Cottbus as part of the Vth Corps. Desertions in the unit – always a problem, continued to rise and SS NCOs were given instructions to kill anyone trying to desert and to shoot all recaptured would-be deserters.[38]

By April 15, the *1st Belorussian Front* was poised along the Oder River some 40 miles east of the German capital. The *Front*, under Marshal Georgi Zhukov, fielded 768,000 soldiers and over 3100 tanks and self-propelled assault guns. Opposing this juggernaut were elements of the German 9th Army with less than 500 fully operational armored vehicles. Southeast of Berlin, the bulk of the 9th Army had been bypassed by the *1st Belorussian Front* to the north and the *1st Ukrainian Front* to the south and, surrounded in the heavily forested lake district of the Spreewald, had to break out of the encirclement to the west or risk total destruction. The German 9th Army was surrounded on April 21, 1945; the 36th SS Division was positioned along the south near Peitz between the 342nd Infantry Division and the 214th Infantry Division, as the Vth Corps with the 21st Panzer Division, 35th and 36th SS Divisions and 275th and 342nd Infantry Divisions were assigned to the 9th Army from the 4th Panzer Army. On the 28th of April Theodor Busse, the commander of the 9th Army, met with his subordinate commanders at the small village of Hammer to discuss the breakout plan. The XIth SS Corps would face west and begin the breakout, attempting to split the junction of the 3rd Guards and 28th Armies. Once the pocket began moving, the corps would cover the northern flank of the breakthrough. The Vth Corps, including the 36th SS Division, would cover the southern flank of the breakout and take over the spearhead of the breakout when needed. The Vth SS Mountain Corps would cover the breakout from the east and cover the rear of the pocket. The situation within the 36th SS Division was even worse. On April 19 about thirty troops deserted to the Red Army near the town of Horno. Forty others crossed the line near Heinersbrück.[39]

The breakout started at dusk and almost immediately army Brigadier General Rudolf Sieckenius, commander of the 391st Security Division of the XIth SS Corps, sensed the hopelessness of the situation and committed suicide near Märkisch-Buchholz. *SS-Obergruppenführer* Matthias Kleinheisterkamp, commander of the XIth SS Corps, is reported to have gone forward in his armored staff car with three officers that night when he was ambushed and killed by Soviet forces near Halbe. Some of the 9th Army managed to break west but the Vth SS Mountain Corps became trapped in the cauldron. The hard-pressed German effort continued into May with some 9th Army elements finally reaching the 12th Army to the west. But most of the 9th Army never made it. Of Busse's original 200,000 soldiers only 40,000 reached the 12th Army.

The 36th SS Division started its pullback as well. The division headquarters re-established its position west at Peitz and then moved through Schlepzig-Lübbenau to Neuendorf. Desertions and battle casualties continued to rise and on April 24 the unit realistically ceased to be a coherent

The Monster Dies

fighting unit. By April 25 stragglers reached Märkisch-Bucholz. *SS-Standartenführer* Buchmann, commander of Waffen-Grenadier Regiment 72 had only a handful of troops. *SS-Obersturmbannführer* Ehlers, commander of Waffen-Grenadier Regiment 73 reported thirty-six. The artillery and engineer units were simply listed as missing in action. During the day it is believed that survivors of the 73rd Regiment hanged Ehlers from a tree. On April 29 the division reached Baruth.

By May 1st the fighting continued with small groups of division soldiers fighting for their lives at the villages of Menniken and Kummersdorf. The final remaining 36th SS Division troops disbanded south of Magdeburg as they attempted to reach western allied lines. Some were successful like *SS-Obersturmbannführer* Kurt Weisse, who was now serving as the division operations officer. Weisse donned the uniform of an army private and went into British captivity. On March 5, 1946 he escaped.[40] However, many other troops were reported massacred by Soviet troops.[41] Undoubtedly, many of those killed were innocent concentration camp inmates and other disciplined soldiers who were forced into the unit – but who had personally avoided involvement in war crimes. As happened numerous times on the eastern front, a soldier wearing an SS collar insignia was often a prisoner who was shot.

Dirlewanger's destiny was just as gruesome. After being wounded in mid-February, he temporarily disappeared. One source says that by this date Soviet Marshall Georgi Zhukov had placed a bounty for the capture or death of Dirlewanger.[42] We do not know if Dirlewanger knew of this bounty, but it is a good assumption that he was aware that his fate would be terrible indeed if apprehended by either the Soviets or the Poles. Another source states that Dirlewanger returned to Esslingen on sick-leave in April 1945 after having visited Gottlob Berger in Berlin in mid-March. This same source states that Dirlewanger brought a truck to the home of his parents in Esslingen and loaded it with plunder that Dirlewanger stored there.[43] He then headed south, closer to neatrul Switzerland or the Alpine Redoubt – the area on the Obersalzberg to which Hitler originally intended to retreat and lead Germany's final struggle. Sometime before June 1945 he appeared in the southern German town of Altshausen. The following account was compiled by Rudolf Multer and sent to the author in February 1996. It is to be published in his book *1945/1995 – Fifty Years Ago*, by Oberschwäbische Verlagsanstalt Drexler & Co.:[44]

The Cruel Hunters

[At the end of the war, the people of Altshausen] had to suffer innumerable legal violations and brutalities by the Mayor, Johannes Franz Rohrer, from Stuttgart, who was living in Altshausen after he had been wounded a year ago while in the Luftwaffe and Kurt Möller, a master technician at the firm of Hilgers, Altshausen, which manufactured parts for the V-2, who was functioning as his right hand. They were installed by the French Occupation Forces. Möllers, who in early 1945 had been fired by Hilgers because of internal confrontations and who shortly thereafter was drafted into the Army at Ellwangen, left his troop, roamed around in the woods, and when the French arrived, he appeared again in Altshausen. On May 1, 1945, co-workers at the firm of Hilgers, the carpenter Alois Ackermann, the Engineer Hans Joachim Eichler, Dr.Eng. Manfred Thomä and the Manager Friedrich Martin Hilgers, who had been arrested in Altshausen and been denounced to the French, were murdered. They were gathered in a car under the pretense that they were to be transferred

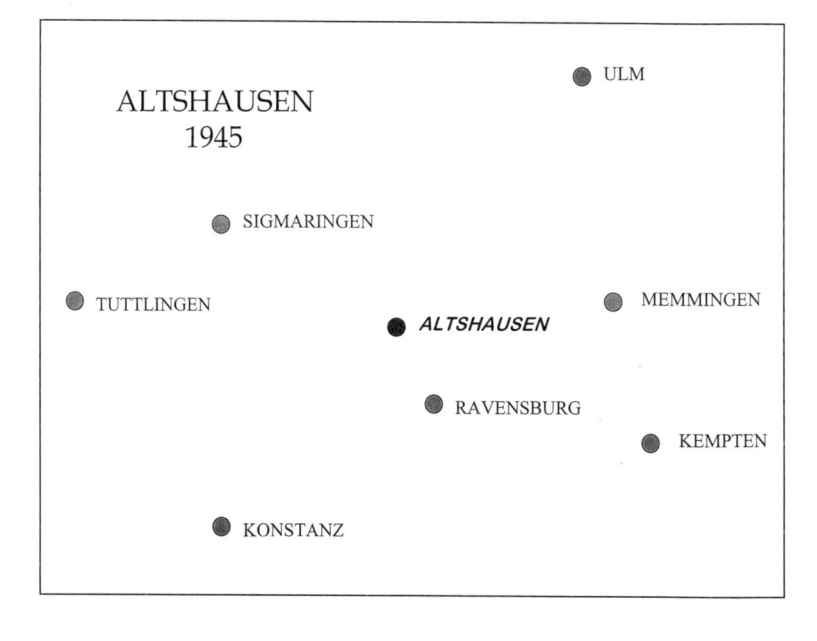

ALTSHAUSEN 1945

● ULM

● SIGMARINGEN

● TUTTLINGEN   ● MEMMINGEN
               ● *ALTSHAUSEN*

         ● RAVENSBURG
                        ● KEMPTEN

     ● KONSTANZ

The Monster Dies

to the KZ in Ravensburg. However, they never arrived there. In the Altshausen retention center there were an average of 10 to 12 people gathered in a very small area. They were guarded by former inmates of the concentration camps, and especially at night they were beaten and mistreated. The prisoners received food from DRK-Helper [German Red Cross Assistant] Betty Angele who was granted permission to enter the retention center. Only after a French soldier came to Altshausen in July of 1945 to visit his girl friend, were the missing people found in the "Oberholz V," close to the Ebenweiler Strasse, after he had pointed this out: they had been beaten to death and were buried in the forest close-by. After they were dug up by the grave digger Thaddäus Hund, they found their last resting place in the Altshauser cemetery in October of 1945.

Also under the use of force, the infamous former Chief of the SS-Penal brigade, Colonel of the Waffen-SS, Dr. Oskar Dirlewanger, died on June 7, 1945, while in the Altshauser Detention Center. Oskar Dirlewanger, who was born on September 26, 1895 in Würzburg, became the Director of the Labor office of Heilbronn in 1933. He entered the Waffen-SS early, however, in 1935 he was sentenced to 2-1/2 years of prison because of misuse of a minor, and for that reason he had to abandon his SS-uniform. After he served his sentence, Dirlewanger volunteered and served in the Legion Condor. Dr. Dirlewanger who was an Oberst in the Waffen-SS-Reserves, was taken back into the Waffen-Ss in 1940, first with the rank of Lieutenant and he was ordered to create a unit where imprisoned poachers and later-on guilty SS-people and people from the prisons could prove their value. The road of the Dirlewanger unit lead from Oranienburg to Lubin-Minsk-Kiev-Privitz-Nousohl-Warsaw and was marked by numerous war crimes. Dr. Dirlewanger was accused of these crimes at the Nürnberg War Crimes Process. The accusation was withdrawn after his death was confirmed to the courts. On the morning of June 8, 1945, the French demanded that a coffin be placed in front of the Altshausen Detention Center. They themselves took care of the placing into the coffin. Two guards and a security officer were on guard so that the coffin was not going to be opened until the funeral at 11 o'clock which was ordered by the local commander *Capitain* Hoffmann and was presided over by Pastor Romer. There he was told by Hoffmann that the person to be interred was SS-Colonel Dr. Oskar Dirlewanger. The respective death certificate at the local registration office was signed by Hoffmann on June 19, 1945. As cause of death, the pastor put the following remark into the death registry: "Died after having been mistreated by the guards." On the same day, the death certificate was signed by former Gestapo employee Gustl Münch, who also was supposed to have died on June 8, 1945 while in custody.

......How and why Dirlewanger had come to the area of Altshausen could not be cleared up. According to authentic reports, Dirlewanger was flown out of the "Berlin Pocket" by a Fieseler Storch [light observation aircraft] after his unit was disbanded. At that time, relatives of Dirlewanger lived in Göppingen and Stuttgart. In addition, it must not be discounted that there could have been a connection with a Christian Häberle, then residing in Altshausen, who was ordered to Dirlewanger's unit because of "Black market butchering" and who was working there as a cook. It is noteworthy that on June 30, 1960 a Dr. Dirlewanger of Bern [Switzerland], the President of Transportation of the Swiss Railroad, made inquiries regarding Dr. Oskar Dirlewanger at the town hall of Altshausen. Responding to an inquiry by the *Ministere des Affaires*

The Monster Dies

Etrangeres – Archives et Documentation – in Paris, it was reported on June 15, 1995 that personal data was to be kept secret for 100 years and that no information could be given.

Dirlewanger's true fate would continue to be a mystery for an additional fifteen years, but his exploits would receive much attention at the Nürnberg War Crimes Trials.

ENDNOTES

[1] Trevor-Roper, Hugh, ed. *Final Entries 1945: The Diaries of Joseph Goebbels.* (New York: G.P. Putnam's Sons, 1978), p. 254.
[2] Landwehr, Richard. *Fighting for Freedom: The Ukrainian Volunteer Division of the Waffen-SS.* (Silver Spring, Maryland: Bibliophile Legion Books, 1985), p. 142.
[3] Höhne. *The Order of the Death's Head.*, p.545.
[4] Landwehr. *Fighting for Freedom.*, pp. 142-145.
[5] Vajicek, Radko. "Allied Airfield Behind Enemy Lines." *World War II.* (Leesburg, VA: Cowles Magazines, May, 1996), p. 56.
[6] Landwehr. *Fighting for Freedom.*, pp. 148-150.
[7] Ibid., pp. 155-158.
[8] Personalakt Oskar Dirlewanger.
[9] International Military Tribunal Nürnberg. *Trial of the Major War Criminals before the International Military Tribunal.* (Nürnberg, Germany: Allied Control Authority for Germany, 1948), Volume XX, p. 382.
[10] National Archives of the United States, Washington D. C. Microcopy T-175, Records of the Reich Leader of the SS and Chief of German Police Roll 70.
[11] Meyer. *Nacht über Hamburg.*, p.126.
[12] Ibid., pp. 216-217.
[13] Klausch. *Antifaschisten in SS-Uniform.*, p.206.
[14] Personalakt Hans Karnop, Washington, D.C: National Archives Microfilm Publication A3343, Records of SS Officers from the Berlin Document Center, Roll SSO-154A.
[15] Personalakt Erich Brandt, Washington, D.C: National Archives Microfilm Publication A3343, Records of SS Officers from the Berlin Document Center, Roll SSO-099.
[16] Personalakt Georg Wild, Washington, D.C: National Archives Microfilm Publication A3343, Records of SS Officers from the Berlin Document Center, Rolls SSO-245B.
[17] Mehner. *Die Geheimen Tagesberichte.*, Band 11, pp. 232, 260.
[18] Michaelis. *Die Grenadier Divisionen der Waffen SS.*, p.184.
[19] Personalakt Erich Buchmann, Washington, D.C: National Archives Microfilm Publication A3343, Records of SS Officers from the Berlin Document Center, Rolls SSO-114, 115.
[20] Ibid.
[21] Michaelis. *Die Grenadier Divisionen der Waffen SS.*, p.189.
[22] Michaelis. *Die Grenadier Divisionen der Waffen SS.*, pp. 184-186. Not much is known about Wille. Born in Pola May 16, 1912, in the former Austrian-Hungarian Empire, he entered the SS in September 1935. His SS number was 309,491. He survived the war.
[23] Mehner. *Die Geheimen Tagesberichte.*, Band 11 (1 September 1944 - 31 December 1944), pp. 280, 282, 285, 290, 308, 313, 315, 323, 335.
[24] Tessin, Georg. *Verbände und Truppen der deutschen Wehrmacht und Waffen-SS, 1939 - 1945.* (Osnabrück, FRG: Biblio Verlag, 1980), Band 5, p.36.
[25] Seaton. *The Russo-German War 1941-45.*, pp. 498-499.
[26] Bender, Roger James and Taylor, Hugh Page. *Uniforms, Organization and History of the Waffen-SS, Vol. 2.*, pp. 14-20.

The Cruel Hunters

[27] Personalakt Oskar Dirlewanger.
[28] Ibid.
[29] Abschrift, SS-Uscha. Andreas Schillinger, 3.1.45, Washington, D.C: National Archives Microfilm Publication T354, Roll 650.
[30] Mehner. *Die Geheimen Tagesberichte.*, Band 12 (1 January - 9 May 1945), pp. 174, 180, 186, and 191 plus situation maps.
[31] Klausch. *Antifaschisten in SS-Uniform.*, p. 303.
[32] Personalakt Theodor Krätzer, Washington, D.C: National Archives Microfilm Publication A3343, Records of SS Officers from the Berlin Document Center, Roll SSO-205A.
[33] Windrow. *The Waffen-SS.*, p.26.
[34] Klausch. *Antifaschisten in SS-Uniform.*, p.302.
[35] Preradovich, Nikolaus von. *Die Generale der Waffen-SS.* (Berg am See, FRG: Kurt Vowinkel-Verlag, 1985), pp. 192-193.
[36] Personalakt Fritz Schmedes, Washington, D.C: National Archives Microfilm Publication A3343, Records of SS Officers from the Berlin Document Center, Roll SSO-083B.
[37] Ibid.
[38] Landwehr, Richard. *Siegrunen: The Waffen-SS in Historical Perspective*, Volume 57 (Fall 1994). (Brookings, OR: Landwehr, 1994), p.29.
[39] Ibid., p.31.
[40] Klausch. *Antifaschisten in SS-Uniform.*, p.314.
[41] Landwehr. *Siegrunen.*, pp. 31-33.
[42] Zentner, Christian and Friedemann Bedürftig. *The Encyclopedia of the Third Reich.* English translation edited by Amy Hackett. (New York: Macmillan Publishing, 1991), Volume 1, p.200.
[43] Klausch. *Antifaschisten in SS-Uniform.*, pp. 302-303.
[44] Newspaper articles and Rudolf Multer's account contained in a letter to the author from Dieter Heske, Hauptamtsleiter der Gemeinde Altshausen, February 1996.

7

JUDGEMENT AT NUREMBERG

Has any court ever convicted an organization?
- Henry Morgenthau, Jr.[1]

The *Sonderkommando* was frequently mentioned in the proceedings at the International Military Tribunal at Nürnberg. However, no former soldiers of the commando were brought up on charges, mainly because it was believed that all officers and non-commissioned officers had perished at the end of the war south of Berlin. The only exception to that belief was that of Oskar Dirlewanger himself, who in 1946 was conjectured to be still at large. However, he was not tried *in absentia*. The bulk of the testimony concerning the unit was used by the prosecution to build a case against the SS at large, and the Waffen-SS in particular.

The indictments at Nürnberg were designed to charge both individuals – such as Göring, Kaltenbrunner, Hess, etc., and organizations such as the SS, the Gestapo and the Nazi "Leadership Corps." Lawyers for the defense attempted to separate sub-organizations within the SS (Waffen-SS versus Allgemeine-SS) to limit the condemnation to the general SS, the overall body of the SS, as distinct from the Waffen-SS. While the *Sonderkommando* itself was not put on trial, its origins and relationship to both *Allgemeine-SS* and Waffen-SS were examined in detail. The prosecution inferred that Dirlewanger belonged to the Waffen-SS, defense witnesses maintained it did not.[2]

Testimony relating to Dirlewanger and his activities figured in three separate International Military Tribunals at Nürnberg. The first was the most famous of the three – the Trial of the Major War Criminals before the International Military Tribunal. Later, testimony about Dirlewanger was introduced at the Trials of War Criminals before the International Military Tribunal, *United States of America vs. Otto Ohlendorf, et al.*, Case No. 9. Finally, more evidence concerning Dirlewanger was presented in the Trials of War Criminals before the International Military Tribunal, *The Ministries Case*, Case No. 11.

On January 7, 1946, Erich von dem Bach-Zelewski testified before the International Military Tribunal at Nürnberg. Von dem Bach had basically entered into a plea bargain arrangement with the western allies, in order to avoid prosecution by the Soviet Union. Von dem Bach was under no illusion as to his fate were that to happen – the hangman's noose in Minsk or Warsaw. So von dem Bach walked the line in his testimony, giving enough information to partially satisfy the allies, but not so much as to warrant a renewed interest in prosecuting von dem Bach himself. It was a thin line – as some of the worst excesses in the anti-partisan conflict occurred after von dem Bach was named Chief of Anti-Partisan Units, not to mention his suppression of the Warsaw Uprising. Himmler's speech to SS leaders at Posen on October 4, 1943 explain von dem Bach's role:[3]

> In the meantime I have also set up the department of Chief of the Anti-Partisan Units. Our comrade *SS-Obergruppenführer* von dem Bach is Chief of the Anti-Partisan Units. I considered it necessary for the *SS-Reichsführer* to be in authoritative command in all these battles, for I am convinced that we are best in a position to take action against this enemy struggle, which is a decidedly political one. Except where the units have been supplied and which we had formed for this purpose were taken from us to fill in gaps at the front, we have been very successful. It is notable that, by setting up this department we have gained for the SS in turn a division, a corps, an army, and the next step, which is the headquarters of an army or even of a [army] group – if you wish to call it that.

The following testimony by von dem Bach relates to the Dirlewanger *Sonderkommando*:[4]

> COLONEL POKROVSKY (PROSECUTOR): Do you know anything about the existence of a special brigade consisting of smugglers, poachers, and persons released from prison?
>
> VON DEM BACH-ZELEWSKI: When all the troops really suitable for anti-partisan warfare had been withdrawn, an anti-partisan battalion under the command of Dirlewanger was formed and attached to Army Group Center at the end of 1941 or the beginning of 1942. This battalion was gradually strengthened by the addition of reserve units until it reached the proportions, first, of a regiment and later, of a brigade. This "Dirlewanger Brigade" consisted for the most part of previously convicted criminals; officially it consisted of so-called poachers, but it did include real criminals convicted of burglary, murder, *et cetera*.
>
> COLONEL POKROVSKY: How do you explain the fact that the German Army Command so willingly strengthened and increased its forces by adding criminals to them and then using these criminals against the partisans?
>
> VON DEM BACH-ZELEWSKI: I am of the opinion that this step was closely connected with a speech made by Heinrich Himmler at Weselsburg at the beginning of 1941, prior to the campaign against Russia, when he spoke of the purpose of the Russian campaign, which was, he said, to decimate the Slav population by 30 million, and that it was in order to achieve this purpose that troops of such inferior caliber were introduced.

Defense lawyers then questioned von dem Bach concerning Dirlewanger and his unit in an attempt to distance their activities from the Waffen-SS and from von dem Bach.[5]

> DR. STAHMER (DEFENSE LAWYER): Did you not know that you were particularly commended by Hitler and Himmler and decorated mainly for your ruthless and efficient actions in the war against the partisans?
>
> VON DEM BACH-ZELEWSKI: No, I received no decoration for the war against the partisans. I received all my decorations beginning with the clusters to the Iron Cross [2nd Class], at the front and from the Wehrmacht. I will gladly give you names.
>
> DR. EXNER (DEFENSE LAWYER): Do you know anything about the Dirlewanger regiment?
>
> VON DEM BACH-ZELEWSKI: That was the Dirlewanger Brigade, which I described in detail to the prosecutor a short time ago.
>
> DR. EXNER: Yes. Was that brigade at any time under your command?
>
> VON DEM BACH-ZELEWSKI: Yes, in 1941.
>
> DR. EXNER: Was it a formation of the Army or the SS?
>
> VON DEM BACH-ZELEWSKI: No, it was not a formation of the Waffen-SS; it was supplied by the Allgemeine-SS, that is, by the Berger office.
>
> DR. STAHMER: The Brigade Dirlewanger was an SS brigade, wasn't it?

VON DEM BACH-ZELEWSKI: The Brigade Dirlewanger did not belong to the Waffen-SS. It was an organization which could possibly be classified as part of the Allgemeine-SS. It was not supplied and kept up by the Waffen-SS, but by the Berger office.

DR. STAHMER: Was the commander of the Brigade Dirlewanger a member of the SS?

VON DEM BACH-ZELEWSKI: Yes.

DR. STAHMER: Didn't you yourself suggest that criminals should be organized and used for fighting the partisans?

VON DEM BACH-ZELEWSKI: No.

DR. THOMA (DEFENSE LAWYER): If I understood you correctly, you disapproved of the manner in which the fighting against the partisans was carried on, involving many innocent people; and you disapproved also of the existence of the Dirlewanger Regiment and of the speech of Reichsführer-SS Himmler?

VON DEM BACH-ZELEWSKI: Yes.

Von dem Bach was obviously lying in many parts of this testimony alone. He won the Bar to the Iron Cross 2nd Class on August 31, 1941 and the Bar to the Iron Cross 1st Class on May 20, 1942. Both awards were given to him as a Higher SS and Police Leader – not a front-line position. He won the German Cross in Gold on February 23, 1943 – once again for services rendered in the rear areas. Dirlewanger had been under von dem Bach's command several times during the war, most notably at Warsaw. Von dem Bach did not have to recommend Dirlewanger for any award – which we have seen that he did – if he truly disapproved of the conduct of the unit. And as has been seen by wartime reports, the unit was in fact a part of the Waffen-SS. After one of Bach's court appearances, former *Reichsmarschall* Hermann Göring became so incensed at von dem Bach's testimony that he shouted "Schweinehund"[6] at him.[7]

Konrad Morgen, Dirlewanger's nemesis from 1941, submitted several affidavits to the prosecution concerning the activities of the *Sonderkommando*. On January 28, 1947 Morgen deposed as follows:[8]

> During my activity as a judge in the Government General it struck me that whenever the Lublin Gestapo reported that in that area Polish workers had been beaten, looting had occurred, etc., that this had frequently been done by members of a unit with a certain A.P.O. number. The frequency of the cases also struck me. On making inquiries, I learned that a road building formation was stationed in the neighborhood of Lublin and that this unit was recruited from all poachers being held in the prisons. The formation operated under the orders of *SS-Obergruppenführer* Berger, Chief of the SS Main Office. I mentioned this to the then Chief of the Gestapo, a *SS-Sturmbannführer* Johannes Mueller, who previously had been Chief of the Gestapo in Warsaw and told me dreadful things about Dirlewanger: that he caught Jews, imprisoned them and either had them shot or else released only if they could pay a certain amount of money; that he caused an entire section of Lublin to be surrounded, systematically looted and subsequently had the plunder sold by Jews; that shocking atrocities such as "scientific" experiments, tortures etc. were performed on Jews. I ascertained that Dirlewanger had been sentenced to 4 years: penal servitude for immoral acts to minors and had gone to Spain during the Civil War there where he probably came to Himmler's notice. I also learned that Dirlewanger later on collected in his formation, in addition to the aforementioned poachers, criminals and prisoners from concentration camps. He was said finally to have had some

2,000 men in his formation, which was known as the Dirlewanger Brigade. He also collected men who had been sentenced to death and subsequently pardoned, and it was this Division which came to be detailed for especially dangerous military enterprises. After I had collected enough evidence I at once approached *SS-Obergruppenführer* Krüger in order to submit to him an order for the arrest of Dirlewanger, together with a report on the matter. Krüger was not authorized to take action, although extremely roused, and in my very presence he phoned *SS-Obergruppenführer* Berger and demanded the immediate removal of Dirlewanger and his men from the Government General, which actually took place. I should like to add that Dirlewanger personally went to the concentration camps and there enlisted volunteers. I heard stories about the terrible life Dirlewanger was leading, that he was drunk all day long, whipping and shooting at random.

Morgen revised his testimony about a year later on December 19, 1947. In his three-page affidavit he described his attempts to prosecute Dirlewanger and the interference given by Gottlob Berger.[9]

I, Dr. Konrad MORGEN, give the following affidavit and state:

During my legal activities in the general government at the Police court VI during the year 1941, I noticed that the incoming penal reports frequently referred to members of a certain field post address concerning misdeeds against Polish civilians. I have pursued the reports in legal proceedings and found that they were members of a unit whose chief was *SS-Sturmbannführer* Dirlewanger and that this unit consisted of previously convicted persons and poachers. I got in touch with the Chief of the Gestapo in Lublin, *SS-Sturmbannführer*

Müller, in whose proximity parts of this unit were located. The unit was stationed at near Lublin. Other divisions were near Riga. Müller informed me that the Brigade Dirlewanger was a pest and ruled arbitrarily, took jews into custody, conducted blackmail, plunders and executions and, among other things, set fire to the Ghetto of Lublin. All these things took place constantly as well as many other unlawful activities and hair-raising cruelties. There was not one crime which did not occur there. I remember from the files that Jewish women were killed by being injected with strychnine; the remains were used for making soap. Further, ransom of 15,000 Zloty was demanded, and whoever could not pay was shot. I reported this matter to the convening authority, *SS-Obergruppenführer* Krüger and was told by him that this whole unit was under the command of *SS-Obergruppenführer* Gottlob Berger. The idea to form this unit was Berger's.

After having combined the material received from Müller with my own findings concerning the crimes, I got in touch with people of the Dirlewanger Unit and found that these people had already been convicted to several years of imprisonment due to moral crimes involving minors. [A later correction was made, to read that ...from personnel files...., that he had already been convicted to several years of imprisonment due to moral crimes involving minors.]

In mid-1941 [later corrected to read: In mid-41 or early 1942], I presented to *SS-Obergruppenführer* Krüger a warrant of arrest against Dirlewanger. Krüger informed me that he was not in charge, but Berger was, and he would call him immediately. He did this in my presence and informed Berger about the situation, demanding that this "bunch of criminals" should have to be removed within eight days from the general government. By order of Berger, the unit then transferred to

Russia which deprived me of the possibility to pursue the matter further.

All files concerning these crimes were given by me to Gottlob Berger as the appropriate legal authority and, therefore, Berger was informed about the criminal doing of this brigade. I know that Berger did nothing to stop the crimes of the Dirlewanger Brigade. To the contrary: nothing happened to Dirlewanger, he was even promoted. I found out during the last years of the war that the brigade was enlarged and at the end was as large as a division. In addition, while on checks of concentration camps, I saw that drafting boards of the Dirlewanger Brigade were there and that volunteers from among the inmates agreed to join. It is known to me that these comprehensive criminal proceedings which I initiated were not the only ones, but that again and again more criminal proceedings were filed. This battalion Dirlewanger, which later became a Division, reported directly to Berger, but it was not an SS-unit, and, therefore, no SS-Court was allowed. During research which I conducted it became known to me that Gottlob Berger was closely acquainted with Dirlewanger and that Dirlewanger sent to Berger large amounts of food and stolen goods.

Former *SS-Obergruppenführer* Karl Wolff, who helped create the *Sonderkommando* in 1940, testified on April 12, 1947 to matters concerning the Dirlewanger brigade. He was asked the following questions by interrogator Schneider:[10]

> SCHNEIDER: Could these items perhaps be meant for this Dirlewanger Brigade? Was this Dirlewanger Brigade under Berger's command, or who else?
>
> WOLFF: I am not in a position to answer this. I know the Dirlewanger unit as a probationary unit very well,

because I was present when the Führer gave his permission for establishing it, from so-called honorable poachers.

SCHNEIDER: Whose idea was it to form this brigade?

WOLFF: It is my opinion that first it was only a battalion.

SCHNEIDER: Whose idea was it to form this unit?

WOLFF: I think it was Himmler. He approached the Führer to give a redeeming chance to these poachers who because of the severity were sentenced to unfitness for serving in the army. The Führer who was opposed to hunting and during dinner often made derogatory remarks about very cowardly hunters picked this up enthusiastically.

SCHNEIDER: Whom did the Führer give the permission to form this unit?

WOLFF: Himmler discussed that with him and recommended it, and the Führer agreed to the idea.

SCHNEIDER: Himmler, what did he do?

WOLFF: That was something in general, I must think it over more carefully. I want to give you a clear reply and I am not interested in keeping something secret, because I am not burdened with it in any way. Most probably he gave it to Berger who was to work on recruiting for the SS.

SCHNEIDER: You say it does not burden you in any way. In what respect did the subject Dirlewanger not burden you?

WOLFF: I don't know. If you ask me about something....

SCHNEIDER: Himmler has given the unit to Berger, isn't that what you just said?

WOLFF: I said most probably.

SCHNEIDER: At that time the task existed to recruit people for this occasion from among poachers?

WOLFF: Yes, sir.

SCHNEIDER: Only from among poachers?

WOLFF: Yes, only from among poachers. After this unit was very successful at the front, the Dirlewanger unit also recruited other SS-members who had been sentenced so they could redeem themselves at the front.

SCHNEIDER: Wasn't it supposed to only concern poachers?

WOLFF: Yes.

SCHNEIDER: During which year? Approximately 1939, 1940?

WOLFF: No, only during the war. I think after 1941.

SCHNEIDER: Berger was the legal officer in his main office?

WOLFF: Yes, sir.

SCHNEIDER: Could you please explain what that means?

WOLFF: Whenever a member of a main office did something wrong, then the matter was examined by the SS-judge responsible for the respective main office and a sentence was pronounced according to the severity of the case; the sentence was then presented to the chief of the main office acting as legal chief for his confirmation.

SCHNEIDER: Now one question, was the Dirlewanger unit under Berger? If that was the case, then Berger was the legal chief of the Dirlewanger unit?

WOLFF: I cannot make a complete judgment about this. It is most probably because the Dirlewanger unit was so-to-say a unit in occupied enemy territory, while Berger was sitting in his office in Berlin. It speaks against every military experience that a chief of a main office who does not command a unit can be its legal authority.

SCHNEIDER: If this Dirlewanger unit was not under Berger, to whom was it responsible in the field?

WOLFF: When this Dirlewanger unit was active in fighting bandits, then it was under the command of the chief of the bandit fighter units, the respective one with whom they were fighting.

SCHNEIDER: Then it can be assumed that the chief of the bandit fighting units had the right to punish Dirlewanger, and not Berger?

WOLFF: Yes sir.

Paul Hausser also testified at the Trial of the Major War Criminals before the International Military Tribunal at Nürnberg. Born October 7,

Judgement at Nuremberg

1880 in Brandenburg, Hausser was one of the most respected commanders in the Waffen-SS. He retired from the *Reichswehr* as a major general in 1932, and joined the SS two years later. During World War II he commanded SS Division "*Das Reich*", the SS Panzer Corps, and the 7th Army. One of the highest decorated soldiers in the Reich, he was a recipient of the Knight's Cross with Oak Leaves and Swords.[11] Hausser's image was that of a true "front-line" soldier, never personally involved in anti-partisan operations. In the following testimony he described partisan warfare and the Waffen-SS:[12]

> The fight against partisans is a general military and political police measure, which can be assigned to any troop; front-line troops of the army and of the Waffen-SS were used only in exceptional cases, for instance when they were in the rear areas. There were usually no partisan fights in the operational areas; they mostly took place in the rear areas only. This fighting was mainly the task of the security division of the army and special defense battalions, and besides these of police troops. Units of the Waffen-SS at the front were not especially trained for this kind of fighting and were assigned this duty just as little as panzer divisions of the army, for instance. In the East, units of my divisions were never used in the fight against partisans at any time. Therefore it was not a special task for SS units, and they were not especially trained or instructed for this purpose.

The explanation was not allowed to stand by itself and the prosecution attempted to press Hausser for conflicting details:[13]

> MAJOR JONES (PROSECUTOR): Those were crimes of the SS [during the Warsaw Uprising], were they not witness?
>
> HAUSSER: That was not the Waffen-SS. They were

241

always only a group of men who belonged to Himmler and who had nothing whatsoever to do with the fighting troops. We never fought at Warsaw.

MAJOR JONES: Are you denying that the Waffen-SS took part in the destruction of Warsaw?

HAUSSER: I have not been there and therefore cannot make any comments. But to my knowledge, there was no fighting there; it was a riot which was quelled, as several witnesses have testified.

MAJOR JONES: It was a revolt – and then mass extermination by the SS troops; that's what happened in Warsaw, wasn't it?

HAUSSER: The Waffen-SS participated only to a very small extent because the Waffen-SS was in combat.

MAJOR JONES: Now, Dirlewanger was the commander of the units operating in Warsaw, was he not?

HAUSSER: Dirlewanger was the commander of a picked troop of men from the concentration camps. He had no connection with the Waffen-SS. I did not meet him personally, nor his troops, so I can give no further testimony from my own knowledge.

MAJOR JONES: Were the officers of his units SS officers?

HAUSSER: I cannot give you information as to that, for I do not know these units.

There are several inconsistencies in Hausser's testimony which may have been from a faulty memory or perhaps an evasion of the truth. He initially denied that there was anything more than a riot at Warsaw, although he had to have known the rough magnitude of casualties on both sides that proved this was substantially more than a mere riot. Then he said that the Waffen-SS did not fight at Warsaw; he subsequently testified that the Waffen-SS had participated in Warsaw "to a very small extent." We do not know if Hausser ever met Dirlewanger during the war. We do know from officer efficiency reports that he knew at least one SS officer in the late 1930s who went on to serve with Dirlewanger.[14]

Gottlob Berger was brought to trial in the Trials of War Criminals before the International Military Tribunal, *The Ministries Case*, Case No. 11. He had a tough task to perform to contradict the deposition of von dem Bach-Zelewski. In addition to his testimony recounted earlier, he described events in the East with some intriguing hints as to the fate of Dirlewanger:[15]

> DR. FROESCHMANN (DEFENSE LAWYER): I want to know how much you know about these atrocities.
>
> BERGER: During the year 1942 until early summer 1943 I did not hear of a single document which might have indicated that this *Sonderkommando* had fought with particular brutality in the East. It was known that in the case of these battles that were always conducted in marshes and woods, they were carried out man against man, one against the other, and therefore the fighting was very brutal. It has been determined unequivocally that for more than three months nobody stayed in this unit without being a casualty – either dead or wounded. Dirlewanger himself was wounded seven times. I have no reason to defend him because if he were a man, and please permit me to say this, if he were a regular fellow, then he would have reported now and would not fight in a western army as a highly respected officer. It would have been easy for him to get here under the protection of his uniform.

DR. FROESCHMANN: What army is he fighting in? You don't want to answer that question?

BERGER: No. But this is an affair that is important and that is why I want to mention it.

DR. FROESCHMANN: From this document the prosecution might conclude that you considered the Dirlewanger unit as your own unit. What do you have to say about this document?

BERGER: Dirlewanger was very attractive. He was one of those people whom one had to guard and supervise constantly. When, by his personal courage and bravery, he had risen in the ranks, the Chief of the Anti-Partisan Units – and Himmler, too – honored him in a special way. If something went well in the case of these operations, then both people mentioned [von dem Bach and Himmler] spoke about it, and [said] say, "my unit, that was the one that saved the situation." But if something went wrong or if he [Dirlewanger] conducted himself in an untoward manner, if he had drunk too much, then I was responsible for it. This ironic pathos [bathos], "my unit," that can be discerned from the entire letter, "my unit."

Berger also testified at Nürnberg as to the organization and actions of the *Sonderkommando* itself.[16]

DR. FROESCHMANN: Did these regulations [concerning rehabilitation of convicts in the *Sonderkommando*], among other things, provide that these men had a chance after proving themselves to have their status and the right to bear arms restored to them?

Judgement at Nuremberg

BERGER: Yes.

DR. FROESCHMANN: And is it further true that from the day they went into action these men were regarded as being drafted by the so-called emergency service law?

BERGER: Yes.

DR. FROESCHMANN: Finally, is it true that the dependents of these men as a result received family allotments?

BERGER: Yes.

DR. FROESCHMANN: Is it further true that according to the implementation regulations, according to suitable service, the sentence was then quashed through the channels of the Reich Ministry of Justice?

BERGER: Yes. That was the essential point.

DR. FROESCHMANN: And which agency responsible for the quashing of such sentences?

BERGER: How far did your activity go and how far did your competencies go with regard to the Dirlewanger Brigade?

BERGER: Since personal connections and official connections are being mixed up at random here, I would like to explain this clearly. My competency with the exception of the question of rehabilitation, the quashing of the sentences, the allotments for families, stopped at the moment that the people entered the barracks and were enrolled and considered as having been called up in the normal manner as a result of the emergency service law.

DR. FROESCHMANN: Were the later recruits to this brigade also your affair?

BERGER: After this affair I didn't need to bother about recruits. That was a matter that ran all by itself as long as poachers existed.

There were numerous inconsistencies in Berger's testimony. Berger had been far more involved with Dirlewanger and the *Sonderkommando* than his testimony would indicate. As we have seen, in 1941 Berger recommended Dirlewanger for promotion. In early 1942 he helped disengage the *Sonderkommando* from Poland and helped reassign them to Russia. In 1943, Berger defended Dirlewanger's actions to *Reichskommissar* Kube. In mid-1944 Berger helped equip the *Sonderkommando* with 88mm guns. As for recruiting, Berger was decisively involved in procuring recruits for the Dirlewanger for the entire duration of the war – the "matter" simply did not run by itself. Gottlob Berger had been linked with Oskar Dirlewanger for almost thirty years, and with the *Sonderkommando* since its inception. He could not escape this link. The tribunal summed up the activities of the *Sonderkommando* in the judgment against Gottlob Berger in 1948. It read in part:[17]

> While in the field the unit [*Sonderkommando*] was not under his tactical direction, it was organized by him, trained by the man whom he selected, the idea was his, he kept it and its commander under his protection, he was repeatedly informed of its savage and uncivilized behavior, which he not only permitted to continue, but attempted to justify; he fought every effort to have it transferred or dispersed, recommended its commander for promotion and covered him with the mantle of his protection. That one of the purposes for which the brigade was organized was to commit crimes against hu-

manity, and that it did so to an extent which horrified and shocked even Nazi commissioners and Rosenberg's Ministry for the Eastern Territories, who can hardly be justly accused of leniency toward the Jews, and people of the eastern territories, is shown beyond a doubt. Berger's responsibility is quite as clear. He is guilty with respect to the matters charged against him regarding the actions of the Dirlewanger unit, and we so find.

Gottlob Berger was sentenced to twenty-five years which was subsequently reduced due in part, by testimony that he had helped allied prisoners of war. He died of natural causes – January 5, 1975 in Gerstetten.

The Trials of War Criminals before the International Military Tribunal, *United States of America vs. Otto Ohlendorf, et al.*, Case No. 9, was popularly called "The *Einsatzgruppen* Case." The proceedings lasted eight months, beginning on July 3, 1947 when indictments were filed against twenty-three defendants. The following statement written by *SS-Brigadeführer* Walter Stahlecker during the war illuminates the way in which the anti-partisan effort blended with the Final Solution:[18]

> The network of information, thus built up yielded much information for the *Einsatzgruppe A*, thus enabling them to surround more narrowly the quarters of the partisans. In particular, information was obtained concerning the villagers who had given food or provisional shelter to partisans. On the basis of these reports a great many villages were combed out. After a village had been surrounded, all the inhabitants were forcibly shepherded into one square. The persons suspected on account of confidential information and other villagers were interrogated, and thus it was possible in most cases to find the people who had helped the partisans. These were either shot off hand or if further interrogations promised useful information, taken to headquarters. After the interrogation they were shot. In order to obtain a deterring effect, the houses of those who helped

the partisans were burned down on several occasions. The population which had congregated was told of the reasons for the punitive measures. At the same time they were threatened that the whole village would be burned down if the partisans were helped once more and if partisans appearing in the village were not reported as quickly as possible. *The tactics, to put terror against terror, succeeded marvelously.*[19]

By their own words the *einsatzgruppen*, and those who helped them, passed into infamy.

ENDNOTES

[1] Smith, Bradley F. *Reaching Judgment at Nürnberg.* (New York: Basic Books, Inc., 1977), p.20.

[2] The author is currently working on another project, concerning concentration camp officers, to determine if such a differentiation between Waffen-SS and Allgemeine-SS was, in fact, a distinction without a difference.

[3] International Military Tribunal. *Nürnberg Trials of War Criminals before the International Military Tribunal, Volume XIII, The Ministries Case, Case No. 11.*, pp. 321-322. Gottlob Berger, during cross examination, maintained that the transcript of Himmler's speech was inaccurate. Prosecutors introduced forty-four records to confirm the validity of the speech to include a phonographic recording.

[4] International Military Tribunal Nürnberg. *Trial of the Major War Criminals before the International Military Tribunal.*, Volume IV, pp. 475-495.

[5] Ibid.

[6] German equivalent to "son of a bitch".

[7] Reitlinger. *The House Built on Sand.*, p.237.

[8] National Archives Record Group 238, NO 1908, Office of Chief Counsel for War Crimes, Sworn affidavit by SS-Hauptsturmführer Dr. Konrad Morgen, January 28, 1947.

[9] National Archives Record Group 238, NO 5741, Office of Chief Counsel for War Crimes, Career affidavit by SS-Hauptsturmführer Dr. Konrad Morgen, December 19, 1947.

[10] National Archives Record Group 238, M-1019/R80/1029, Office of Chief Counsel for War Crimes, Interrogation of SS-Obergruppenführer Karl Wolff, April 12, 1947.

[11] Schneider. *Their Honor was Loyalty!*, pp. 147-150.

[12] International Military Tribunal Nürnberg. *Trial of the Major War Criminals before the International Military Tribunal.*, Volume XX (30 July - 10 August 1946), p. 365.

[13] International Military Tribunal Nürnberg. *Trial of the Major War Criminals before the International Military Tribunal.*, Volume XX (30 July - 10 August 1946), pp. 382-383.

[14] Franz Magill

[15] International Military Tribunal Nürnberg. *Trials of War Criminals before the International Military Tribunal, Volume XIII, The Ministries Case*, Case No. 11., pp. 546-547.

[16] Ibid., pp. 535-536.

[17] Ibid., pp. 545-547.

[18] International Military Tribunal Nürnberg. *Trials of War Criminals before the International Military Tribunal, Volume IV, United States of America vs. Otto Ohlendorf, et al., Case No. 9.*, p.168.

[19] Emphasis added by author. Stahlecker was killed in 1942.

EPILOGUE

Stop! It upsets me to think about it.
- Heinrich Himmler, 1941[1]

After the war, reports were rampant that Oskar Dirlewanger had survived. Alan Clark maintained that Dirlewanger bribed his way past the Allied net after the war and further elaborated this story in 1965 in *Barbarossa: The Russian-German Conflict, 1941-45*:[2]

> Dirlewanger, probably the worst of the lot, was surrounded with the remnants of his brigade at Halbe in April 1945. In one of the most gruesome massacres of the Eastern campaign the whole unit and a large number of German civilians were put to the sword by the Russians. Dirlewanger is rumored to have escaped by hiding under a pile of bodies. He surfaced in Egypt in 1955, and currently lives in fine style in a villa in Cairo, although it is rumored that the Israelis periodically send him explosive packages.

There is no evidence that Dirlewanger returned to his unit after turning command over to *SS-Brigadeführer* Fritz Schmedes in February. It is far more likely that Dirlewanger remained in a convalescent hospital before wandering to Altshausen which remained under German control until mid-April when it was overrun by Allied forces.

The Cruel Hunters

In 1952 the German-language New York weekly *Aufbau* cited a Munich newspaper, *Echo der Woche*, as the source of a report that Dirlewanger was staying at the villa "Aida" in Heliopolis, Egypt as the guest of the Mufti of Jerusalem. According to the story, several other Nazi personalities were present including Adolf Eichmann![3]

In 1960 German officials, responding to the growing rumors that Dirlewanger was still alive and living in Egypt, contemplated exhuming the corpse at Altshausen. German newspapers began following the story in April 1960. The following is a newspaper article published on April 20, 1960, in the *Schwarzwälder Bote*.[4]

"Geheimnis um ein Soldatengrab"
Secret Surrounding a Soldier's Grave

Who was buried in Altshausen in 1945 instead of Colonel Dirlewanger?

Altshausen (District Saulgau). In the cemetery of Altshausen over a grave which is hardly taken care of, there stands a grayish wooden cross; fifteen years' time has wiped out the name and dates on it. A mistletoe bush spreads its branches over it, and a caring hand has planted a few pansies on the hill. The old grave digger maintains he knows what he is talking about: under exclusion of the public and being guarded by two French soldiers, SS-Colonel Dr. Oskar Dirlewanger was buried by him there in June of 1945. Even though he never saw the corpse in the coffin, he believes that the colonel of Penal Battalion 999 found his last resting place here. He was taken prisoner in Altshausen. The death certificate at the town hall certifies that the officer who came from Würzburg and who was born in 1895 died a natural death. At the occasion of the Nürnberg Trials during which charges against Dirlewanger were to be made, the French made it public that the SS-Colonel had died and was buried in Altshausen.

But now news came that Dirlewanger is still living today, was in Württemberg in 1956 and 1957 where he was photographed, and that he was carrying a Syrian passport. It is being assumed that the colonel at that time, after having been taken prisoner by the French, was pushed aside and worked in their services. At this time, Dirlewanger is supposed to be living in Cairo.

This is how the grave site at the Altshauser cemetery suddenly became the vocal point of many questions. Who was put to rest there if Dirlewanger is still alive? During those tumultuous days at the collapse, the son of a elevated employee of the Herzog-Haus of Württemberg vanished from the castle of Altshausen. From there he had gone to a close-by farm and never returned from this excursion. Never again there was a trace of this Dr. Schickhardt. Despite all the research, he remained missing. As it is now assumed by important factions, instead of SS-Colonel Dirlewanger, this Dr. Schickhardt was buried, without the secret surrounding him to have been lifted.

We have heard that in the near future an exhumation is to take place in order to find the truth about the rumors which are now in circulation.

The public clamor continued. Officials exhumed the corpse in mid-November. The regional newspaper *Schwäbische Zeitung* reported the event on November 19.[5]

"In aller Stille exhumiert"
Quietly Exhumed.

Federal judges pursue the rumors surrounding
SS-Colonel Dirlewanger
By a member of our editorial staff

M.S. Altshausen, District Saulgau. Very quietly at the cemetery of Altshausen, a coffin was exhumed last Saturday which had been buried there just as quietly fifteen and a half years ago. If possible, the exhumation is supposed to clear up whether it was the notorious *SS-Strafbrigadeführer* Dr. Oskar Dirlewanger who was buried there, and whose death and funeral on June 7 and 8, 1945 was registered in the death reports of the municipal administration and the parish office.

If the legal/medical examination of the remains as ordered by the Upper State Administration in Ravensburg leads to the conviction that the dead man was not the SS-Colonel, then the rumors which have not been silenced in years could surface again according to which Dr. Oskar Dirlewanger has been sighted several times and was in good health.

The exhumation which took place in strict silence to which all participants were sworn does come as a surprise because the pertinent places at the State courts declared just half a year ago, on April 21st, after having been questioned about it, that there should be put no importance to the rumors and it was not at all possible to order an exhumation. Therefore, one should be curious as to which circumstances prompted the State courts to change their minds. It is not the least to be discounted that the research surrounding the case of Dirlewanger were prompted by remarks which are connected with the *SS-Obersturmbannführer* Adolf Eichmann who is imprisoned in Israel.

As we have further learned, at the exhumation in Altshausen, representatives of the State courts and legal/medical experts from Freiburg were present. Two inmates of the near-by district penitentiary helped the grave digger do his job. This same grave digger buried this coffin in June of 1945 under French guard. The local priest was then told by the French town com-

Epilogue

mander that the dead man was Dirlewanger who supposedly died "a natural death" while under French arrest.

It is a fact that this was one of the approximately ten to twelve German inmates who had been shot or beaten to death by the French guards. Only after the rumors surfaced again and again that Dirlewanger was sighted in Egypt, Syria or even in Württemberg, people in Altshausen remember that the coffin of Dirlewanger was not to be opened by order of the French authorities. This order, however, could be connected with the fact that the French did not want the Germans to see what they had done to the victim. The version which was spread here and there that a load of bricks were buried instead of Dirlewanger has been countered by the exhumation this past Saturday.

When the grave was opened, a relatively well preserved coffin was found in which there was a skeleton. A first examination pointed to the stature of the deceased: he must have been of considerable height because the corpse was obviously forced into the coffin.

Pieces of cloth or similar objects were no longer to be found. Therefore, the closer examination in Freiburg had to rely on checking of the teeth and possible damage to the bones which could be compared to Dirlewanger's war wounds. In any case, the legal medical examiners will also consider the possibility whether the remains are those of administrator Dr. S. from Rottweiler who at that time had been taken prisoner by the French and who since then had vanished without leaving any trace.

German officials announced the results of their forensic examination in early December. Again the *Schwarzwälder Bote* (Black Forest Messenger) carried the news:[6]

"Dirlewanger ist tot"
Dirlewanger is dead
Skeleton was identified, leaving no doubt.

RAVENSBURG. As the State legal authorities at the Judicial Court of Ravensburg report, the director of the Institute for Judicial Medicine in Freiburg, Professor Dr. Weyrich, has come to the conclusion in his report that the corpse which had been exhumed in Altshausen is identical with Dr. Oskar Dirlewanger. The certification refers to general identical facts as far as height of the corpse is concerned and especially the eleven wounds which Dirlewanger suffered during World War I and later. Among them were four wounds to bones which could all be identified, without any doubt, through structure and changes of the bones of the skeleton.

The grave of Oskar Dirlewanger no longer exists at the Altshausen cemetery. According to information from the warden of the cemetery, the remains of Oskar Dirlewanger were not returned to Altshausen after the examination in Freiburg. It is unknown what happened to them.[7] And, despite the apparent thoroughness of the investigation, rumors of Dirlewanger's survival continued.

Michael Bar-Zohar in his 1967 book *The Avengers* disagreed with the findings of the exhumation. He asserted that the body found in the coffin was not that of Dirlewanger, but rather the corpse of a young man who had eleven bullet wounds. Bar-Zohar went on to assert that a well-informed source stated that Dirlewanger joined the French Foreign Legion after the war. Shortly thereafter, Dirlewanger's unit departed France to sail to Indochina. During the voyage, Dirlewanger and five German comrades, including a man named Eichenberger (Eichelberger), dove overboard as the ship passed through the Suez Canal. On reaching friendly soil, Dirlewanger then became a technical advisor to the Egyptian Army and changed his name to Hassan Souleiman.[8]

Epilogue

In 1981 Glenn B. Infield wrote in *Skorzeny: Hitler's Commando* this account of Dirlewanger in Egypt in 1951:[9]

> Skorzeny felt at ease among Egyptian officials with this attitude. His first task was to organize a staff of former SS and Wehrmacht officers to train the Egyptian army and security forces. He selected carefully, making certain that each officer he brought to Egypt was a diehard Nazi, an expert military tactician, and was anti-Semitic. Among those recruited by Skorzeny were SS General Oskar Dirlewanger, who had commanded a brigade composed of poachers, criminals and men under the sentence of a court-martial during the Warsaw ghetto uprising and whose actions against the Jews had earned him the nickname "Butcher of Warsaw"...

Infield interviewed Skorzeny in preparation for writing the book; we do not know if Skorzeny was telling the truth or what motivated him to fabricate the story. We do know that Dirlewanger was not present during the Jewish Warsaw Ghetto Uprising in 1943, nor was the *Sonderkommando*. Dirlewanger certainly was a butcher in Warsaw in 1944, but his activities there are more accurately characterized as being against the Polish people as a whole, rather than Jews in particular. We also know that Dirlewanger was never promoted to the general officer ranks – his last promotion being to *SS-Oberführer*, or senior colonel.

Even such a distinguished scholar as Raul Hilberg promulgated the legend of Dirlewanger surviving the war. In his *The Destruction of the European Jews (Revised and definitive edition)*, published in 1985 – which is widely considered to be the definitive work on the Holocaust, he mentioned that Dirlewanger was reported in Cairo in 1952. Hilberg at that time probably left the fate of Dirlewanger in doubt so as to not discourage future investigations into his demise – on the off chance that Dirlewanger did not die at Altshausen. A few years ago, Dr. Hilberg came to the conclusion that Dirlewanger most probably died in French captivity, and stated this opinion in a letter to the author in 1996.[10]

Stories of Dirlewanger's survival continued into the late 1980s. In 1987, J. Lee Ready in *The Forgotten Axis: Germany's Partners and Foreign Volunteers in World War II* reported that Dirlewanger went into hiding at the end of the war, and later retired in safety to Egypt.[11]

We are also left with Berger's testimony at Nürnberg. When he stated "...if he were a regular fellow, then he would have reported now and would not fight in a western army as a highly respected officer. It would have been easy for him to get here under the protection of his uniform" to what was Berger referring? It is a bold statement, one which could be verified by allied intelligence agencies, but was not subsequently addressed by the prosecution. The various Nürnberg trials took place from 1945 and 1948, well before reports of Dirlewanger in the Middle East. It simply does not seem possible that, even had Dirlewanger survived the war, he could have been employed in this manner. He would not have had anything to offer the allies – no in-place espionage net as Reinhard Gehlen possessed.

Aaron Breitbart, a senior research associate at the Simon Wiesenthal Center, believes Dirlewanger perished at Altshausen. In an April 30, 1996 letter to the author he stated:[12]

> We are aware of those who disagree with the identification of the remains uncovered in 1960 as those of Dirlewanger, but in the absence of reasonable evidence to the contrary, [we] are of the opinion that the identification was probably correct.

Rudolf Multer of Altshausen remains, to me, the most knowledgeable source on Dirlewanger's death. In addition to researching the actual site of Dirlewanger's death – the "Hopfendarre" – hop drying house, he has examined all other details. In a letter to the author Rudolf Multer, who lived in the area during these turbulent times, stated that many of Altshausen's citizens were happy and relieved when German authorities kept Dirlewanger's remains in Freiburg. His research into the documents listing Dirlewanger's death reveal that the SS officer probably died at 7:30 PM on June 7, 1945.[13]

Epilogue

An eyewitness account supports this theory. In 1958, former Luftwaffe lieutenant, Anton Füssinger, gave the following report to the criminal police in the city of Ravensburg:[14]

> While being in the local prison of Altshausen, I was with two other prisoners in the same cell from June 1 to June 5, 1945. We introduced ourselves by giving our family names. One of the two introduced himself as Gustl Minch from Oberndorf, the other one as Dirlewanger without any additional comment. However, when on the second day he was addressed by a Polish concentration camp inmate who was among the guards with "Colonel," I asked him what that meant. In reply to that he told me that this means "*Oberst.*" Later, after we had been together for a while longer, he told me in reply to further questions that he was a member of the Waffen-SS. To the accusation by concentration camp inmates that he was commander of a concentration camp because his name was written on a tablet at the entrance to the concentration camp, he declared in our presence that he was not commander of a concentration camp, but merely temporarily with his battalion there for guard duty. [This possibly refers to the time in Lublin, 1940-41.]
>
> I am unable to make definite statements regarding the guards. When I was handed in for arrest in the local prison on June 1, 1945, a French soldier with a red cap stood at the door as a guard. During the five days during which I was imprisoned, I was not allowed to leave it. However, during the arrest I have seen no Frenchmen, only armed and uniformed Poles. During the following days, none of us in the cell was beaten during the day with one exception. On the second day during which I was with Minch in the same cell, a Jewish boy of about 16 years who lived in Ebersbach, District Saulgau, and, while guarded by the Poles, he was al-

lowed to hit us three prisoners in the face until he had enough or was unable to hit us any longer. This he did, and all three of us ended up with highly swollen faces. I myself was only hit once by the Poles with a wooden piece; this was on the same day because I refused to repeat three times that I was a German pig. On the other side, Dirlewanger and Minch were taken out of the cell during that night and I assume they were beaten by the Poles in the hallway. I have heard the beatings and the terrible cries of the beaten men. During daylight I could then see that Minch and Dirlewanger had open and bleeding wounds in the face and in addition, they were covered with bleeding stripes over the whole body.

During the night of June 4th to June 5, 1945, Dirlewanger and Minch were taken out of the cell separately three times and beaten in the same manner in the hallway. After the two returned to the cell after the third time, they were in no position to say anything or to get up because of the injuries sustained. A short time later, the guards came again to the cell and demanded again that they come along. The guards beat both with the rifle butt in the heads so that both ended up with deep bleeding wounds. After that, both were kicked with in the lower bodies and in my opinion, Minch suffered some broken ribs. After this all happened, the guards left both unconscious lying in the cell. During all that time, I sat in a corner and did not dare to move because I was afraid that I would also be beaten in the same manner. It is my opinion that both must have died as a consequence of the injuries suffered during these beatings. However, I did miss to ascertain whether they were really dead. Approximately 30 minutes later, Minch was pulled along the floor out of the cell by a guard, I don't know where to. From that time on, I did not see Minch anymore. Dirlewanger remained in the cell. However, he did not move nor say anything. In the morning of

Epilogue

June 5th at about 8:30 AM I was taken out of the cell and released. During the time we were under local arrest, we got warm food only once. The food was brought to us in a big pail by a French soldier and we had to eat from the pail without a spoon.

I am surprised that according to the death reports by the French Command, Dirlewanger was only to have died on June 7, 1945 and Minch only on June 8, 1945. It is known to be incorrect when it is stated as reasons for their death in the reports that they died a natural death. I can make the statement anytime in the courts under oath that Minch as well as Dirlewanger must have died due to the injuries which they have suffered during the beatings by the Polish guards.

Dirlewanger told me that while driving through Altshausen, he was recognized by a Jew who had been a concentration camp inmate and that he was arrested because of it. We then exchanged our home addresses with the expressed promise that none of us would divulge it during interrogations. We did this at the request of Dirlewanger because he said he did not believe that we would escape this arrest alive.

I believe that Dirlewanger did die in June 1945 in Altshausen. How he got there is somewhat of a mystery. It is possible that he was flown out of Berlin in the final days of the war; but it is more likely that he returned to the Stuttgart area by more conventional transportation to continue his recovery from the wounds he received in February and prepare for his further escape. Then, with the allies advancing in the spring of 1945, he may well have gone to Altshausen in an attempt to blend in to avoid postwar prosecution – perhaps to be close to the Swiss border in case he needed sanctuary – or conceivably Dirlewanger believed in the myth of the German Redoubt in the Alps, where Nazis would fight to the bitter end. The French probably did murder him and have successfully covered up the facts of the incident; it could have been an interrogation that went too far or possibly Polish nationals, working for the French, could have spotted their old nemesis and meted out justice.

The best evidence that Dirlewanger did not survive is that his flawed character traits could not have remained dormant. If Dirlewanger had not been killed at Altshausen in 1945, but had escaped to Egypt, Syria or even remained in Germany, he would, in my opinion, have returned to the perverse conduct he demonstrated in the 1930s and the war years. While his behavior could be shielded by Nazi authorities such as Gottlob Berger and Erich von dem Bach-Zelewski, such conduct in the post-war environment would have ultimately led the authorities to him with resultant publicity and judicial action. Police authorities may be convinced to look the other way with regard to political extremists, but they are never deterred when the innocent youth of an area are being preyed upon. Dirlewanger was a serial sex pervert and murderer. Only death would have stopped his predations.

Nevertheless, I am convinced many of the other soldiers in the *Sonderkommando* survived. Several of the officers who were assigned to the unit from Berlin, returned to the German capital during the war – before the desperate fighting at the end of the war. Since there was not a concerted effort to find these individuals for judicial proceedings after the war, it is probable that many blended back into civilian life. A former Waffen-SS soldier, a tank commander and winner of the Knight's Cross, had this to say in a letter to the author in 1996 about the *Sonderkommando*:[15]

> Now I would like to answer your question regarding Dirlewanger. All soldiers, even those in the Waffen-SS, distanced themselves already during the war from the Dirlewanger Brigade. This brigade consisted only of sentenced members of the Wehrmacht and the Waffen-SS and they were used in fighting against the partisans. In those battles, under strict leadership, soldiers who had been sentenced could prove their worth! Since the missions against partisans were especially cruel and hard (just like we are seeing it today in the former Yugoslavia), as far as I know, no soldier was delighted to end up on those missions, because partisans had their own laws and neither honored the Geneva Convention nor the rules of war among cultured na-

Epilogue

> tions. Therefore, it will be impossible to find a soldier who belonged to the Dirlewanger Brigade or who was in combined battles with the brigade. During the long years of the war and in the 50 years afterwards, I have never had the chance to talk to a member of this Dirlewanger Brigade or even to have met one. In addition, these soldiers never mentioned that they had belonged to this unit because everybody knew that it was not a good reputation to have fought in this organization. I cannot give you more information personally or through another member of this group. If I should some time and some where meet a comrade who knows more about the Dirlewanger Brigade or who has obtained more information, I will let you know. I wish you good luck with this very difficult task because this subject was not and could not be researched and evaluated by a German soldier. When the subject is mentioned, there is a reluctance to even talk about it.

While it is clear this particular Waffen-SS veteran made no attempt to distance the *Sonderkommando* from the overall SS, some authors attempted to continue the myth that the *Sonderkommando* was not truly part of the Waffen-SS. Hellmuth Auerbach, writing in 1962, summarized the unit as follows:[16]

> While it is true that Dirlewanger and the SS men sent to his unit on probation were members of the Waffen-SS and the unit was carried as a field formation on a Waffen-SS list of 30 June 1944 prepared by the Statistical Science Institute of the *Reichsführer-SS*, it nevertheless was not considered a full-fledged formation of the Waffen-SS because its members (with the exception of those who came from the Wehrmacht) were, so to speak, only second-class SS members just like the Latvian, Croatian and similar non-German "*Waffen-Grenadier-Divisionen der SS.*"

The Cruel Hunters

Auerbach's argument about "second class citizens" and the "non-German" SS divisions is specious. Many of the "non-German" SS divisions had numerous recipients of the Knight's Cross, Germany's premier award for bravery and military achievement. The recipients of the award were not considered "second-class." The 5th SS Panzer Division "*Wiking*", which had many Scandinavians in the ranks, had fifty-four winners of this award – second highest of all SS divisions! The 11th SS Volunteer Panzer Grenadier Division "*Nordland*", another foreign volunteer division, had thirty recipients. The 19th SS Grenadier Division, composed mainly of Latvians, had eleven winners of this award. The 23rd SS Volunteer Panzer Grenadier Division "*Nederland*", consisting of many Dutch volunteers, had twenty winners of the award. By way of comparison, the German army's veteran 3rd Panzer Division had seventeen winners of the Knight's Cross as did the 96th Infantry Division. The prestigious 1st Mountain Division had twenty-nine awardees while the 5th Jäger Division – a unit constantly in the fray, had thirty-four. The 110th Infantry Division had ten winners while the 125th Infantry Division had six. This award was not given lightly – for most recipients it represented soldierly honor and achievement. So much for the supposed poor reputation of the fighting capabilities of non-German soldiers – they often displayed great bravery.

Other publications have made even more debatable claims. Richard Landwehr's historical newsletter, *Siegrunen: The Waffen-SS in Historical Perspective*, states that the *Sonderkommando* "may well have been the best anti-partisan troop to ever fight in any war at any time." [17] Perhaps it was the most vicious but, considering that Soviet partisans continued to operate in White Russia throughout the German occupation, it was certainly not the best or most efficient.

What is not debatable is the horrific conduct of the Dirlewanger unit during the entire war. Conceived by an idea that the German race was born to subjugate inferior people in the east, manned by many individuals from the lowest criminal strata of society and led by a perverted officer, it went on an unparalleled rampage of destruction for over two years in the woods and swamps of central Russia. Fighting in a bitter anti-partisan struggle – where no quarter was given on either side, the *Sonderkommando* also participated in Hitler's war against the Jews by

Epilogue

aiding and abetting Himmler's *einsatzgruppen*. It is little wonder that many German veterans of the war – who conducted themselves with honor – continue to avoid the subject of Dirlewanger and the activities of his unit.

Many other nations avoided the subject of Dirlewanger, almost causing his history to be forgotten. The Americans and British had no real motive to pursue Dirlewanger – he served exclusively on the eastern front. The French had no desire to resurrect Dirlewanger's memory – they probably had murdered him in 1945. The Russians made no intense effort to search for survivors of the *Sonderkommando* – as the Red Army believed it had killed most of them south of Berlin in 1945. Even Israel had bigger targets to hunt – and perhaps did not realize the direct role the *Sonderkommando* had in anti-Jewish operations due to the nature of Dirlewanger's operational reports. But whether the words were "cleansed", "special action", "special handling", "evacuated" or "processed", the result was the slaughter of thousands of innocent men, women and children.

And so Dirlewanger and his *Sonderkommando* passed into the dark corner of history. Medieval in their outlook on war and certainly not indicative of many German military formations in their lack of chivalry, they none-the-less remain a reflection of a segment of mankind gone mad in the inferno of World War II on the eastern front. May we not see the likes of these cruel hunters again.

ENDNOTES

[1] Padfield. *Himmler: Reichsführer-SS.*, p. 352.
[2] Clark. *Barbarossa: The Russian-German Conflict, 1941-45.*, p. 460.
[3] Letter to the author from Raul Hilberg, June 2, 1996.
[4] "Geheimnis um ein Soldatengrab", *Schwarzwälder Bote*, April 20, 1960.
[5] "In aller Stille exhumiert", *Schwäbische Zeitung*, No 267, November 19, 1960.
[6] "Dirlewanger ist tot", *Schwarzwälder Bote*, December 2, 1960. I have attempted to research Professor Dr. Weyrich to determine his background. While there is no reason to believe that the forensic investigation was not properly conducted, I was interested to see if Dr. Weyrich had been in the SS during the war. A review of the SS officer personnel files at the National Archives reveal that two Dr. Weyrichs served in the SS officer ranks. Dr. Karl Weyrich, born March 17, 1898 in Zweibrücken, had SS number 116,222 and a Nazi Party number of 3,277,155. He entered the SS September 15, 1933 and was an SS-Untersturmführer. Dr. Günter Weyrich, born July 6, 1898 in Ried, had SS number 304,524 and Nazi Party number 6,351,864. He entered the SS on March 1, 1938 and held the rank of SS-Obersturmführer. I do not know if the Dr. Weyrich at Freiburg was one of these two men. The odds are, he was not. But if he had been in the SS, the results of the exhumation should be called into question. Source of information on Drs. Weyrich: Personalakt Günter Weyrich, Washington, D.C: National Archives Microfilm Publication A3343, Records of SS Offic-

The Cruel Hunters

ers from the Berlin Document Center, Roll SSO-240B and Personalakt Karl Weyrich, Washington, D.C: National Archives Microfilm Publication A3343, Records of SS Officers from the Berlin Document Center, Roll SSO-240B.

[7] Letter to the author, February 1996 from Dieter Heske, Hauptamtsleiter der Gemeinde Altshausen.

[8] Bar-Zohar, Michael. *The Avengers*. Translated from the French by Len Ortzen. (New York: Hawthorn Books INC., 1967), pp. 145-146. Bar-Zohar did not footnote his work, so we are unable to review the validity of his sources.

[9] Infield, Glenn B. *Skorzeny: Hitler's Commando*, (New York: St. Martin's Press, 1981), p. 207.

[10] Letter to the author from Raul Hilberg, June 2, 1996.

[11] Ready. *The Forgotten Axis.*, p.496.

[12] Letter to author April 30, 1996 from the Simon Wiesenthal Center.

[13] Letter to the author from Rudolf Multer, May 24, 1996.

[14] Michaelis, Rolf. *Der Weg zur 36. Waffen-Grenadier-Division der SS*. (Rodgau, FRG: Verlag für Militärhistorische Zeitgeschichte, 1991), pp.14-16.

[15] Letter to the author, January 1996 from a former member of the SS and Knight's Cross winner, whom the author has known for about a decade.

[16] Stein. *The Waffen-SS: Hitler's Elite Guard at War.*, p. 270.

[17] Landwehr. *Siegrunen.*, Volume 57 (Fall 1994), p.29.

APPENDICES

APPENDIX 1
SS RANKS

SS-Reichsführer (Reichsführer-SS)	Reichs Leader
SS-Oberstgruppenführer	General
SS-Obergruppenführer	Lieutenant General
SS-Gruppenführer	Major General
SS-Brigadeführer	Brigadier General
SS-Oberführer	Senior Colonel
SS-Standartenführer	Colonel
SS-Obersturmbannführer	Lieutenant Colonel
SS-Sturmbannführer	Major
SS-Hauptsturmführer	Captain
SS-Obersturmführer	First Lieutenant
SS-Untersturmführer	Second Lieutenant
SS-Sturmscharführer	Sergeant Major
SS-Hauptscharführer	Master Sergeant
SS-Oberscharführer	Sergeant First Class
SS-Scharführer	Staff Sergeant
SS-Unterscharführer	Sergeant
SS-Rottenführer	Corporal
SS-Sturmmann	Acting Corporal
SS-Oberschütze	Private First Class
SS-Schütze	Private

Appendices

APPENDIX 2
SONDERKOMMANDO OFFICERS

The following is a partial list of known SS officers who served in the *Sonderkommado* during the war. All officers listed have annotations listed in their personnel file confirming they were in the unit. The list is not complete, and does not include Ukrainian and Russian officers.

SS-Untersturmführer Heinrich Amann
SS-Untersturmführer Antonius Ammerlaan
SS-Hauptsturmführer Werner Blessau
SS-Hauptsturmführer Waldemar Bodammer
SS-Obersturmführer Erich Brandt
SS-Standartenführer Erich Buchmann*
SS-Hauptsturmführer Hans Bünger
SS-Oberführer Oskar Dirlewanger†
SS-Untersturmführer Dr. Heinz Dransfeld
SS-Haupsturmführer Ewald Ehlers†
SS-Hauptsturmführer Josef Falter
SS-Obersturmführer Otto Gast
SS-Hauptsturmführer Kurt Gramatke
SS-Hauptsturmführer Josef Grohmann
SS-Sturmbannführer Ernst Heidelberg
SS-Obersturmführer Egyd Ingruber
SS-Hauptsturmführer Josef Karnop
SS-Obersturmführer Theodor Krätzer
SS-Untersturmführer Helmut Lewandowski
SS-Obersturmbannführer Franz Magill
SS-Hauptsturmführer Ludwig Mann
SS-Obersturmführer Franz de Martin††
SS-Obersturmbannführer Andreas Mayer-Mader†
SS-Obersturmführer Fritz Missmahl
SS-Hauptsturmführer Wolfgang Plaul
SS-Untersturmführer Siegfried Polack†
SS-Sturmbannführer Karl Praefke
SS-Hauptsturmführer Wilhelm Reiner

SS-Obersturmführer Hans Schäftlmeier
SS-Brigadeführer Fritz Schmedes*
SS-Hauptsturmführer Will Schneier
SS-Hauptsturmführer Hans Schreier
SS-Untersturmführer Max Schreiner†
SS-Hauptsturmführer Jan Schreuder
SS-Untersturmführer Karl Staib
SS-Hauptsturmführer Rudolf Stöweno†
SS-Obersturmführer Adalbert Trattenschegg†
SS-Obersturmführer Dr. Friedrich Turek
SS-Untersturmführer Fritz Wagner
SS-Obersturmführer Othmar Walchensteiner†
SS-Sturmbannführer Erwin Walser*
SS-Obersturmführer Hans Georg Weber
SS-Untersturmführer Heinrich Wehninck
SS-Sturmbannführer Kurt Weisse*
SS-Untersturmführer Georg Wild
SS-Obersturmführer Waldemar Wilhelm
SS-Hauptsturmführer Bruno Wille
SS-Untersturmführer August Zeller†
SS-Untersturmführer Paul Zimmermann

* Killed during or shortly after the war
† Definitely survived the war
†† Assigned to *Sonderkommando* but may not have reported to unit

Appendices

APPENDIX 3
SONDERKOMMANDO ENLISTED PERSONNEL

The following is a partial list of known SS and other service personnel who served in the *Sonderkommado* during the war. It is not complete, and does not include Ukrainian and Russian personnel.

Ackermann, Alfred	Bax, Erich	Böll, Richard
Adami, Willi	Bayer, Ludwig	Böning, Willy
Afmann, Walter	Becker, Hans	Bork, Wilhelm
Ahrens, Friedrich	Behnke, Bernhard	Bormann, Walter
Albrecht, Josef	Behr, Wilhelm	Bornhold, Otto
Anderegg, Karl	Behrendt, Erich	Böttcher, Otto
Anderer, Alfons	Behrens, Johann	Braasel, Walter
Anderl, Josef	Behrens, Willy	Bracht, Willi
Andree, Adolf	Beier, Hermann	Brauer, Heinz
Appold, Waldemar	Beling, Otto	Brehm, Fritz
Arndt, Heinrich	Belitz, Heinrich	Brehm, Harry
Arning, Hans	Beller, Eugen	Breiler, Willy
Asbach, Walter	Bender, Herbert	Brencher, Wilhelm
Aschauer, Karl	Beniger, Ludwig	Bretschneider, Horst
Asum, Anton	Benkert, Karl	Breuer, Jacob
Augert, Franz	Berghoff, Kurt	Brey, Jakob
Augustin, Walter	Berke, Otto	Brune, Otto
Aumaier, Wolfgang	Berner, Emil	Brusberg, Gustav
Axthelm, Artur	Bernhardt, Ewald	Buckwitz, Willy
Backer, Bernhard	Bertheld, Willy	Budnewski, Max
Baderschneider, Karl	Beschem, Andreas	Budnick, Walter
Bahn, Otto	Beutler, Reinhold	Bujara, Ewald
Balke, Fritz	Beyer, Julius	Bungert, Arthur
Bandendiek, Karl-Erich	Beyer, Walter	Bunn, Friedrich
Barainsky, Josef	Binzer, Georg	Bürner, Wilhelm
Barsch, Rudolf	Bischoff, Franz	Busch, Josef
Bartels, Theodor	Bissey, Eduard	Busch, Walter
Barth, Karl	Bitsch, Oskar	Büsching, Ernst
Barth, Paul	Blau, Willi	Busse, Karl
Barthelmess, Georg	Böck, Adolf	Buttjereit, Otto
Barz, David	Boczki, Edgar	Buttmeister, Stefan
Bauch, Karl	Böhm, Gustav	Büttner, Rudolf
Bauer, Hans	Böhme, Friedrich	Christ, Andreas
Bauholzer, Josef	Böhnisch, Gerhard	Chwalczyk, Josef
Baumhöfer, Walter	Bölke, Walter	Chwalinski, Albert

The Cruel Hunters

Cichon, Georg	Eichhorn, Walter	Fries, Hermann
Ciesewski, Alfred	Eickhoff, Hugo	Fritsch, Hans
Credner, Ernst	Eiding, Eduard	Fuchs, Hans-Martin
Credner, Günther	Eisert, Gerhard	Fuchs, Josef
Cwiklak, Martin	Elias, Adolf	Fuchs, Martin
Czeczor, Erich	Engelage, Fritz	Funke, Erich
Danderke, Otto	Engelhard, Karl	Gabriel, Max
Dankl, Hans	Engelhardt, Willi	Gabriel, Rudolf
Decker, Josef	Engelmann, Otto	Gaede, Hans
Demand, Josef	Engels, Heinrich	Gaertner, Peter
Dett, Jakob	Enzinger, Franz	Galle, Willi
Didszuleid, Walter	Ernst, Franz	Gamsjaeger, Johann
Diegsa, Erich	Ernst, Richard	Garmasch, Michael
Dietrich, Kurt	Erretkamps, Peter	Geest, Otto
Dietrich, Paul	Escher, Dr. Walter	Gehring, Gottlieb
Dinkgräfe, Johann	Esser, Peter	Gehrke, Gustav
Dittmer, Fritz	Ewald, Nikolaus	Geisler, Karl
Dobrak, Erich	Fänger, Willi	Gelbrich, Kurt
Dohrand, Heinrich	Faistauer, Josef	Gerards, Heinrich
Doll-Wimmer, Josef	Faust, Rudolf	Gersbach, Karl
Dorfer, Ferdinand	Feierfeil, Andres	Geschler, Engelbert
Döring, Johann	Feiertag, Heinz +	Giesel, Hermann
Doering, Richard	Fentzahn, Walter	Glauber, Mathias
Drimmer, Herbert	Feuchter, Kurt	Glomb, Willi
Drzymala, Claus	Fey, Heinrich	Glück, Richard
Dühler, Karl	Finking, Kurt	Göhmann, Robert
Dumke, Erich	Finnis, Josef	Golenia, Willy
Dunkel, Alfred	Fischer, Walter	Gorn, Erwin
Dzietko, Wilhelm	Flesch, Karl	Gosch, Hans
Dzunbowski, Willi	Fliege, Karl	Goschler, Engelbert
Ebel, Fritz	Fliessenschuh, Karl	Gossens, Peter
Eberhardt, Walter	Flohr, Heinrich	Grabenhofer, Josef
Ebert, Gerhard	Flossk, Heinz	Grabs, Otto
Ebert, Robert	Föger, Rudolf	Graf, Georg
Echner, Karl	Förderer, Rene	Gräf, Alfred
Eckert, Max	Förster, Fritz	Gräfe, Max
Eckner, Heinrich	Förster, Wilhelm	Grams, Josef
Eder, Franz	Förstner, Bruno	Gräser, Walter
Edler, Georg	Franke, Rudolf	Griebel, Georg
Egger, Oswald	Frankl, Max	Griegusch, Willi
Eich, Heinrich	Friedrich, Gustav	Gröbner, Georg
Eichenauer, August	Friedrich, Paul	Gröck, Richard

Appendices

Grönwald, Wilhelm
Gründner, Rudolf
Grunert, Willi
Grünwald, Franz
Grzella, Albert
Gschwind, Adolf
Günther, Ernst
Günther, Willy
Gumpert, Gerhard
Gustav, Otto
Güthing, Arno
Güthner, Josef
Gutknecht, Johann
Gutmann, Franz
Guttke, Oskar
Haberer, Josef
Haberland, Kurt
Hagen, Heinrich
Hagen, Helmut
Hahn, Karl
Hahn, Otto
Hähnle, Erich
Haibl, Georg
Hanika, Franz
Hanke, Walter
Hansen, Eugen
Hartl, Alois
Hartl, Michael
Hartwig, Heinz
Hase, Johann
Hasselfeldt, Martin
Hau, Ernst
Haupt, Karl
Hausser, Albert
Heff, Otto
Heger, Georg
Heimig, Willi
Heimsch, Arthur
Heine, Karl
Hellcamp, Gerhard
Henneberg, Fritz
Henning, Rudi

Henschtschel, Fritz
Henze, Gerhard
Herkt, Otto
Herrle, Johan
Herweler, Peter
Herze, Walter
Herzog, Fritz
Hesener, Alfons
Hessler, Leopold
Heuschneider, Leopold
Heyer, Heinrich
Heyke, Alexander
Himmelbauer, Karl
Hinckel, Oskar
Hobelsberger, Franz
Hoch, Friedrich
Hochwartner, Josef
Höfer, Georg
Hoffmann, Friedrich
Hoffmann, Helmut
Höltke, Walter
Holzwart, Adolf
Homberg, Julius
Homes, Rudolf
Hommel, Alfred
Höpfner, Gerhard
Hora, Gustav
Hörath, Karl
Hornig, Erich
Huber, Alois
Hübner, Josef
Hunger, Fritz
Hunke, Franz
Huppertz, Hubert
Iber, Vincenz
Illibauer, Rudolf
Illing, Paul
Iskam, Robert
Iwik, Hermann
Jäger, Florian
Jäger, Heinrich
Jakowski, Gustav

Jankowski, Franz
Janusch, Kurt
Janzinski, Albert
Jochheim, Karl
Jokiel, Erhard
Jokiel, Ewald
Jülich, Anton
Jung, Carl
Junghenn, Karl
Kälber, Friedrich
Kahlisch, Willy
Kalbe, Theodor
Kalix, Herbert
Kaminski, Gustav
Karalus, Gerhard
Karl, Heinz
Kaschner, Hugo
Kathrein, Alois
Keck, Willi
Kehl, Heinrich
Kehr, Karl
Kellkamp, Johannes
Kellner, Herbert
Kerstan, Heinrich
Keusch, Gerhard
Kirsch, Max
Kirstein, Anton
Kitzmann, Georg
Klak, Ladislaus
Klapproth, Herrmann
Klaus, Willi
Klees, Hans
Klein, Nikolaus
Klekamp, Johannes
Klem, Josef
Kley, Max
Klingenberg, Hermann
Knes, Paul
Knöpfel, Emil
Koas, Otto
Koch, Erich
Koch, Franz

Ködel, Erich
Kohl, Heinrich
Köhler, August
Kohle, Otto
Kolesnik, Wladimir
Koller, Franz
Komerewski, Leo
König, Emil
König, Paul
Koos, Arthur
Korsch, Werner
Koschka, Franz
Koschmieder, Alfred
Kosowski, Herbert
Kostelnik, Bruno
Kowalick, Wilhelm
Kramer, Franz
Kramer, Paul
Krasshoff, Rudolf
Kraus, Alois
Kraus, Heinrich
Krause, Heinz
Krause, Erich
Krause, Siegfried
Krenz, Emil
Kretschmar, Paul
Krieb, Erwin
Kriegel, Heinz
Krieger, Waldemar
Krüger, Fritz
Kruk, Marion
Krümmel, Walter
Krumpholz, Werner
Kubinski, Franz
Küchler, Max
Küchler, Otto
Kugler, Walter
Kuhfehl, Albert
Kuhlmann, Heinrich
Kühn, Erich
Kuhnert, Martin
Kuhnert, Walter

Kunze, Paul
Kunzmann, Heinz
Kuschy, Heinrich
Kynast, Wilhelm
Laabs, Erich
Labermeier, Andreas
Labette, Gerhard
Labott, Gerhard
Lack, Hermann
Lalla, Paul
Lande, Otto
Lang, Erwin
Lange, Georg
Lange, Walter
Laprath, Georg
Latz, Artur
Lau, Paul
Laubach, Heinrich
Lauckner, Willy
Laue, Hermann
Lebin, Erich
Lechner, Alfons
Ledermann, Walter
Lehmann, Robert
Lehnhard, Gustav
Lehrmann, Ewald
Leibel, Erwin
Leidzak, Johann
Lempa, Viktor
Lessing, Peter
Leuendorf, Werner
Liebenberger, Josef
Liebig, Wilhelm
Liebkowski, Wilhelm
Liers, Rudolf
Litz, Reinhardt
Lodz, Michael
Löffler, Walter
Lorenz, Hermann
Lorenz, Otto
Löw, Rudolf
Lowitz, Rudolf

Ludwig, Eygolf
Lüders, Walter
Lühr, Hans
Lupitz, Otto
Mai, Mattias
Mammitsch, Alfred
Martin, Alexander
Martin, Hans
Märtin, Wilhelm
Masel, Alfred
Maske, Erich
Mathies, Georg
Matthes, Werner
Mattyseck, Georg
Mautsch, Franz
Mayer, Berthold
Medow, Herbert
Meier, Franz
Meier, Hans
Meier, Wilhelm
Meinert, Rudi
Mennel, Paul
Mensel, Herbert
Meyer, Bruno
Meyer, Friedrich
Meyer, Hans
Meyer, Herbert
Meyer, Kurt
Meyer, Willy
Miketta, Hans
Milau, Heinrich
Mildner, Heinrich
Mill, Ernst
Milow, August
Mitze, Fritz
Möhle, Heinrich
Moll, Theodor
Möller, Johannes
Möller, Karl
Möller, Paul
Mölzer, Alfred
Moritz, Alfons

Appendices

Moy, Maximilian
Mühlberg, Erich
Mühlmann, Otto
Müller, Albert
Müller, Friedrich
Müller, Gustl
Müller, Herbert
Müller, Johann
Müller, Karl
Müller, Kurt
Müller, Ludwig
Müller, Martin
Müller, Willi
Murgner, Ehrhardt
Musckogel, Christian
Muster, Herbert
Nageldorn, Johann
Nägele, Josef
Nagell, Harald
Nawrath, Victor
Nentwig, Helmut
Netterdon, Karl
Neubauer, Emil
Neumann, Erich
Neumann, Heinz
Neumann, Konstantin
Neuwerth, Franz
Nickel, Gustav
Nickel, Rudolf
Niemeyer, Richard
Nikolai, Hugo
Nolting, Helmut
Nuthmann, Max
Oberfeldner, Alois
Opalla, Paul
Ortelt, Albert
Osinski, Johan
Osnabrugge, Max
Ott, Leo
Otto, Friedrich
Otto, Herbert
Panten, Franz

Pantlen, Julius
Päper, Walter
Paul, Erich
Peters, Albert
Peters, Johann
Pfab, Hans
Pfaffenrodt, Helmuth
Pfeifer, Alfred
Pfeiffer, Walter
Pfisterer, Friedrich
Pflugbeil, Erwin
Philippin, Heinrich
Pichinger, Johann
Pieper, Willi
Pireck, Rudolf
Planitzer, Franz
Plate, Wilhelm
Plattner, Othmar
Plugbeil, Erwin
Pohl, Hans
Pohl, Willi
Pohland, Heinrich
Pohlmann, Otto
Pollmüler, Hermann
Poprawa, Kurt
Posselt, Ernst
Pototschnig, Johann
Pötzel, Hermann
Pranschke, Max
Prehm, Ernst
Prell, Eigen
Pres, Adam
Prosche, Helmut
Pucher, Franz
Purzer, Richard
Pütz, Heinrich
Pütz, Heinrich
Quetschke, Willi
Rahe, Ewald
Rainer, Friedrich
Raml, Fritz
Recknagel, Walter

Reel, Fritz
Reels, Karl
Rehbein, Gerhard
Reichel, Otto
Reineck, Hermann
Reinhard, Siegfried
Reinhardt, Adolf
Reinicke, Ernst
Reiss, Horst
Reiter, Erich
Reiter, Wilhelm
Rentmeister, Albert
Resch, Franz
Rett, Willi
Reuter, Adolf
Richter, Paul
Richter, Walter
Richter, Willi
Riedel, Herbert
Ring, Karl-Heinz
Rischow, Otto
Rizzi, Ernst
Rogalski, Hans
Röde, Karl
Röhe, Henri
Rölich, Klaus
Rose, Erich
Rosenberger, Ludwig
Rossa, Willi
Roth, Edwin
Ruch, Otto
Ruch, Wilhelm
Ruch, Willi
Rüdiger, Hermann
Rühle, Richard
Ruppe, Wilhelm
Ruppert, Otto
Ruwee, Paul
Sanne, Hermann
Schabitz, Otto
Schacht, Rudolf
Schäfer, Johann

273

Schahreine, Walter
Schaible, Heinz
Schall, Wilhelm
Schaltka, Willy
Schaltysch, Leonhard
Scharain, Paul
Schauert, Hubert
Scheber, Josef
Scheid, Alfred
Schelbert, Albert
Schenkel, Robert
Scheppach, Georg
Schillinger, Andreas
Schlaak, Benno
Schleicher, Josef
Schlicht, Alfred
Schlotterbeck, Karl
Schmalkoke, Werner
Schmeiker, Werner
Schmidt, Heinz
Schmidt, Karl
Schmidt, Ludwig
Schmidt, Melchior
Schmidt, Otto
Schmidt, Richard
Schmidt, Robert
Schmidt, Rudolf
Schmidt, Siegesmund
Schmidthaber, Johann
Schneider, Werner
Schneidt, Kurt
Schober, Josef
Scholz, Werner
Schönenberger, Josef
Schopf, Ludwig
Schöpfer, Alfred
Schraen, Ernst
Schramm, Josef
Schreiner, Max *
Schreuder, Jakob
Schröder, Heinrich
Schöning, Gustav

Schröter, Alfred
Schubert, Michael
Schüle, Robert
Schüler, Alfred
Schüler, Georg
Schultheiss, Jakob
Schulz, Adolf
Schulze, Albert
Schulze, Ewald
Schumacher, Lothar
Schumann, Friedrich
Schur, Ernst
Schütz, Georg
Schütze, Willi
Schwanberger, Georg
Schwann, Willy
Schwarz, Arthuer
Schwarz, Arthur
Schweichler, Horst
Selke, Erich
Selzer, Erich
Senner, Fritz
Siegel, Kurt
Siemon, Fritz
Silbermann, Karl
Simoner, Adolf
Smoliner, Alois
Sorge, Paul
Sörnitz, Herbert
Soudier, Josef
Spachtenhausen, Johann
Spern, Heinrich
Sperzel, Adam
Sporn, Heinrich
Staab, Ernst
Staib, Karl *
Stammnitz, Bruno
Starke, Alfred
Starzak, Konstantin
Steier, Hermann
Stein, Max
Steinert, Willi

Steinhauff, Willi
Steinig, Kurt
Sten, Jürgen
Stendatis, Rudolf
Sterzl, Erich
Stiedl, Otto
Stöckert, Franz
Stotzer, Paul
Stracke, Heinz
Streubel, Reinhard
Strumpf, Gustav
Strumpf, Gustav
Stuber, Erwin
Stübner, Walter
Suchalski, Alex
Teichmann, Hans
Theissen, Walter
Theobald, Rudolf
Thiel, Kurt
Thiele, Willy
Thielecke, Calis
Thielen, Leonhard
Thiemann, Albert
Thieme, Egen
Thomas, Franz
Thomsen, Kurt
Tölkner, Richard
Trautmann, Horst
Treitl, August
Trimborn, Peter
Tröger, Paul
Türk, Heinrich
Uhle, Heinrich
Ulmer, Eugen
Ungetüm, Fritz
Valtin, Emil
Varschen, Bruno
Veith, Franz
Veitschegger, Victor
Viel, Reinhold
Vierke, Karl
Voge, Hermann

Appendices

Voge, Otto	Weinert, Paul	Wohlgemuth, Willy
Vogel, Werner	Weischnegg, Walter	Wolf, Ewald
Voigt, Wilhelm	Weiss, Walter	Wolf, Fritz
Voss, Georg	Werner, Josef	Wolfrath, Hans
Wacheim, Philipp	Weseloh, Otto	Woytinek, Walter
Wackernagel, Günther	Weygand, Karl	Wunder, Willi
Wächter, Wilhelm	Wicker, Richard	Wurnitsch, Ambros
Wagner, Josef	Wicky, Wilhelm	Würth, Richard
Wagner, Walter	Widera, Paul	Zaddech, Willy
Wallner, Johann	Wiediger, Heinz	Zahn, Herbert
Walter, Friedrich	Wiegratz, Heinrich	Zalle, Eugen
Wamser, Karl	Wiesen, Peter	Zalsky, Gottlieb
Wandel, Max	Wieshaupt, Fridolin	Zenger, Karl
Wandschneider, Karl	Wilhelm, Karl	Zepke, Walter
Wangelin, Ludwig	Wilke, Otto	Ziek, Otto
Wanzke, Erich	Will, Otto	Zientarski, Rudolf
Weber, Johann	Willgut, Oswald	Zillmann, Gustav
Weber, Karl	Wilm, Bruno	Zimmermann, Albin
Wedel, Eduard	Wilts, Hans	Zimmermann, Paul *
Wegner, Walter	Wimmer, Franz	Zische, Herbert
Weidemann, Robert	Winkler, Karl	Zollmann, Gustav
Weiffenbacher, Josef	Witschel, Franz	Zöllner, Walter
Weinert, Kurt	Wittenberg, Fritz	Zosel, Hans

* Promoted to officer rank while serving in the Sonderkommando
+ Promoted to officer rank after serving in the Sonderkommando

APPENDIX 4
FATE OF DIRLEWANGER PROTAGONISTS

von dem Bach-Zelewski, Erich – Chief of Anti-Partisan Warfare and Commander of German units during Warsaw Uprising; died March 8, 1972

Berger, Gottlob – Chief SS Main Office and benefactor of Dirlewanger; died January 5, 1975

Brack, Viktor – official in Reich Chancellery, helped Dirlewanger overturn civilian conviction; hanged June 2, 1948

Brandt, Rudolf – on Himmler's personal staff, issued instructions to the Replacement Office of the Waffen-SS to transfer Dr. Oskar Dirlewanger into the Waffen-SS; hanged June 2, 1948

Breithaupt, Franz – Chief of main SS court, recommended Dirlewanger for promotion; killed in a car accident, 1945

Frank, Hans – Governor General of occupied Poland; hanged Nürnberg October 16, 1946

Fegelein, Hermann – SS general, urged Hitler to withdraw *Sonderkommando* from Warsaw; executed on Hitler's orders in Berlin, April 1945

Freisler, Roland – President of People's Court, helped form *Sonderkommando*; killed February 3, 1945 in Berlin during an Allied bombing raid.

Freissner, Johannes – Colonel-General, Dirlewanger's superior in Hungary; died June 26, 1971.

Globocnik, Odilo – Dirlewanger's superior in Poland 1940-41; suicide May 31, 1945

Appendices

Glücks, Richard – Head of the concentration camp inspectorate, provided replacements to *Sonderkommando*; suicide May 14, 1945

Goering, Hermann – Chief of the Luftwaffe, supported convicts reinforcing the *Sonderkommando*; suicide October 1946

von Gottberg, Curt – Battle Group von Gottberg leader 1942-43; suicide May 9, 1945

Himmler, Heinrich – SS-Reichsführer; suicide May 23, 1945

Hitler, Adolf – Führer, made decision to form *Sonderkommando*; suicide Berlin April 30, 1945

Hoefle, Hermann – Dirlewanger's superior in quelling the Slovakian Uprising; hanged 1947

Jeckeln, Friedrich – Higher SS and Police Leader Northern Russia 1941-44; hanged Minsk February 3, 1946

Korsemann, Gerret – Higher SS and Police Leader White Russia; died 1958.

Krüger, Friedrich – Higher SS and Police Leader General Government 1939-44, threatened to jail Dirlewanger; suicide May 10, 1945

Kube, Wilhelm– General Commissioner White Russia 1941-43, complained of Dirlewanger's conduct in White Russia; assassinated Minsk September 23, 1943

Kutschera, Franz – Battle Group Kutschera leader in 1942; assassinated Warsaw, February 1, 1944

Murr, Wilhelm – Gauleiter of Württemberg, jailed Dirlewanger in 1937; suicide May 14, 1945

Naumann, Erich – Commander *Einsatzgruppe B*; hanged June 8, 1951

Nebe, Artur – Chief Reich Criminal Office, helped form *Sonderkommando*; executed by the SS March 2, 1945

Reinefarth, Heinz-Friedrich – Dirlewanger's superior in Warsaw; died May 7, 1979

Richert, Johann-Georg – commander 286th Security Division; hanged Minsk January 30, 1946.

Sauckel, Fritz – chief of slave labor, ordered Eastern Muslim regiment to reinforce the *Sonderkommando* in 1944; hanged Nürnberg October 16, 1946

Schwedler, Hans – commander of death's head units, recommended Dirlewanger for promotion; suicide 1945

Stahel, Rainer – city commander of Warsaw at the start of the Uprising; died November 30, 1955 in Soviet prisoner of war camp at Woikowo.

Thierach, Otto – Reich Minister of Justice 1942-1944, provided Dirlewanger with criminals through judicial system; suicide October 26, 1946

Trabandt, Wilhelm – commander of 1st SS Brigade during anti-partisan operations with Dirlewanger; suicide.

Wolff, Karl – Himmler's principal adjutant, formed the *Sonderkommando*, died July 15, 1984.

Appendices

APPENDIX 5
DIRLEWANGER UNIT DESIGNATIONS

Wilddiebkommando Oranienburg – June 1940 to July 1940

Sonderkommando Dr. Dirlewanger – July 1940 to September 1, 1940

SS-Sonderbataillon Dirlewanger – September 1, 1940 to September 1943

Einsatz-Bataillon Dirlewanger – numerous occasions in 1943 and 1944

SS-Regiment Dirlewanger – September 1943 to December 19, 1944

SS-Sonderregiment Dirlewanger – various times in 1943 and 1944

SS-Sturmbrigade Dirlewanger – December 19, 1944 to February 14, 1945

36. Waffen-Grenadier Division der SS – February 14, 1945 to May 1, 1945

APPENDIX 6
GERMAN ANTI-PARTISAN OPERATIONS WITH SONDERKOMMANDO DIRLEWANGER

OPERATION	START DATE	ENEMY KILLED
Operation Adler	July 1, 1942	1,381
Operation Greif	August 14, 1942	
Operation Nordsee	September 2, 1942	
Operation Regatta	October 4, 1942	
Operation Karlsbad	October 14, 1942	2,984
Operation Frieda	November 6, 1942	
Operation Franz	December 28, 1942	1,349
Operation Erntefest I	January 19, 1943	1,970/82*
Operation Erntefest II	January 30, 1943	144*
Operation Hornung	February 11, 1943	9,662
Operation Lenz Süd	March 31, 1943	
Operation Lenz Nord	April 8, 1943	
Operation Zauberflöte	April 17, 1943	
Operation Draufgänger I	April 28, 1943	

Appendices

Operation Draufgänger II	May 1, 1943	680*
Operation Günther	June 28, 1943	291*
Operation Hermann	July 7, 1943	
Operation Kottbus		9,500
Operation Frühlingsfest	April 11, 1944	7,000/65*

* Number reported killed by just the *Sonderkommando*
Operation locations shown on maps at start of appropriate chapters.

APPENDIX 7
COMPOSITION OF SONDERKOMMANDO DIRLEWANGER

The following chart shows the rough composition of the *Sonderkommando* troops during various stages of the war. Not all soldiers were sent to the unit as punishment; a steady cadre of SS personnel, with comparatively clean records, served in the formation. The percentages of poachers decreased during the conflict as losses mounted. Most foreign troops served during the period the unit fought in central Russia. Concentration camp inmates do not include poachers, but do include other types of common criminals as well as political prisoners. Regular army troops were only incorporated as the unit assumed division status in 1945.

	July 40 - June 42	July 42 - June 43	July 43 - June 44	July 44 - Nov 44	Dec 44 - Feb 45	Feb 45 - May 45
Regular	5%	5%	5%	5%	5%	5%
Poachers	94%	60%	15%	5%	5%	5%
Foreign Troops	0%	15%	30%	10%	5%	5%
SS & Army Penal Troops	1%	20%	15%	40%	45%	40%
Concentration Camp Inmates	0%	0%	35%	40%	40%	15%
Regular Army Troops	0%	0%	0%	0%	0%	30%

APPENDIX 8
GLOSSARY

Allgemeine SS – the general SS, the overall body of the SS, distinct from the Waffen-SS.

Bund deutscher Mädel or **BdM** – the league of German girls; the feminine branch of the German youth movement. Within this organization, girls ten to fourteen years old belonged to the Jungmädel.

Einsatzgruppe – battalion-size mobile extermination group on the eastern front, primarily Security Police and SD officials.

Einsatzkommando – subordinate command of an einsatzgruppe, normally company-size.

Endlösung – final solution, the German euphemism used here to indicate the extermination of the Jewish race.

Gauleiter – highest ranking Nazi Party official in a district. Germany was composed of forty-two Nazi Party districts.

Gestapo – Geheime Staatspolizei, the secret police dedicated to the preservation of the Nazi regime.

Hauptamt SS Gericht – the SS Legal Department.

HSSPF – Höhrere SS und Polizeiführer, Higher SS and Police Leader, Himmler's regional commander in an area. Directly responsible to Himmler for the implementation of all measures related to the security of the state and the treatment of dangerous elements within their realm.

Kripo – Kriminalpolizei, criminal police under the control of the SD.

KZ – Konzentrations Lager, concentration camp.

OKH – Oberkommando des Heeres, the Army High Command.

OKW – Oberkommando der Wehrmacht, Armed Forces High Command.

Orpo – Ordnungspolizei, order police, consisting of uniformed police forces in the Third Reich. While separate from the Gestapo and Criminal Police, they handled routine police business and sometimes assisted in carrying out mass executions.

Osttruppen – Eastern troops who served with the Germans.

RFSS – Reichsführer-SS, Reich Leader Heinrich Himmler

SA – Sturmabteilung; Storm Detachment, the early private army of the Nazi party.

SD – Sicherheitsdienst, the intelligence branch of the SS.

Sicherheitspolizei – Security Police; a fusion of various criminal police forces and state political police separate from the SS, but closely linked to the SD.

Sonderkommando – special commando, used here to indicate the Dirlewanger unit.

SS-Führungshauptamt or **SS-FHA** – SS Leadership Main Office, the headquarters of the Waffen-SS; designed to control the organization of field units of the SS and to monitor the training and replacement units of the Waffen-SS. It additionally looked after training schools of the Waffen-SS. The **SS-FHA** was independent of the SS Main Office.

SS-Hauptamt or **SS-HA** – SS Main Office, evolved in the mid-1930s and controlled such functions as personnel, administration, medical, physical training, education, communications and so forth.

Appendices

SS und Polizeiführer or **SSPF** – SS and Police Leader, district commander subordinate to an HSSPF.

Totenkopf – Death's Head, units which guarded concentration camps. Also the 3rd Waffen-SS Division.

Verfügungstruppe – the first Waffen-SS field troops.

Waffen-SS – SS field troops.

Wirtschafts und Verwaltungshauptamt or **WVHA** –, Economics and Administration Head Office of the SS charged with the administration of the concentration camps.

SOURCES

Published Documents

Angolia, John. *For Führer and Fatherland: Military Awards of the Third Reich*. San Jose, CA: R. James Bender Publishing, 1976.

Arad, Yitzhak. *Belzec, Sobibor, Treblinka: The Operation Reinhard Death Camps*. Bloomington, IN: Indiana University Press, 1987.

Arad, Yitzak, Shmuel Krakowski and Shmuel Spector. *The Einsatzgruppen Reports*. New York: Holocaust Library, 1989.

Auerbach, Hellmuth. "Die Einheit Dirlewanger," *Vierteljahrshefte für Zeitgeschichte*, X, No. 3 (July 1962).

Bar-Zohar, Michael. *The Avengers*. Translated from the French by Len Ortzen. New York: Hawthorn Books INC., 1967.

Bender, Roger James and Taylor, Hugh Page. *Uniforms, Organization and History of the Waffen-SS, Vol. 2*. Mountain View, CA: R. James Bender Publishing, 1971.

Bielecki, Tadeusz and Szymanski, Leszek. *Warsaw Aflame: The 1939-1945 Years*. Los Angeles, CA: Polamerica Press, 1973.

Breitman, Richard. *The Architect of Genocide: Himmler and the Final Solution*. New York: Alfred A. Knopf, 1991.

Buchheim, Hans. "Die Höheren SS und Polizeiführer," *Vierteljahrshefte für Zeitgeschichte*, III, No. 4 (October 1963).

Büchler, Yehoshua, "Kommandostab Reichsführer-SS: Himmler's Personal Murder Brigades in 1941." *Holocaust and Genocide Studies* Volume 1 Number 1, Oxford, Great Britain: Pergamon Press, 1986.

Clark, Alan. *Barbarossa: The Russian-German Conflict, 1941-45*. New York: William Morrow and Company, 1965.

Cooper, Matthew. *The Nazi War Against Soviet Partisans*. New York: Stein and Day, 1979.

Crow, Duncan. *Armored Fighting Vehicles of Germany*. New York: Arco Publishing Company, 1973.

Deschner, Gunther. *Warsaw Rising. Ballantine's Illustrated History of the Violent Century – Politics in Action Number 5*. New York: Ballantine Books, 1972.

"Dirlewanger ist tot", *Schwarzwälder Bote*, December 2, 1960.

Dörr, Manfred und Franz Thomas. *Die Träger der Nahkampfspange in Gold*. Osnabrück, FRG: Biblio Verlag, 1986.

Sources

Engelmann, Joachim und Horst Scheibert. *Deutsche Artillerie 1934-1945: Eine Dokumentation in Text, Skizzen und Bildern*. Limburg/Lahn, FRG: C.A. Starke Verlag, 1974.

Feig, Konnilyn G. *Hitler's Death Camps: The Sanity of Madness*. New York: Holmes & Meier, 1979.

Der Freiwillige (Bundesverband der Soldaten der ehemaligen Waffen-SS e.V.) 4500 Osnabrück, Germany (Postfach 3023): Münin Verlag.

Fröbe, Rainer and others. *Konzentrationslager in Hannover: KZ-Arbeit und Rüstungsindustrie in der Spätphase des Zweiten Weltkriegs*. Hannover, FRG: Lax, 1985.

" Geheimnis um ein Soldatengrab", *Schwarzwälder Bote*, April 20, 1960.

Gilbert, Martin. *Atlas of the Holocaust*. Tel-Aviv: Steimatsky's Agency Limited, 1982.

Guderian, Heinz. *Panzer Leader*. Washington, D.C.: Zenger Publishing Company, 1979.

Gutman Yisrael and Berenbaum, Michael. *Anatomy of the Auschwitz Death Camp*. Bloomington, IN: Indiana University Press, in association with the United States Holocaust Memorial Museum, 1994.

Halcomb, Jill. *The SA: A Historical Perspective*. Columbia, S.C.: Crown/Agincourt Books, 1985.

Hanson, Joanna K. M. *The Civilian Population and the Warsaw Uprising of 1944*. Cambridge, England: Cambridge University Press, 1982.

Hartung, Lothar. *Verleihungs-Urkunden des 3. Reiches*, Fürstentum, Liechtenstein: Infora Research Est., 1982.

Headland, Ronald. *Messages of Murder: A Study of the Reports of the Einsatzgruppen of the Security Police and the Security Service*. 1941-1943. London: Associated University Presses, 1992.

Hilberg, Raul. *The Destruction of the European Jews (Revised and definitive edition)*. New York: Holmes & Meier, 1985.

Hinze, Rolf. *Das Ostfront-Drama 1944: Rückzugskämpfe Heeresgruppe Mitte*. Stuttgart, FRG: Motorbuch Verlag, 1988.

Höffkes, Karl. *Hitlers politische Generale: Die Gauleiter des Dritten Reiches*. Tübingen, FRG: Grabert Verlag, 1986.

Höhne, Heinz. *The Order of the Death's Head: The Story of Hitler's SS*. New York: Coward-McCann, Inc., 1970.

"In aller Stille exhumiert", *Schwäbische Zeitung*, No 267, November 19, 1960.

Infield, Glenn B. *Skorzeny: Hitler's Commando*, New York: St. Martin's Press, 1981.

International Military Tribunal Nürnberg. *Trial of the Major War Criminals before the International Military Tribunal.* Nürnberg, Germany: Allied Control Authority for Germany, 1948.

International Military Tribunal Nürnberg. *Trials of War Criminals before the International Military Tribunal, Volume IV, United States of America vs. Otto Ohlendorf, et al., Case No. 9.* Washington, DC: U.S. Government Printing Office, 1949.

International Military Tribunal Nürnberg. *Trials of War Criminals before the International Military Tribunal, Volume XIII, The Ministries Case, Case No. 11.* Washington, DC: U.S. Government Printing Office, 1952.

Keilig, Wolf. *Die Generale des Heeres.* Friedberg, FRG: Podzun-Pallas-Verlag, 1983.

Klausch, Hans-Peter. *Antifaschisten in SS-Uniform.* Bremen, Germany: Edition Temmen, 1993.

Koehl, Robert Lewis. *The Black Corps: The Structure and Power Struggles of the Nazi SS.* Madison, WI: University of Wisconsin Press, 1983.

Krausnick, Helmut & Hans Buchheim, Martin Broszat and Hans-Adolf Jacobsen. *Anatomy of the SS State.* New York: Walker and Company, 1968.

Krannhals, Hanns von. *Der Warschauer Aufstand 1944.* Frankfurt am Main: Bernhard & Grafe verlag, 1964.

Landwehr, Richard. *Fighting for Freedom: The Ukrainian Volunteer Division of the Waffen-SS.* Silver Spring, Maryland: Bibliophile Legion Books, 1985.

Landwehr, Richard. *Siegrunen:The Waffen-SS in Historical Perspective*, Volume 57 (Fall 1994). Brookings, OR: Landwehr.

Le Tissier, Tony. *The Battle of Berlin 1945.* New York: St. Martin's Press, 1988.

Littlejohn, David and Dodkins, COL C..M. *Orders, Decorations, Medals and Badges of the Third Reich.* Mountain View, CA: R. James Bender, 1968.

Lochner, Louis P. *The Goebbels Diaries, 1942-1943*. New York: Doubleday & Company, 1948.

Lukas, Richard C. *The Forgotten Holocaust: The Poles under German Occupation, 1939-1944*. Lexington, KY: The University Press of Kentucky, 1986.

Mehner, Kurt. *Die Geheimen Tagesberichte der Deutschen Wehrmachtführung im Zweiten Weltkrieg 1939-1945*. Osnabrück, FRG: Biblio Verlag, 1988.

Mehner, Kurt. *Die Waffen-SS und Polizei, 1939-1945*. Norderstedt, Germany: Militair-Verlag Klaus D. Patzwall, 1995.

Meyer, Gertrud. *Nacht über Hamburg*. Frankfurt/Main, FRG: Röderberg Verlag, 1971.

Michaelis, Rolf. *Der Weg zur 36. Waffen-Grenadier-Division der SS*. Rodgau, FRG: Verlag für Militärhistorische Zeitgeschichte, 1991.

Michaelis, Rolf. *Die Grenadier Divisionen der Waffen SS*, Band III. Erlangen, Germany: Michaelis Verlag, 1995.

Munoz, Antonio J. *Forgotten Legions: Obscure Combat Formations of the Waffen-SS*, Boulder, CO: Paladin Press, 1991.

Niepold, Gerd. *Battle for White Russia: The Destruction of Army Group Center June 1944*. London: Brassey's Defense Publishers, 1987.

Orpen, Neil. *Airlift to Warsaw: The Rising of 1944*. Norman, OK: University of Oklahoma press, 1984.

Padfield, Peter. *Himmler: Reichsführer-SS*. New York: Henry Holt and Company, 1990.

Prados, John. "Warsaw Rising: Revolt of the Polish Underground, 1944." *Strategy & Tactics*. Lake Geneva, WI: Dragon Publishing, Number 107, May-June 1986.

Preradovich, Nikolaus von. *Die Generale der Waffen-SS*. Berg am See, FRG: Kurt Vowinkel-Verlag, 1985.

Proctor, Raymond L. *Hitler's Luftwaffe in the Spanish Civil War*. Westport, Connecticutt: Greenwood Press, 1983.

Ready, J. Lee. *The Forgotten Axis: Germany's Partners and Foreign Volunteers in World War II*. Jefferson, North Carolina, 1987.

Reitlinger, Gerald. *The House Built on Sand: The Conflicts of German Policy in Russia, 1939-1945*. New York: The Viking Press, 1960.

Reitlinger, Gerald. *The SS: Alibi of a Nation 1922-1945*. London: Arms and Armour Press, 1984.

Schneider, Jost. *Their Honor was Loyalty!* San Jose, CA: R. James Bender Publishing, 1977.

Seaton, Albert. *The Russo-German War 1941-45.* Novato, CA: Presidio Press, 1990.

Segev, Tom. *Soldiers of Evil: The Commandants of the Nazi Concentration Camps.* New York: McGraw Hill, 1987.

Seidler, Franz W. "SS-Sondereinheit Dirlewanger. Ein Sträflingsbataillon zum Einsatz im Kampf gegen Partisanen." *Damals,* 7/1977. Giessen, Germany: Damals-Verlag.

Smith, Bradley F. *Reaching Judgment at Nürnberg.* New York: Basic Books, Inc., 1977.

Snyder, Louis L. Encyclopedia of the Third Reich. New York: McGraw-Hill, 1976.

Spielberger, Walter J. and Uwe Feist. *Sonderpanzer: German Special Purpose Vehicles,* Armor Series Volume 9. Fallbrook, CA: Aero Publishers, 1968.

Stein, George H. *The Waffen-SS: Hitler's Elite Guard at War, 1939-1945.* Ithaca, N.Y: Cornell University Press, 1966.

Sydnor, Charles W. Jr. *Soldiers of Destruction: The SS Death's Head Division, 1933-1945.* Princeton, NJ: Princeton University Press, 1977.

Thomas, Nigel and Peter Abbott. *Partisan Warfare 1941-45,* Osprey Men at Arms Series 34, London: Osprey Publishing Ltd, 1983.

Tieke, Wilhelm. *Das Ende zwischen Oder und Elbe: Der Kampf um Berlin 1945.* Stuttgart, FRG: Motorbuch Verlag, 1981.

Tessin, Georg. *Verbände und Truppen der deutschen Wehrmacht und Waffen-SS, 1939 – 1945.* Osnabrueck, FRG: Biblio Verlag, 1980.

Trevor-Roper, H. R. ed. *Blitzkrieg to Defeat: Hitler's War Directives 1939-1945.* New York: Holt, Rinehart and Winston, 1964.

Trevor-Roper, H. R. ed. *Hitler's Table Talk, 1941-1944.* London, England: Weidenfeld and Nicolson, 1953.

Vasicek, Radko. "Allied Airfield Behind Enemy Lines." *World War II.* Leesburg, VA: Cowles Magazines, May, 1996.

Weingartner, James J. "Law and Justice in the Nazi SS: The Case of Konrad Morgen." *Central European History,* 16. Atlantic Highlands, NJ: Humanities Press, 1983.

Sources

Windrow, Martin. *The Waffen-SS*, Osprey Men at Arms Series 34, London: Osprey Publishing Ltd, 1982.

Yerger, Mark C. *Riding East: The SS Cavalry Brigade in Poland and Russia 1939-1942*. Atglen, PA: Schiffer Publishing, 1996.

Zawodny, J. K. *Nothing But Honor: The Story of the Warsaw Uprising, 1944*. Stanford, CA: Hoover Institution Press, 1978.

Zentner, Christian and Friedemann Bedürftig. *The Encyclopedia of the Third Reich*. English translation edited by Amy Hackett. New York: Macmillan Publishing, 1991.

Ziemke, Earl F. *Stalingrad to Berlin: The German Defeat in the East*. Washington, D.C: Center of Military History, United States Army, 1968.

Archival Documents
National Archives Record Group 238, NO 1908, Office of Chief Counsel for War Crimes, Sworn affidavit by SS-Hauptsturmführer Dr. Konrad Morgen, January 28, 1947.

National Archives Record Group 238, NO 2366, Office of Chief Counsel for War Crimes, Letter from SS-Hauptsturmführer Dr. Konrad Morgen to SS-Sturmbannführer Pohl, November 2. 1941.

National Archives Record Group 238, NO 5741, Office of Chief Counsel for War Crimes, Career affidavit by SS-Hauptsturmführer Dr. Konrad Morgen, December 19, 1947.

National Archives Record Group 238, M-1019/R80/1029, Office of Chief Counsel for War Crimes, Interrogation of SS-Obergruppenführer Karl Wolff, April 12, 1947.

Archival Microfilm Sources
National Archives of the United States, Washington D.C. Microcopy RG 238, M-1019, Interrogations of Nürnberg witnesses, (Reels 6 and 80).

National Archives of the United States, Washington D. C. Microcopy T-175, Records of the Reich Leader of the SS and Chief of German Police (Reels 18, 70, 140, 198, 205, 225, 226, 235, 236).

National Archives of the United States, Washington D. C. Microfilm T-354, Records of the Waffen-SS, (Reels 161, 648, 649, 650).

National Archives of the United States, Washington D. C. Microfilm Publication A3343 Series SSO, Records of SS Officers from the Berlin Document Center, (Reels 013, 058, 076, 081, 096, 099, 104, 114, 115, 118, 154, 174, 175, 196, 199, 004A, 016A, 017A, 024A, 027A, 033A, 074A, 126A, 148A, 154A, 186A, 205A, 259A, 278A, 288A, 298A, 302A, 320A, 324A, 341A, 343A, 345A, 383A, 388A, 391A, 019B, 020B, 068B, 083B, 100B, 101B, 124B, 149B, 163B, 187B, 188B, 189B, 217B, 219B, 222B, 225B, 232B, 240B, 245B, 246B, 247B, 019C, 023C)

Unpublished Documents

Letter to the author from Aaron Breitbart of the Simon Wiesenthal Center, April 30, 1996.

Letter to the author from Dieter Heske, Hauptamtsleiter der Gemeinde Altshausen, February 1996.

Letter to the author from Raul Hilberg, June 2, 1996.

Letter to the author from Rudolf Multer, May 24, 1996.

Letter to the author, from a former member of the SS and Knight's Cross winner, January 1996.

NOTES

NOTES

NOTES

NOTES

NOTES

INDEX

Amann, Heinrich, 131, 163
Angele, Betty, 225
Appold, Waldemar, 100
Auerbach, Hellmuth, 261
Augustin, Walter, 143

Bach, Von dem, 177, 184, 196, 230
Bach-Zelewski, Erich von dem, 14, 76, 78, 91, 92, 94, 98, 134, 153, 177, 230, 243, 260
Bar-Zohar, Michael, 254
Bassewitz-Behr, Georg Henning von, 94
Baur, Hans, 144
Bax, Erich, 143
Beniger, Ludwig, 144
Benkert, Karl, 100
Berger, Gottlob, 14, 25, 33, 36, 39, 45, 51, 54, 55, 57, 62, 63, 65, 71, 72, 74, 79, 101, 115, 144, 154, 159, 162, 164, 179, 199, 207, 223, 235, 243, 246, 247, 260

Bernhard, Friedrich, 77
Binzer, Georg, 144
Blessau, Werner, 131, 156, 157
Bodammer, Waldemar, 94
Böhme, Friedrich, 131
Bór-Komorowski, General, 175-176
Brack, Viktor, 35, 39
Bradfisch, Otto, 88
Brandenburg, Walter, 166
Brandt, Erich, 204, 205
Brandt, Rudolf, 52, 71
Brehm, Fritz, 144
Breitbart, Aaron, 256
Breithaupt, Franz, 14, 55, 56
Brencher, Wilhelm, 143
Brune, Otto, 130
Brusberg, Gustav, 130
Buch, Walter, 142
Buchmann, Erich, 206, 223
Bujara, Ewald, 144
Bünger, Hans, 196
Bunn, Friedrich, 153

Burckhardt, Karl, 77
Busse, Karl, 153
Busse, Theodor, 222

Chrusciel, Antoni "Monter", 175, 190
Cichon, Georg, 153
Ciesewski, Alfred, 144
Cjhonkow, Nestor, 163
Clark, Alan, 249
Credner, Günther, 146

Dett, Jakob, 163
Dirlewanger, Oskar, 12, 14, 15, 16, 19, 26, 28, 34-35, 46, 51, 56, 65, 73, 80, 93, 108, 118, 123, 134, 142, 154-155, 164, 177, 191, 202, 211, 223-225, 229, 246, 249, 252, 254, 263
Doll-Wimmer, Josef, 130
Dorfer, Ferdinand, 153

Eggers, Georg-Wilhelm, 165
Ehlers, Ewald, 195, 223
Ehrlinger, Erich, 90
Eichler, Hans Joachim, 224
Eichmann, Adolf, 252
Eicke, Theodor, 56
Ernst, Franz, 144

Faust, Rudolf, 144
Fegelein, Hermann, 17, 97, 98
Feiertag, Heinz, 79, 123, 144, 164, 169
Flesch, Karl, 144
Flohr, Heinrich, 164
Franco, Francisco, 35, 163

Frank, Hans, 63, 201
Freisler, Roland, 42
Freitag, Fritz, 100
Friessner, Johannes, 211
Fuchs, Martin, 164
Füssinger, Anton, 257

Gaertner, Peter, 73
Gamsjaeger, Johann, 153
Gast, Otto, 145, 170
Gehlen, Reinhard, 256
Gerards, Heinrich, 164
Geschler, Engelbert, 164
Globocnik, Odilo, 14, 59, 62-65
Glücks, Richard, 121-122, 144
Goldwianik, Ivan, 163
Göring, Hermann, 80, 142, 229, 234
Gorn, Erwin, 153
Gossens, Peter, 134
Gottberg, Curt von, 95, 111, 113, 130, 132, 134, 143, 147, 167, 172
Grabs, Otto, 144
Gramatke, Kurt, 131
Gröbner, Georg, 143
Grohmann, Josef, 124, 168
Guderian, Heinz, 17, 176

Haberland, Kurt, 153
Hähnle, Erich, 144
Halder, Franz, 91
Hanser, Eugen, 143
Hausser, Paul, 240, 241, 243
Heidelberg, Ernst-Günther, 158
Heimsch, Arthur, 143
Heissmeyer, August, 65

Index

Henze, Gerhard, 134, 143
Herff, Maximilian von, 113, 211
Herrmann, Paul, 91
Heuschneider, Leopold, 164
Heydrich, Reinhard, 85
Hilberg, Raul, 255
Hilgers, Friedrich Martin, 224
Himmler, Heinrich, 12, 15, 42, 44, 51, 52, 56, 61, 64, 71, 74, 77, 89, 91, 111, 115, 121, 142, 144, 153, 155, 176, 179, 202, 213, 230
Hitler, Adolf, 15, 25, 26, 34, 36, 45, 57, 62, 77, 110, 172
Hoefle, Hermann, 200
Holtwjanik, Ivan, 163
Hölz, Max, 16
Hörath, Karl, 100

Illing, Paul, 134
Infield, Glenn B., 255
Ingruber, Egyd, 107, 108, 117, 131
Iskam, Robert, 74

Jalinskij, Wasil, 163
Jeckeln, Friedrich, 131, 134, 142, 144
Jokiel, Erhard, 144
Jüttner, Hans, 65

Kaelber, Friedrich, 144
Kalbe, Theodor, 143
Kalix, Herbert, 153
Kaminsky, Bratislav, 187
Karnop, Johannes, 204
Kehl, Heinrich, 164
Kellkamp, Gerhard, 146

Keusch, Gerhard, 153
Kleinheisterkamp, Matthias, 222
Klekamp, Johannes, 153
Knoblauch, Kurt, 77
Koch, Erich, 164
Komorowski, Bór, 196
Korsemann, Gerret, 95, 124
Kostelnik, Bruno, 134
Krannhals, Hanns von, 19
Krätzer, Theodor, 216
Kraus, Georg, 170
Krause, Heinz, 163
Krause, Siegfried, 144
Krüger, Friedrich, 14, 60, 64-65
Krüger, Fritz, 143
Kube, Wilhelm, 14, 141, 142, 246
Kuhlmann, Heinrich, 144
Kutschera, Franz, 96

Labette, Gerhard, 164
Lammerding, Heinz, 125, 144
Lammers, Hans, 16
Lange, Walter, 144
Lebin, Erich, 144
Ledermann, Walter, 164
Lempa, Viktor, 144
Leuendorf, Werner, 143
Lewandowski, Helmut, 172
Liebermann, Franz, 172
Liers, Rudolf, 145
Lohse, Hinrich, 143
Loritz, Hans, 57
Lowitz, Rudolf, 134
Lühr, Hans-Friedrich, 131, 155
Luther, Martin, 44

Magill, Franz, 96, 99, 106

Mammitsch, Alfred, 145, 158
Mayer-Mader, Andreas, 162
Mehlen, Thido, 131
Melnitschenko, Ivan, 163
Meyer, Willy, 123, 134
Miketta, Hans, 144
Möhle, Heinrich, 144
Möller, Kurt, 224
Morgen, Konrad, 60, 61, 72, 121, 213, 234
Multer, Rudolf, 223, 256
Murr, Wilhelm, 34

Naumann, Erich, 88, 89
Nebe, Artur, 43, 45, 154
Nickel, Rudolf, 96
Nitschipuronitsche, Colonel, 84

Ohlendorf, Otto, 88
Orlov, Sergei, 114

Panow, Vladimir, 114
Pauly, Max, 203
Pfab, Hans, 144
Pfaffenrodt, Helmut, 134
Pfeiffer, Walter, 75
Planitzer, Franz, 144
Plaul, Wolfgang, 168
Praefke, Karl-Joachim, 117-118, 134
Pres, Adam, 163

Radkowski, Alexander, 163
Raml, Fritz, 144
Rascher, Sigmund, 74
Reel, Fritz, 144
Reinefarth, Heinz, 188

Reiner, Wilhelm, 120, 121
Reinhard, Siegfried, 144
Reinhardt, Georg-Hans, 92
Rett, Willi, 144
Richert, Johann-Georg, 77
Richter, Heinz, 88, 89
Richter, Walter, 143
Ritter von Thoma, Colonel, 40
Röhm, Ernst, 26
Romanenko, Pawel, 163
Roschko, Nikolai, 163
Rosenberg, Alfred, 142, 144, 162
Rossa, Willi, 143
Ruch, Wilhelm, 101
Ruebe, Adolf, 87
Ruppert, Otto, 113

Sakhno, Leonid, 163
Sauckel, Fritz, 163
Schäftlmeier, Hans, 164
Schall, Wilhelm, 134
Scheber, Josef, 164
Schenckendorff, Max von, 93
Scheppach, Georg, 134
Schillinger, Andreas, 215
Schimana, Walter, 114
Schindhelm, Hans-Gerhard, 88, 90
Schlicht, Alfred, 153
Schmalkoke, Werner, 73
Schmedes, Fritz, 216, 249
Schmidt, Karl, 143
Schopf, Ludwig, 145
Schreiner, Max, 144, 183
Schulz, Adolf, 113
Schuschnigg, Kurt, 44
Schütze, Willi, 144
Schwedler, Hans, 55

Index

Selzer, Erich, 144
Skorzeny, Otto, 169
Slobodjanik, Stepan, 163
Smoliner, Alois, 144
Souleiman, Hassan, 254
Spern, Heinrich, 164
Stahel, Rainer, 178
Stahlecker, Walter, 247
Staib, Karl, 183, 187
Stalin, Josef, 44, 170
Steinhauer, Joseph, 131
Stöweno, Rudolf, 124, 144
Strumpf, Gustav, 144
Stübner, Walter, 113
Susuija, Ivan, 163

Teretschenko, Ivan, 163
Teretschuk, Piotr, 163
Thiel, Kurt, 164
Thieme, Egeon, 163
Thierack, Otto, 16
Thomä, Manfred, 224
Tiso, Josef, 199
Tölkner, Richard, 163
Trattenschegg, Adelbert, 194
Treuenfeld, Karl von, 84-85

Ulmer, Eugen, 144

Voigt, Wilhelm, 73
Von Thoma, Colonel Ritter, 35
Vormann, Nikolaus von, 92

Wächter, Wilhelm, 134
Wagner, Eduard, 85
Walchensteiner, Othmar, 145
Waldowski, Leonid, 91
Wallner, Johann, 113
Walser, Erwin, 120, 131
Walter, Friedrich, 134
Weber, Hans Georg, 101
Weber, Karl, 144
Wegner, Walter, 144
Wehninck, Heinrich, 143
Wehser, Ralf, 72, 80
Weisse, Kurt, 124, 125, 223
Westphal, Carl, 43
Wicky, Wilhelm, 113
Wiesenthal, Simon, 256
Wiesshaupt, Fridolin, 101
Wild, Georg, 204, 205
Wilhelm, Waldemar, 94, 134
Wille, Bruno, 208
Winkler, Karl, 153
Wittje, Kurt, 65
Wolff, Karl, 42, 237

Zahn, Herbert, 144
Zalsky, Gottlieb, 79
Zeller, August, 142, 144
Zhukov, Georgi, 223
Zimmermann, Paul, 134, 183, 187